JOURNALIST SAFETY AND SELF-CENSORSHIP

This book explores the relationship between the safety of journalists and self-censorship practices around the world, including local case studies and regional and international perspectives.

Bringing together scholars and practitioners from around the globe, *Journalist Safety and Self-Censorship* provides new and updated insights into patterns of self-censorship and free speech, focusing on a variety of factors that affect these issues, including surveillance, legislation, threats, violent conflict, gender-related stereotypes, digitization and social media. The contributions examine topics such as trauma, risk and self-censorship among journalists in different regions of the world, including Central America, Estonia, Turkey, Uganda and Pakistan. The book also provides conceptual clarity to the notion of journalist self-censorship, and explores the question of how self-censorship may be studied empirically.

Combining both theoretical and practical knowledge, this collection serves as a much-needed resource for any academic, student of journalism, practising journalist, or NGO working on issues of journalism, safety, free speech and censorship.

Anna Grøndahl Larsen holds a PhD from the Department of Journalism and Media Studies, Oslo Metropolitan University. She is currently a senior lecturer at the Department of Media and Communication at the University of Oslo. Her research interests include journalism and political communication, comprising topics such as extremism, terrorism and the media.

Ingrid Fadnes is a journalist and researcher connected to the Media, War and Conflict research group at Oslo Metropolitan University. Fadnes was a member of the organizing committee of the Safety of Journalists conference at Oslo Metropolitan University 2017, 2018 and 2019.

Roy Krøvel is Professor of Journalism at Oslo Metropolitan University and the Sámi University of Applied Sciences. Krøvel is a civil engineer with specialization in risk management and holds a PhD in History.

JOURNALIST SAFETY AND SELF-CENSORSHIP

*Edited by Anna Grøndahl Larsen,
Ingrid Fadnes and Roy Krøvel*

LONDON AND NEW YORK

First published 2021
by Routledge
2 Park Square, Milton Park, Abingdon, Oxon OX14 4RN

and by Routledge
52 Vanderbilt Avenue, New York, NY 10017

Routledge is an imprint of the Taylor & Francis Group, an informa business

© 2021 selection and editorial matter, Anna Grøndahl Larsen, Ingrid Fadnes and
Roy Krøvel individual chapters, the contributors

The right of Anna Grøndahl Larsen, Ingrid Fadnes and Roy Krøvel to be identified
as the authors of the editorial material, and of the authors for their individual chapters,
has been asserted in accordance with sections 77 and 78 of the Copyright, Designs
and Patents Act 1988.

All rights reserved. No part of this book may be reprinted or reproduced or utilised
in any form or by any electronic, mechanical, or other means, now known or
hereafter invented, including photocopying and recording, or in any information
storage or retrieval system, without permission in writing from the publishers.

Trademark notice: Product or corporate names may be trademarks or registered trademarks,
and are used only for identification and explanation without intent to infringe.

British Library Cataloguing-in-Publication Data
A catalogue record for this book is available from the British Library

Library of Congress Cataloging-in-Publication Data
Names: Fadnes, Ingrid, editor. | Larsen, Anna Grøndahl, editor. | Krøvel, Roy, editor.
Title: Journalist safety and self-censorship / edited by
Ingrid Fadnes, Anna Grøndahl Larsen, Roy Krøvel.
Description: London ; New York : Routledge, 2020. |
Includes bibliographical references and index. |
Identifiers: LCCN 2020003838 | ISBN 9780367409647 (hardback) |
ISBN 9780367409623 (paperback) | ISBN 9780367810139 (ebook)
Subjects: LCSH: Journalists–Violence against. | Journalists–Crimes against. |
Journalism–Political aspects. | Freedom of the press. | Censorship.
Classification: LCC PN4751 .J68 2020 | DDC 070.4/33–dc23
LC record available at https://lccn.loc.gov/2020003838

ISBN: 978-0-367-40964-7 (hbk)
ISBN: 978-0-367-40962-3 (pbk)
ISBN: 978-0-367-81013-9 (ebk)

Typeset in Bembo
by Newgen Publishing UK

CONTENTS

List of contributors   *vii*

1   Introduction: Safety for journalists and self-censorship   1
      Ingrid Fadnes, Roy Krøvel and Anna Grøndahl Larsen

2   Journalism and self-censorship in the insecure democracies of
      Central America   13
      José Luis Benítez

3   Red lines of journalism: Digital surveillance, safety risks and
      journalists' self-censorship in Pakistan   29
      Sadia Jamil

4   Chilling or cosy effects? Zimbabwean journalists' experiences
      and the struggle for definition of self-censorship   47
      Nhamo Anthony Mhiripiri

5   *Lèse-majestè* and journalism in Turkey and Europe   65
      Aytekin Kaan Kurtul

6   Online surveillance and the repressive Press Council
      Bill 2018: A two-pronged approach to media
      self-censorship in Nigeria   80
      Olunifesi Adekunle Suraj

vi Contents

7 The "triple effect" silencing female journalists online: A
   theoretical exploration   100
   Marte Høiby

8 A way to silence journalists? Estonian female journalists'
   experiences with harassment and self-censorship   114
   Signe Ivask

9 Risk perception and negotiation of safety among Ugandan
   female journalists covering political demonstrations   130
   Aisha Sembatya Nakiwala

10 Fear, trauma and local journalists: Implications for media
   development and peacebuilding   148
   Michelle Betz and Paul Beighley

11 Safety and self-censorship: Examining their linkage to social
   media use among Uganda journalists   164
   Florence Namasinga Selnes

12 Defending the watchdog: How local NGOs build journalists'
   resilience by combating threats to their safety and security   181
   Gerald Walulya

13 Conclusion: Researching self-censorship caused by inadequate
   safety of journalists. Causes, solutions and future research   197
   Ingrid Fadnes, Roy Krøvel and Anna Grøndahl Larsen

Index   *204*

CONTRIBUTORS

Paul Beighley holds an MD from the University of Texas Health Science Center in San Antonio. He is currently the medical director for the Adult Mental Health Division of the State of Hawaii on the Big Island of Hawaii. He retired from the US Foreign Service at the rank of minister counsellor after a career serving the mental health needs of the diplomatic community both domestically and abroad, and maintains an interest in promoting mental health support for journalists working internationally.

José Luis Benítez holds a PhD from Ohio University. He is currently an independent media and journalism researcher and consultant. His research interests include journalism and freedom of expression in Central America, communication and transnational migration, and media and communication policies.

Michelle Betz holds an MJ from Carleton University in Canada. She is a senior media development expert specializing in issues of media and conflict, journalism safety and press freedom. She consults for a range of international organizations and UN agencies. Her research interests include psychosocial issues and support for local journalists and safety issues more broadly.

Ingrid Fadnes is a journalist and researcher connected to the Media, War and Conflict research group at Oslo Metropolitan University. Fadnes was a member of the organizing committee of the Safety of Journalists conference 2017, 2018 and 2019.

Marte Høiby is an associate professor in journalism at the Department of Journalism and Media studies, Oslo Metropolitan University. Høiby teaches mainly on topics related to journalism and globalization, gender, conflict reporting, threats

viii Contributors

to journalists and field security. In parallel with her academic work, Høiby has given workshops and safety training to journalists in Latin America, Asia and Africa.

Signe Ivask holds a PhD from the Department of Social Sciences, University of Tartu. She is currently a lecturer in journalism and a research fellow in the sociology of journalism at the Institute of Social Studies at the University of Tartu. Her research interests include stress and burnout of journalists, working routines in the newsroom and communication between journalists and audience.

Sadia Jamil holds a PhD from the School of Communication and Arts, University of Queensland, Australia. She is currently postdoctoral fellow in humanities and social sciences at Khalifa University of Science and Technology, Abu Dhabi, UAE. Her research interests include journalism, new media and political communication, and freedom of expression and press freedom.

Roy Krøvel is Professor of Journalism at Oslo Metropolitan University and at the indigenous Sami University College. Krøvel is a civil engineer with a specialization in risk management and holds a PhD in History.

Aytekin Kaan Kurtul is a PhD student and junior lecturer in law at Middlesex University, London. His main fields are public comparative law, public international law and international human rights law, and his research interests include freedom of political expression, academic freedom, the rights of the child and Westphalian sovereignty.

Anna Grøndahl Larsen holds a PhD from the Department of Journalism and Media Studies, Oslo Metropolitan University. She is currently a senior lecturer at the Department of Media and Communication at the University of Oslo. Her research interests include journalism and political communication, comprising topics such as extremism, terrorism and the media.

Nhamo Anthony Mhiripiri holds a PhD from the Centre for Communication Media and Society, University of KwaZulu-Natal. He is currently associate professor and chairperson of the Department of Media and Society Studies at the Midlands State University. His research interests include media law and ethics, business and financial reporting, critical media theory and film studies.

Florence Namasinga Selnes holds a PhD in media and communication from the University of Oslo, Norway. She holds an MPhil. in media studies and first degree in mass communication. She has worked as a lecturer in journalism, media and communication at Makerere University. She currently works as a media and communication researcher. Her research interests include journalism and ICTs, social media, political communication, gender and ICTs.

Contributors **ix**

Aisha Sembatya Nakiwala holds a PhD from the Department of Journalism and Communication, Makerere University. She is currently lecturer at the same university. Her research interests include media, communication and social change, comprising topics such as women's mediated narratives, gender in the media, communication and social protection, as well as community participation, health and social change.

Olunifesi Adekunle Suraj holds a PhD in information science, from the African Regional Centre for Information Science, University of Ibadan, Nigeria. He is currently senior lecturer at the Department of Mass Communication at the University of Lagos. His research interests include media development and freedom of expression comprising topics such as new and social media, internet governance, safety of journalists, media and information literacy.

Gerald Walulya is a lecturer at the Department of Journalism and Communication, Makerere University, Uganda. He holds a PhD in media and communication from the University of Oslo, Norway. His research interests are political communication and journalism.

1

INTRODUCTION

Safety for journalists and self-censorship

Ingrid Fadnes, Roy Krøvel and Anna Grøndahl Larsen

Introduction

Unsafe working conditions for journalists are a growing concern on a global level. Every day we see forms of censorship and other means and actions that may directly or indirectly contribute to repressing free speech and freedom of the press, including surveillance, criminalization of encryption and anonymity, acts of terror, anti-terror laws, hate speech and harassment (Carlsson & Pöyhtäri, 2017). While a murder of a journalist today rarely goes unreported, we know less about practices of self-censorship among journalists, where journalists for safety reasons choose to avoid certain topics, angles, perspectives and so forth in their reporting. Addressing vital issues pertaining to freedom of speech and the press, the present book concerns the relationship between the safety of journalists and self-censorship. Drawing together local case studies from around the world, as well as regional perspectives, the book's main objective is to help us better understand the safety of journalists and self-censorship in both country-specific contexts and from regional perspectives. Together, the contributions in this book add to our understanding of the causes and consequences of self-censorship in different contexts and under different circumstances, as well as what can be done to improve the safety of journalists.

Organizations like the Committee to Protect Journalists (CPJ), Reporters Sans Frontières, Article 19, International Media Support, International Press Institute, IFEX, and local and regional unions increasingly focus on the safety of journalists. In recent years, we have also seen an increased academic focus on the topic. In 2014, UNESCO developed a ten-point research agenda in line with the UN Plan of Action. The agenda has stimulated scientific studies on the very broad and complex matter of journalistic safety. Several higher educational institutions, such as the Center for Freedom of the Media at the University of Sheffield, the University of Gothenburg, the University of Helsinki and Oslo Metropolitan University, have followed up the agenda (Fadnes, Orgeret & Krøvel, 2019). In the search for more knowledge and discussion of self-censorship and the "chilling effect", the 4th Annual International Conference on the Safety for Journalists in 2018 at Oslo Metropolitan University – OsloMet, organized to coincide with UNESCO's International Day to End Impunity for Crimes against Journalists, had a particular focus on this subject. In the call for abstracts the conference asked:

> We need to know more about self-censorship and how it works in relation to journalists' security and freedom of expression in general. How can you talk about self-censorship? How can you know that self-censorship exists? What can make journalists better equipped to secure themselves without having to tie themselves up and jeopardize freedom of speech? What role do state authorities or journalist associations play here?

Studies from around the world were presented at the conference, whose participants included scholars from Bangladesh, Colombia, Egypt, Estonia, Ethiopia, Finland, France, Germany, India, Malta, Mexico, Namibia, Nepal, Nigeria, Norway, Pakistan, Turkey, Uganda, UK, USA and Zimbabwe. This book is coming out of this conference. Bringing together scholars and practitioners from around the world, the book provides new and updated empirical insights into issues concerning the safety of journalists and self-censorship, including attention to a variety of factors – such as surveillance, legislation, threats, gender, violent conflict and digitization – that may affect patterns of self-censorship and in turn impact free speech. In addition to providing empirical insights into safety concerns facing journalists in different geographical contexts, and how these influence journalists' ability to do their job, the book seeks to contribute theoretically and methodologically to the conceptualization and empirical study of self-censorship. Self-censorship is a contested concept, and practices of self-censorship are more challenging to identify than direct censorship. It is our aim to contribute to conceptual clarity – to illustrate and discuss how self-censorship may be studied empirically.

In the following, we discuss the notion of self-censorship, and define self-censorship as used in this book. We then highlight current challenges related to the safety of journalists and self-censorship, before briefly discussing issues concerning responsibility and solutions in addressing self-censorship. Finally, the chapters in the volume are presented.

Self-censorship – a definition

Self-censorship may result from different motivations and can have both positive and negative consequences. This entails that self-censorship should not be regarded as inherently bad. This openness of the notion of self-censorship is illustrated by looking at both dictionary and scholarly definitions of the concept. Merriam-Webster, for example, defines self-censorship as "the act or action of refraining from expressing something (such as a thought, point of view, or belief) that others could deem objectionable". The Cambridge English Dictionary defines self-censorship as "control of what you say or do in order to avoid annoying or offending others, but without being told officially that such control is necessary". Similarly, scholarly definitions within journalism studies include understandings of self-censorship as "the individual self-restriction of one's freedom of speech" (Jungblut & Hoxha, 2017, p. 227), and as grounded partly in journalists' professional norms, personal political attitudes and the editorial stance of the news organizations journalists' work for (Lee & Chan, 2009). Based on these general definitions of self-censorship – highlighting self-censorship as avoiding saying or doing certain things in order to avoid offending others, and integrated in everyday practices of journalism – it becomes obvious that self-censorship may not only be deemed illegitimate, but could also be regarded as a necessary and legitimate part of social relations. Thus, self-censorship may be rooted in phenomena such as fear of physical harm *and* in social responsibility (Jungblut & Hoxha, 2017, p. 223). As noted by Miller:

> For people to successfully negotiate their social world, they must have the ability to suppress their private feelings and thoughts, and equally important, to disguise the fact that they are doing so … Self-censorship is also essential to the smooth functioning society. Civilized life would not be possible were people not able and willing to censor their strongest antisocial feelings.
>
> *(2006, p. 2)*

A crucial question, then, is how to assess whether an act of self-censorship should be deemed legitimate or illegitimate, problematic or unproblematic. One way to come closer in answering this question is to look at the motivation behind self-censorship (Jungblut & Hoxha, 2017, p. 229) – that is, the reasons why journalists self-censor in a given situation or context. Skjerdal (2010) distinguishes between what he terms wide and narrow definitions of self-censorship, pointing out that:

> [Self-censorship] stretches from a wide understanding, seeing self-censorship as an everyday practice for any journalist anywhere in the world caused by the inevitable selection and de-selection processes while reporting and editing; to a narrow definition, entailing only those practices which are performed for the sake of excluding information from publicity due to felt threats by public authorities.
>
> *(Skjerdal, 2010, p. 99)*

In other words, in the absence of direct censorship, the news media are always left with a range of choices in terms of what should be published and how to balance various concerns. Journalistic assessments are partly regulated by ethical codes of the press. Yet journalists and newsrooms nevertheless have to make a number of decisions on *what* issues to report and *how* issues should be reported. In other words, selection and omission are inherent parts of journalism. From the myriad of events

4 Fadnes, Krøvel and Larsen

and issues that could be reported every day, journalists routinely make decisions to omit certain topics, angles or perspectives. While many such decisions go uncontested, others are regularly subject to debate and criticism. One perspective to shed light on self-censorship and issues of legitimacy is Cook and Heilmann's (2013, p. 179) distinction between public and private self-censorship. Within their framework, *public self-censorship* "refers to a range of individual reactions to a public censorship regime". Here, "individuals internalize some aspects of the public censor and then censor themselves". In relation to journalism, Jungblut and Hoxha (2017, p. 227) point out that here, in regard to an existing censor "journalists internalize the rules of what they are allowed to cover and self-censor themselves accordingly". This could for example entail that journalists refrain from reporting a story out of fear of harassment or to protect their safety. As discussed further below, it is public self-censorship, or a variant of Skjerdal's narrow definition of self-censorship, that is the focus of this book. *Private self-censorship*, on the other hand, is, according to Cook and Heilmann (2013, p. 179), "the suppression by an agent of his or her own attitudes where a public censor is either absent or irrelevant". They further note that this form of self-censorship "is a process of regulation between what an individual regards as permissible to express publicly, and that which he or she wishes to express publicly" (p. 179). In relation to journalism, this entails that "journalists might censor themselves because of an assessment of different values such as professional (e.g. an important story) and ethical norms (e.g. a story that is important but might ruin someone's life)" (Jungblut & Hoxha, 2017, p. 227).

In defining the forms of self-censorship dealt with in this book, an important question is the reasons *why* journalists and newsrooms choose not to report news or to omit certain perspectives. An example where both reporting and non-reporting (self-censorship) tend to be contested is terrorism reporting. The Council of Europe report of January 2016 warned against the danger that the fight against terrorism and extremism could lead to disproportionately strict measures at the expense of democratic freedom in order to maintain state security. The report came one year after the terrorist attack on the French satirical weekly magazine *Charlie Hebdo* that killed ten of its staff and two police officers. The phrase *Je suis Charlie*, French for "I am Charlie", was adopted after the attack by supporters of free speech and freedom of expression who were reacting to the shootings. A joint editorial from the European newspapers *Le Monde*, *The Guardian*, *Süddeutsche Zeitung*, *El Pais*, *La Stampa*, and *Gazeta Wyborcza* after the attack stated:

> We continue to inform, to inquire, to interview, to comment, to publish – and to draw – about every subject that appears to us legitimate, in a spirit of openness, intellectual enrichment and democratic debate.
>
> *(The Guardian, 7 January 2019)*

However, the hashtag *#Jesuischarlie* sparked a debate about the limits of free speech. Do you have a right to say, write, and draw whatever you want? Shortly after the attack, the *New York Times* published the opinion "I am not Charlie Hebdo", where columnist David Brooks questioned the right to make satirical drawings based on others religion (Brooks, 2015). These, and other debates, point to how editorial assessments on whether and how to report terrorism may be related to perceived symbolic consequences of the reporting (Larsen, 2018; Mortensen, 2018) *and/or* to concerns related to potential safety risks to journalists as a result of the reporting. While non-reporting grounded in both symbolic concerns and safety concerns can be regarded as self-censorship, in this book our focus is primarily on the latter type; namely cases in which journalists avoid certain topics, angles or perspectives that may be in the public interest, due to perceived physical or psychological risks that publishing could entail. Such risks could include online or offline harassment, physical violence, threats, and other risks potentially affecting journalists' professional and personal safety.

A way to further specify our focus is to distinguish between different forms of self-censorship based on who might be directly affected in the case of publishing a story: the journalist and his or her health, economic or social situation; other individuals, like news sources or person who are reported upon; or a group of people, such as the public or the news organization (Jungblut & Hoxha, 2017, p. 229). The chapters in our book primarily focus on the first form – cases in which publishing is perceived to affect the journalists' health, well-being, economic or social situation; but also to some extent the latter – cases in which reporting could negatively affect news organizations. Thus, although intimidation and self-censorship among sources may pose an equally serious challenge for free speech, this discussion is largely left out of this volume.

Fear can be regarded as a key driver behind self-censorship. This entails that self-censorship "occurs when journalists are not driven by editorial concerns, but by fear" (White, 2014, such as fear of losing their job, fear of risking their lives, or fear for their own mental well-being – and where this pushes them to choose to avoid certain topics and perspectives in their reporting (cf. Yesil, 2014). Thus, while our book is grounded on the notion that all forms of self-censorship have broader consequences in terms of free speech, our point of departure is self-censorship due to perceived risks that journalists face. In sum, our book concerns the safety of journalists and self-censorship, defined as *instances in which journalists avoid seeking out information and/or publishing certain topics, angles or perspectives that may be in the public interest, due to perceived physical or psychological risks – from actors internal or external to the newsroom – that publishing could entail.*

While censorship is relatively easily identified and measured, self-censorship is more challenging to identify, name and quantify (cf. Çipuri, 2015). Since self-censorship here is conceptualized as a consequence of perceived risks, identification of actual self-censorship is available through journalists' interpretations and perceptions (Jungblut & Hoxha, 2017, p. 227). Therefore, in-depth interviews and surveys are important methods to explore self-censorship among journalists. Yet, although we are granted empirical access to journalists' interpretations and perceptions, there is the problem of whether journalists recognize or willingly admit practices of self-censorship. Addressing this, several of the chapters in this book, drawing on surveys and interviews with journalists, not only ask them whether or not they self-censor, but ask a range of questions regarding how they perceive various forms of risk, how perceived risks are handled and how this affects their work. In conjunction with, and in addition to focusing on the experience of journalists, chapters in this book also address various structural issues – for example, legislation and gendered expectations – that may push journalists to self-censor. This entails that the chapters provide insights into structural factors that should be addressed in efforts to improve the safety of journalists and freedom of the press. This is important, because as discussed further below and in the chapters that follow, the causes of self-censorship, and therefore also the solutions, should arguably not primarily be understood as the responsibility of individual journalists, but as something that require collective efforts and structural changes at various societal levels.

Journalism and self-censorship – current challenges

Self-censorship in journalism due to safety concerns is increasingly an area of concern for practitioners, organizations, politicians and academics alike. Simultaneously, there are important regional differences, both in terms of the degree to which journalists experience safety risks and in terms of awareness of self-censorship. Journalists in, for instance, African or Latin American countries, have been aware of both censorship and self-censorship for decades since many of the countries has a recent history of military dictatorship resulting in strong control over the media.

Between 2015 and 2018 the Committee to Protect Journalists (2020) registered 226 murdered, 992 imprisoned and 251 disappeared journalists, confirming a critical situation for journalists at the global level. These overall numbers, however, disguise huge geographical differences in terms of the safety of journalists. China, Egypt and Turkey rank high on numbers of imprisoned journalists. Turkey has an increasing number of jailed journalists, with at least 68 journalists imprisoned in 2018 as a direct result of their profession, whereas China has 47 imprisoned journalists (CPJ, 2020). Countries such as Ethiopia have slowly started a process towards more media freedom, going from 16 imprisoned journalists in 2016 to zero in 2018 (CPJ, 2020). Moreover, CPJ (2019a) identifies Belarus, China, Cuba, Equatorial Guinea, Eritrea, Iran, North Korea, Saudi Arabia, Turkmenistan and Vietnam as the most censored countries in the world, where the media are severely restricted, journalists are intimidated into silence and self-censorship is pervasive. In the Reporters without Borders' Press Freedom Index (2019), the Nordic countries, Netherlands, Switzerland, Jamaica, New Zealand, Belgium and Costa Rica rank on top in terms of press freedom, whereas countries like Sudan, Vietnam, China, Eritrea and North Korea rank at the bottom. In terms of overall regional differences, countries in Europe and Oceania tend to experience higher degrees of press freedom than countries in Africa, Latin America and Asia (Reporters without Borders, 2019).

Factors that may affect practices of self-censorship include surveillance, organized crime, violent conflict, gendered expectations, legislation, media ownership, and form of government (e.g. Lee & Chan, 2009; Simon, 2014 Tapsell, 2012;

Waisbord, 2002). As illustrated in several chapters in this book, the relative importance of different factors may vary between countries, regions and time periods. For example, in many countries corruption and organized crime have impacted negatively on press freedom (e.g. CPJ, 2019a; Waisbord, 2002). In a 2010 special report of the Committee to Protect Journalists – "Silence or death in Mexico's press – crime, violence and corruption are destroying the country's journalism" – Joel Simon (former executive director of the CPJ) states: "In this report, we reveal the culture of bribery and extortion that is producing a devastating self-censorship in Mexico".

In Europe, self-censorship has recently received heightened awareness as journalists are targeted both physically – for example, as prime targets for violent groups – and verbally, particularly through digital media. Four years after the attack on *Charlie Hebdo* the 2019 Annual Report of the Council of Europe paints a disturbing picture arguing that press freedom in Europe is more fragile now than at any time since the end of the Cold War, and that:

> Impunity routinely protects those responsible for violent crimes who deliberately target journalists for their work. Legal protections have been progressively weakened and denied. The space for the press to hold government authorities and the powerful to account has been diminished.
>
> *(Council of Europe, February 2019, p. 5)*

At a global level, The International Committee for the Protection of Journalists (CPJ) expresses its concern regarding safety and self-censorship as follows: little by little, drop by drop, the media integrate security concerns into their news routines and some even anticipate or go beyond security service orders or recommendations. They further argue that although journalists may reject any notion of self-censorship, "caution" has become the byword of "ethical" or "responsible" journalism. Simultaneously, the press not only encounters threats and pressure from potential terrorists or extreme voices. As the chapters in this book document, also other actors and voices, including governments and citizens, pressure journalists into cautious reporting.

Technology, social media and self-censorship

Technology and the Internet make up altered premises for journalistic practices and may both enable and delimit free speech. In this sense, Internet and social media can be regarded double-edged swords in terms of the safety of journalists and self-censorship. On the one hand, the digital media environment provides journalists with a range of tools for information-seeking, collaboration and publishing that may serve to increase the range of perspectives and themes published. On the other hand, digital media come with a range of possibilities for surveillance and for directly and openly posting harassing or threatening comments to reporters. Social media like Facebook and Twitter are a direct and incredibly fast channel to spread messages. The networked structured of these and other platforms makes

8 Fadnes, Krøvel and Larsen

the publishing borderless. Thus, while journalists may publish news or commentary aimed at audiences in a specific geographic context, today's networked media environment makes it impossible to write and publish without taking into consideration that publications may be spread, used, interpreted and misinterpreted, at an incredible speed and well beyond the intended audience. This obviously creates both opportunities and challenges for journalists.

Moreover, digital surveillance poses a number of challenges in terms of journalists' privacy, including security and anonymity in communicating with sources. While digital tools provide easier opportunities for seeking out information and sources, the cognizance of possible surveillance of digital platforms may lead to a chilling effect, in which both sources and journalists self-censor. Similar dynamics may occur in countries where legislation bans online sites, such as in Turkey where social media accounts and news websites critical of the government have been banned (Akgül & Kırlıdoğ, 2015).

Another potential way to silence journalists is to use social media platforms or the online comment sections in newspapers to attack individual journalists. The Philippine journalist Maria Ressa addressed the problem in her keynote speech at the 11th Global Investigative Journalism Conference in Hamburg, noting that social media platforms are "now used as a weapon against journalists, where lies laced with anger and hate spread faster than facts". Online abuse and harassment as a form of risk for journalists have increasingly been a problem over the last decade (TrollBusters, n.d.). While the use of social media and online engagement are increasingly important parts of journalistic work, increased interaction on these platforms also entails increased risk of online abuse and harassment. Michelle Ferrier, the founder of Troll-Busters.com, a project offering what they term "pest control for journalists", shares her story of the consequences of being harassed as a journalist:

> ... I changed as a person. I became angrier. More wary and withdrawn. I had police patrolling my neighborhood. I gave up and quit my job to protect my family and young children.
>
> *(About Us, www.troll-busters.com)*

The quote clearly underlines the potential harmful consequences of online harassment in terms of free speech.

In sum, while the Internet and social media provide opportunities in terms of freedom and information and speech, the ways in which they are used and handled by citizens, governments and organizations pose serious challenges for journalism in terms of safety and self-censorship.

Self-censorship and responsibility

While self-censorship due to safety risks delimits free speech and the free flow of information, pertinent questions are how should it be dealt with, and what can we

Safety for journalists and self-censorship **9**

ask from journalists themselves. At the 2018 Free European Media Conference, Matthew Caruana Galizia, Pulitzer Prize-winning journalist and son of the journalist and anti-corruption activist Daphne Caruana Galizia who was killed in October 2017, called for better standards among journalists:

> Tell stories of ethical and unethical behaviour, talk to each other about self-censorship and do not sacrifice your dignity or betray your readers. Set the bar high for yourself and your trade, set standards and hold yourselves to them. Learn from the examples set by others who've been there before you.
> *(Caruana Galizia, 1 March 2018)*

Similarly, after the Paris attacks on November 13, 2015, the general secretary of the European Federation of Journalists, Ricardo Gutiérrez, said "journalists will not cede to fear". These examples illustrate the important notion that increased violence against journalists should not and must not lead to the silencing of journalists. Yet, important questions are who is responsible and where to look for solutions.

It is arguably hard to ask a journalist or an editor to keep the commitment of freedom of speech and a free flow of information to the public when publishing could risk the lives of the ones who put their names on the work. "I am committed to journalism, but first I am committed to survival", a Mexican editor told Mike O'Connor in an article written for CPJ in 2014. The article was written in the aftermath of the killing of the 29-year-old reporter Valentín Valdés Espinosa who was tortured, bound by his hands and feet, and dumped at a motel, where he was shot dead. In 2010, in conjunction with the publication of the CPJ report "Silence or death in Mexico's press", the Mexican newspaper *El Diario* from the northern city Juàrez published an editorial titled: "What do you want from us?", concerning the crossfire Mexican journalists find themselves in. The question "what do you want from us?" was aimed at narco cartels and corrupt politicians responsible for numerous killings of journalists in the region. Murders of Mexican journalists have only increased since 2010 (CPJ, 2020) and several news outlets have ceased publication in recent years due to violence. One of the latest, the Chihuahua daily *El Monitor de Parral* suspended its print edition after it was firebombed on July 30, 2019. The news editor Esteban Villalobos stated after the bombing that the paper's website would continue, "but it will cease to report on crime or publish stories that could 'represent political bias'" (CPJ, 2019b). Should we then blame Villalobos for lacking ethical standards? Or should criticism be directed elsewhere? We return to these and other related questions in the concluding chapter.

The structure of the book – presentation of chapters

The chapters in this book are written by authors situated within the country-specific contexts they are writing about, many of them with both academic and practical expertise concerning safety of journalists and self-censorship. The context-specific situatedness of the authors entails heightened awareness of pertinent issues

10 Fadnes, Krøvel and Larsen

related to self-censorship, which, we argue, strengthen the chapters' analyses. The book furthermore combines country-specific case studies with chapters providing regional and international perspectives on the topics of the safety of journalists and self-censorship, thus drawing together a range of perspectives that affect self-censorship and free speech, in different contexts and at different institutional levels. Through combining theoretical and practical knowledge, the various chapters in the book strengthen our understanding of topics in much need of research and provide a resource not only for academics, but also for journalism students, practising journalists and NGOs working with issues concerning journalism, safety, free speech and censorship.

In Chapter 2, José Luis Benítez applies the notion of insecure democracies to the three Central American countries, Guatemala, Honduras and El Salvador, to shed light on limitations for the work of journalists, and how such constraints may affect self-censorship among journalists.

In Chapter 3, Sadia Jamil investigates the extent to which safety risks and digital surveillance result in journalists' self-censorship in Pakistan, showing that journalists omit both certain frames and certain topics from their reporting due to safety risks and digital surveillance. Despite self-censoring due to digital risks, journalists are not trained in digital safety.

In Chapter 4, Nhamo Anthony Mhiripiri focuses on how Zimbabwean journalists explain factors leading to self-censorship. He notes that Zimbabwean journalists not only self-censor due to external pressures and fear of reprisals but also due to party politics and economic incentives, and argues that such political and economic incentives are routinized in decision-making processes in Zimbabwean newsrooms.

In Chapter 5, Aytekin Kaan Kurtul explores how *lèse-majesté* regimes – i.e. crimes of insulting the head of state – affect the practice of journalism today. Using Turkey as an example, viewing the case of Turkey in light of relevant case law of the European Court of Human Rights, he argues that *lèse-majesté* laws in principle can be exploited anywhere.

In Chapter 6, Olunifesi Adekunle Suraj examines the perceptions of Nigerian journalists towards the Nigerian Press Council Act (2018) and the Nigerian government's online surveillance. A key finding is that journalists consider government online surveillance to be an impediment to their professional duties, and believe that it is not unlikely that their digital presence is tracked and monitored by government security agencies. As a result, journalists avoid reporting on certain topics considered critical of government and avoid activities on social media that may be considered controversial or suspicious.

In Chapter 7, Marte Høiby presents an explorative theoretical approach to understanding the processes at play when women journalists are threatened and harassed online. Drawing on perspectives from areas such as feminist theory and literature on antipress violence, Høiby argues that female journalists' predisposition to online harassment is largely connected to online governance (or lack thereof), an enduring patriarchy and a rise in threats against journalists.

In Chapter 8, Signe Ivask investigates Estonian female journalists' experiences with harassment resulting in self-censorship. The chapter shows that online harassment towards women journalists makes them avoid writing on topics that they know will result in negative feedback, either from particular sources or from a broader public.

In Chapter 9, Nakiwala Aisha Sembatya focuses on perceptions of risk among female journalists covering political demonstrations in Uganda, and how they negotiate such risks. The chapter documents how reporting of political demonstrations is indeed perceived as risky, preventing women journalists from covering such events. Simultaneously, collective resilience strategies, including "speaking out", support and training, may counter self-censorship.

In Chapter 10, Michelle Betz and Paul Beighley discusses trauma, risk and self-censorship among journalists reporting conflict, and proposes strategies to address psychosocial issues and thus prevent self-censorship among journalists.

In Chapter 11, Florence Namasinga Selnes focuses on Uganda and explores how social media not only serve to undermine journalists' safety, but also are used by journalists to bypass suppression driving them into self-censorship.

In Chapter 12, Gerald Walulya explores the role of NGOs in contributing to minimize self-censorship and encouraging resilience among journalists. The chapter highlights five major roles of NGOs in these respects, including advocacy and networking, documentation and research, training, and provision of free legal aid and financial assistance to journalists.

In Chapter 13, the editors conclude by summarizing and discussing the findings of the chapters in terms of causes, consequences and possible solutions to self-censorship among journalists.

References

Akgül, M. & Kırlıdoğ, M. (2015). Internet censorship in Turkey. *Internet Policy Review*, 4(2). DOI:10.14763/2015.2.366

Brooks, D. (2015). I am not Charlie Hebdo. *The New York Times* (8.1.15). Retrieved from: www.nytimes.com/2015/01/09/opinion/david-brooks-i-am-not-charlie-hebdo. html.

Cambridge English Dictionary (n.d.). "Self-censorship". Retrieved from: https://dictionary. cambridge.org/dictionary/english/self-censorship.

Carlsson, U. & Pöyhtäri, R. (eds.) (2017). *The assault on journalism. Building knowledge to protect freedom of expression*. Gothenburg: Nordicom.

Caruana Galizia, M; Tinius Trust (2018). Self-censorship among journalists. Retrieved from https://tinius.com/2018/03/01/self-censorship-among-journalists/.

Cipuri, R. (2015). Reasons of self-censorship landscape for journalists. AAB College.

Cook, P., & Heilmann, C. (2013). Two types of self-censorship: Public and private. *Political Studies*, 61, 178–196.

Council of Europe (2019). *Democracy at risk: Threats and attacks against media freedom in Europa*. Retrieved from: https://rm.coe.int/annual-report-2018-democracy-in-danger-threats-and-attacks-media-freed/1680926453.

CPJ (2014). Journalists in Hong Kong and Taiwan battle Beijing's influence. Retrieved from: https://cpj.org/2014/02/attacks-on-the-press-hong-kong-analysis.php.

CPJ (2018) *Prison Census*. Retrieved from: https://cpj.org/data/reports.php?status=Imprisoned&start_year=2018&end_year=2018&group_by=location.

CPJ (2019a). *10 most censored countries*. Retrieved from: https://cpj.org/reports/2019/09/10-most-censored-eritrea-north-korea-turkmenistan-journalist.php.

CPJ (2019b). Chihuahua daily El Monitor de Parral suspends print edition after firebombing. Retrieved from: https://cpj.org/2019/08/chihuahua-daily-el-monitor-de-parral-suspends-prin.php.

CPJ (2020). Data & research. Retrieved from: https://cpj.org/data/killed/?status=Killed&motiveConfirmed%5B%5D=Confirmed&motiveUnconfirmed%5B%5D=Unconfirmed&type%5B%5D=Journalist&start_year=1992&end_year=2020&group_by=year.

Fadnes, I., Krøvel, R., & Orgeret, K.S. (2019). Where are we now? (Almost) a decade with the UN Plan of Action on the Safety of Journalists and the Issue of Impunity. *Conflict & Communication*, 18(1).

The Guardian (2019). Europa partnership of newspapers speaks out over Charlie Hebdo attack (07.01.19). Retrieved from: www.theguardian.com/commentisfree/2015/jan/07/europa-newspapers-declaration-charlie-hebdo-attack.

Jungblut, M., & Hoxha, A. (2017). Conceptualizing journalistic self-censorship in post-conflict societies. A qualitative perspective on the journalistic perception of news production in Serbia, Kosovo and Macedonia. *Media, War & Conflict*.

Larsen, A.G. (2018). Newsworthy actors, illegitimate voices: Journalistic strategies in dealing with voices deemed anti-democratic and violent. *Journalism*. Online first. DOI: 10.1177/1464884918760865.

Lee, F.L.F., & Chan, J. (2009). Organizational production of self-censorship in the Hong Kong media. *International Journal of Press/Politics*, 14(1), 112–133.

Merriam-Webster (n.d.). Self-censorship. Retrieved from: www.merriam-webster.com/dictionary/self-censorship.

Miller, Dale T. (2006). *An invitation to social psychology: Expressing and censoring the self*. Thomson/Wadsworth.

Mortensen, M. (2018). The self-censorship dilemma: Media coverage of terrorists in the post-factual era. *Journalism Studies*, 19(13), 1957–1968.

O'Connor, M. (2014). *Media self-censor after killing of Mexican reporter*. Retrieved from: https://cpj.org/blog/2010/01/media-self-censors-after-killing-of-mexican-report.php

Reporters without Borders (2019). *2019 World press freedom index*. Retrieved from: https://rsf.org/en/ranking.

Simon, J. (2014). *The new censorship. Inside the global battle for media freedom*. New York: University of Columbia Press.

Skjerdal, T. (2010). Justifying self-censorship: A perspective from Ethiopia. *Westminster Papers in Communication and Culture*, 7(2), 98–121.

Tapsell, R. (2012). Old tricks in a new era: Self-censorship in Indonesian journalism. *Asian Studies Review*, 36(2), 227–245.

Yesil, M. (2014). The invisible threat for the future of journalism: Self-censorship and conflicting interests in an increasingly competitive media environment. *International Journal of Business and Social Science*, 71–78.

Waisbord, S. (2002). Antipress violence and the crisis of the state. *Press/Politics*, 7(3), 90–190.

White, A. (2014). Fear in the news: The difference between self-censorship and ethical journalism. Retrieved from: https://ethicaljournalismnetwork.org/fear-in-the-news-the-difference-between-self-censorship-and-ethical-journalism.

2

JOURNALISM AND SELF-CENSORSHIP IN THE INSECURE DEMOCRACIES OF CENTRAL AMERICA

José Luis Benítez

Introduction

This chapter analyses the conditions and limitations of journalism and press freedom in the Central American countries of Guatemala, El Salvador and Honduras. These nations share similar elements of internal conflict, political polarization and high levels of violence. Corruption and impunity constitute another feature common to these three countries. In Guatemala and El Salvador, former presidents and vice-presidents have been prosecuted and sentenced to prison on charges of corruption and money laundering. In Guatemala, the role of the International Commission against Impunity (CICIG, Spanish acronym), supported by the United Nations, has been crucial. Likewise, the Salvadoran president Nayib Bukele has signed an agreement with the Organization of American States (OAS) in order to establish a special commission to investigate governmental corruption in El Salvador. This fight against corruption and impunity, including the killing of journalists, is more fragile in Honduras, where political, military and economic elites are unwilling to collaborate with the Mission to Support the Fight against Corruption and Impunity in Honduras (MACCIH, Spanish acronym). Moreover, some relevant cases of governmental corruption and human rights abuses in these countries have been unveiled by investigative journalism; but at the same time, the high levels of violence and political polarization promote conditions for engagement in practices of self-censorship among journalists and news media organizations.

In this context, it is important to analyse the structural constraints on journalism and news media organizations and how these factors also influence journalists' motivations for engaging in practices of self-censorship. Furthermore, the understanding of self-censorship requires the consideration of the media environment in general and how this impacts the performance of journalism and the configuration of the media system. Thus, based on academic research and reports

14 José Luis Benítez

on the situation of press freedom in these countries, as well as my own research and professional practice in the region, I propose some considerations and findings on journalism and implications for self-censorship in these insecure democracies of Central America.

In this chapter, I first introduce some considerations about the concept of self-censorship in the context of journalism and its implications for the rights of citizens to obtain quality information from news media organizations. Second, I discuss the importance of understanding self-censorship and press freedom within the broad media environment, particularly the need to evaluate the consequences of media concentration and the prevalence of a private commercial media system in these Central American countries. Third, I explore the notion of "insecure democracies" and how this concept can be applied to these three countries. Likewise, I evaluate key structural limitations to news media organizations and the practice of journalism: legal, political, economic, professional and organizational, and journalists' sociopsychological characteristics. Fourth, I describe some features of the context of violence in Central America, and specific conditions of press freedom in each of these countries: El Salvador, Guatemala, and Honduras. Fifth, I underline common elements that these countries share regarding the levels of violence against journalists and how these conditions might impact the motivations and practices of self-censorship among journalists and news media organizations. In conclusion, the engagement of social, political, academic actors and journalists' associations is crucial to advance the conditions for freedom of the press and improve the safety and security of journalists in this region. Ultimately, the practices of self-censorship among journalists and the lack of plural and diverse media systems have a harmful impact on the citizens' rights to access quality information, public debate and effective exercise of freedom of expression in a democratic society.

Self-censorship and journalism

There is an important distinction between censorship and self-censorship in the realm of journalism. Murat Yesil (2014), points out that *censorship* entails that outside powers such as governments or private companies establish limitations of what to cover and publish. When journalists *self-censor*, they "are not told to do things openly but they censor themselves, hide some facts that they think would be dangerous to write" (Murat Yesil, 2014, p. 72). Thus, one important question is: what are the specific factors that influence journalists' decision to self-censor in the Central American sociocultural and political context? Estévez (2010) emphasizes that self-censorship implies an act of "controlling what one publishes, writes or says in order to avoid annoying or offending others, but without being told that such control is necessary" (p. 13). Self-censorship can also be analysed as a personal or collective practice in the newsroom, because sometimes journalists make joint decisions with the editor to avoid the publication of certain topics and hide information from other colleagues in the newsroom (Hughes and Márquez-Ramirez, 2017).

Some journalistic practices of self-censorship are motivated by protecting interests of the news organizations, and the decision to avoid the coverage of certain topics because of market pressures on the media outlets (Pew Research Center, 2000). In most Central American countries, journalism is confronted with political and economic powers, because there is an "illegitimate and undue influence of corporate and political interests not only in terms of topics, tones, and frames, but also in the most basic issues regarding journalists' freedom of speech and personal security" (Márquez-Ramírez and Guerrero, 2014, p. 51). In this sense, it is crucial to evaluate key structural limitations to the practice of journalism and news media organizations: legal, political, economic, professional and organizational dimensions, and journalists' sociopsychological characteristics such as age, gender, political views and educational level, among factors that influence the decision to engage in self-censorship (Bar-Tal, 2017).

Moreover, in the context of violence and aggression against journalists in Central America, to engage in self-censorship, sometimes, is a tactic for journalists' self-defence and for the protection of their sources (Sánchez, 2017). In these cases, journalists' decision to avoid the coverage or prevent the publication of certain topics is motivated by external forces beyond professional journalism and ethical considerations. As a result, these practices of self-censorship entail that citizens are deprived of their right to receive crucial information, and the conditions for the free flow of information, freedom of the expression and press freedom are weakened in society. Before I evaluate structural limitations for free press and the practice of journalism, it is pertinent to highlight key connections between democracy and journalism, and how these elements might influence the conditions to engage in self-censorship among journalists.

Journalism and democracy

Journalism has been characterized as the "watchdog" of power, implying a connection between journalism and the prevalence of the collective interest in a democratic society. As Coronel (2002) underlines, "the watchdog press is guardian of the public interest; warning citizens against those who are doing harm" (p. 4). Thus, journalism is crucial for providing quality information to the public, uncovering corruption and human rights violations, and strengthening the mechanisms for transparency and accountability in a democratic society. However, this role of journalism as a counterbalance to power is weakened when media organizations are controlled by non-democratic economic and political interests. In Latin America, according to Márquez-Ramírez and Guerrero (2014), media should be characterized as "a media *establishment* that has not necessarily served the interests of media pluralism and democracy, but the legitimation of political elites and the consolidation of media conglomerates in the region" (pp. 10–11). The Central American media landscape has a dominant private or commercial media system, which excludes the existence of public and community media. This situation is contrary to the international standards on freedom of expression proclaimed by UNESCO (2008) and the Inter-American Commission on Human Rights (IACHR), which appeal for plural and diverse media systems where private, public and community media coexist.

Historically, there has been a concern about the independence of the media from government and private control as a fundamental factor for press freedom and democracy. As Thompson (1995) argues, it is undeniable that "the struggle for an independent press, capable of reporting and commenting on events with minimum of state interference and control, played a key role in the development of the modern constitutional state" (p. 68). Nowadays, it is also relevant to discuss the economic and political factors that promote or constrain access to the media by citizens in general, and by a definitely influenced journalism of social actors. In this sense, as UNESCO (2008) underlines:

> It is not just the absence of restrictions on the media that matters, but the extent to which all sectors of society, especially the most marginalized, can access the media to gain information and make their voices heard.
>
> *(p. 4)*

In summary, the absence of a pluralistic and diverse media system is a decisive limitation for the practice of investigative journalism, particularly through a news agenda that promotes government transparency, civic participation and public accountability (Waisbord, 2012). Likewise, the absence of pluralistic media systems has a negative impact on the levels of press freedom and public debate, and generates conditions for journalists' engagement in practices of self-censorship, particularly when media outlets are controlled by a small number of wealthy families and transnational media conglomerates (McChesney, 2004), as is the case in these Central American countries.

Limitations to media and journalism in the insecure democracies of Central America

The concept of "insecure democracies" refers to formal democratic regimes where there is an enduring context of violence and ineffective application of the rule of law. This notion entails the existence of "uneven performance in the rule of law, accountability and representativeness" (Hughes and Márquez-Ramírez, 2017, p. 514). Although elections are recognized as the formal mechanism for contesting national and municipal administration, in insecure democracies key actors such as the police, judicial operators and other public officials are incoherent or unsuccessful in controlling violence and providing solutions for extreme levels of economic inequality and the condition of marginalized sectors of society (Hughes et al. 2017). I argue that the Central American countries of Guatemala, El Salvador, and Honduras can be analysed through this notion of insecure democracies, because formal democratic aspects coexist with structural conditions of violence, institutionalized corruption and territorial control by transnational youth gangs and organized crime. For instance, in Guatemala and El Salvador during the 1990s, at the end of their respective civil wars there were "peace agreements" between the government and guerrilla organizations, which included political and electoral reforms, the protection of human rights and the incorporation of the revolutionary forces into the political system. However, these political pacts omitted a deep discussion about the socioeconomic inequalities and condition of marginalized sectors of society such as indigenous communities, demobilized combatants and youth.

In this context, I evaluate key structural constrains that influence the work of journalists and news media organizations: legal, political, economic, professional and organizational, and journalists' sociopsychological characteristics. Similarly, it is critical to understand how these constrains also promote conditions for journalists' engagement in personal or collective practices of self-censorship in these Central American countries.

Legal constraints

It is vital to highlight the legal framework related to the work of journalists and news media organizations, specifically laws on free access to public information, laws on defamation, insults and calumny, and "gag laws that aim to discourage critical reporting by imposing hefty penalties on journalists and press organizations" (Waisbord, 2002, p. 385). Even though Guatemala, El Salvador and Honduras have approved laws on access to public information, the implementation of these laws faces several challenges in each country. For instance, Guatemala does not have a specialized institution to enforce the fulfilment of this law, and in Honduras the National Congress blocked access to public information with the approval of a new law on secret information. Meanwhile in El Salvador, as in the other two countries, several public officials and municipal authorities are reluctant to comply with the obligation to govern with transparency and accountability mechanisms established in the laws on access to information (IACHR, 2017). Furthermore, the Penal Code of these countries includes laws on insults, defamation and calumny. In Guatemala, criminal defamation laws have been applied against journalists, particularly by public officials and political leaders. For instance, José Rubén Zamora, director of the newspaper *El Periódico*, was named by former president Otto Pérez Molina and the vice-president Roxana Baldetti. In this case, Zamora was accused of coercion, blackmail and insulting the president and vice-president. Likewise, in Honduras, public officials and individuals have brought proceedings against journalists for what they have published or reported (Committee to Protect Journalists, 2016). As a consequence, some Honduran journalists have suffered abusive judicial trials, received unjust prison sentences and the prohibition to exercise their profession after release (RSF, 2019). Nevertheless, the context of Honduras might change after 2019, when the new Penal Code will come into effect that excludes the so-called "crimes against honour" such as defamation, libel and slander. Hence, through this legal reform, these crimes will be part of civil law and will prevent the imprisonment of journalists (Committee to Protect Journalists, 2019). In El Salvador, despite the

18 José Luis Benítez

inclusion of defamation and calumny in the Penal Code, there have been few cases of judicial demands against journalists and news media organizations. Moreover, Honduras and El Salvador have approved anti-terrorist laws that, in some cases, have been used against communicators, journalists and social leaders. In short, as the Inter-American Commission on Human Rights (IACHR, 2012) has claimed, the existence of these laws directly affects press freedom and "the simple threat of being criminally prosecuted for critical expressions concerning matters of public interest may rise to self-censorship, given its chilling effect" (p. 4).

Political constraints

Political pressures have definitely influenced journalism and the configuration of the dominant media system in Latin America, which Guerrero (2014) characterizes as "captured liberal" model because there is a predominance of private commercial media, conditions that block states' regulatory capacities and that afflict the watchdog role of journalism by economic and political interests. Nevertheless, this captured model does not include the reality of the new digital media landscape, where there are innovative opportunities for more diverse journalistic perspectives and news media platforms compared to traditional media (Guerrero, 2014). Furthermore, government advertising has been used in many countries as a mechanism for promoting clientelism and punishing dissident news media organizations (UNESCO, 2018). Thus, in some conditions of political pressure, news media organizations and journalists engage in self-censorship in order to avoid criticism of the government and the loss of government advertising. In this respect, the Inter-American Commission on Human Rights has condemned the use of government advertising as a mechanism for punishment or reward to certain news media organizations, because these practices are based on "discriminatory aims according to the editorial position of the media outlet included in or excluded from such allocation, and with the purpose of imposing conditions on its editorial position or line of reporting" (IACHR, 2012, p. 6).

On the other hand, political polarization has been another constraint for journalism and independent media organizations. In El Salvador, since 1994, when the former guerrilla organization of the *Frente Farabundo Marti para la Liberación Nacional* (FMLN) became a legal political party, the ideological confrontation has been between this party and the right-wing party *Alianza Republicana Nacionalista* (ARENA). Indeed, these two political organizations have ruled the country for the last three decades until 2019, when Nayib Bukele, with the support of a different party and an emergent political movement won the presidential elections. The political polarization in Guatemala has been related to certain political leaders, cases of governmental corruption and the role of the CICIG in the combat of impunity in the country. For instance, the CICIG investigated and provided strong evidence to prosecute the former Guatemalan president Otto Pérez Molina and the vice-president Roxana Baldetti on charges of illicit campaign finance, illegal association, negotiation of bribes for public contracts, and money laundering. Finally, the Guatemalan president Jimmy Morales in 2019 expelled the CICIG from the country and the progress in combating corruption and impunity made by the CICIG was undermined. In Honduras, the political polarization has had a different dimension after the 2009 coup d'état that overthrew former president Manuel Zelaya. The political instability has been accompanied by attacks on journalists, media organizations and community leaders (Rafsky, 2014). This political polarization has been aggravated by the controversial re-election of president Juan Orlando Hernández in 2017, which has been considered as a fraudulent election and illegitimate by the political opposition and other social sectors of the country. In summary, these political constraints, the pressures of governmental advertising and the context of political polarization influence the conditions and motivations for engagement in self-censorship among journalists and news media organizations in these Central American countries.

Economic constraints

The economic constraints can be evaluated from the framework of the political economy of the media in these three Central American countries. These conditions of media ownership and alliances with economic elites are also crucial to understand the possibilities for diverse and plural media systems, and for the development of investigative journalism and a news agenda connected with citizens' information needs and interests. Although it is difficult to obtain up-to-date data on media ownership and advertising investments, there is evidence of the high levels of media concentration in Guatemala, Honduras and El Salvador (Mastrini and Becerra, 2009). In Guatemala, several radio and television stations are controlled directly or indirectly by the Mexican businessman Ángel González, who also has investments in the media market in several Latin American countries, but in Guatemala alone owns at least four television channels and about 20 radio stations (Mastrini and Becerra, 2009). In El Salvador, the broadcasting sector is mainly controlled by the Eserski family through the *Telecorporación Salvadoreña (TCS)*, and most radio stations are owned by a few radio corporation groups such as *Grupo Radio Stereo, Corporación YSKL* and *Radio Corporación* (Mastrini and Becerra, 2009). Similarly, in Honduras the broadcasting media sector is monopolized by few owners challenges in its effective implementation, particularly the Ferrari family, and two of the national media conglomerates are *Televicentro* in the television sector, and *Emisoras Unidas* in the radio market (Mastrini and Becerra, 2009). Simultaneously, in these countries, the public media outlets are mainly used as a platform for reproducing the ideological and political perspective of the government and political party in power. In this media landscape, community radio and television stations are marginalized or blocked to obtain some share of the electromagnetic spectrum, broadcasting licenses and government advertising; in some cases, community media are mistreated and prosecuted by the telecommunications authorities (Benítez, 2014a).

News media organizations in these countries are also affected by the practices of private advertising and the control of advertising agencies by the same owners of media conglomerates (Mastrini and Becerra, 2009). Thus, some businesses tend to place their media advertisements based on ideological and political alliances with certain political parties or with the government, and consequently constrain the possibilities for independent media to obtain a share of the advertising market (Benítez, 2014b). Moreover, commercial advertising can be a good option for news media organizations to gain independence from governments, but in some cases journalists might be constrained because "investigative reporters can uncover wrongdoing as long as these findings do not affect advertisers or the interests of their employers" (Waisbord, 2002, p. 390). In this way, private advertising and business interests play a major role in promoting limitations to press freedom and influencing conditions for journalists' engagement in practices of self-censorship in these countries. Just as Waisbord (2002) underlines, if there is a lack of newsroom autonomy in the conditions of market and advertising pressure, "fearing irate publishers and board members, reporters are driven to self-censorship" (p. 391).

Professional and organizational constraints

There are several constraints related to professional and organizational elements within the newsroom and media organizations, such as the media outlet's editorial policies, peer pressure, and the absence or lack of implementation of a code of ethics. In these Central American countries, some news media organizations, because of external pressures or perception of potential threats, decided to avoid investigative reporting on topics such as organized crime, youth gangs, drug trafficking, corruption and human rights abuses (Sánchez, 2017). Thus, organizational policies might impact on journalists' engagement in practices of self-censorship and the coverage of sensitive issues. Another factor is the dynamics of peer pressure among journalists within the newsroom and particular national contexts. Indeed, some practices of self-censorship intend to protect in-group relationships and professional reputation (Bar-Tal, 2017). For instance, the decision to avoid the coverage of certain stories is based on the fear of embarrassment or potential damage to a professional career (Pew Research Center, 2000). Moreover, in a work environment with weak stability and insecure labour conditions for journalists, as Waisbord (2002) argues, "self-censorship becomes a survival mechanism to maintain job security" (p. 391). The absence or lack of implementation of a code of professional ethics is another limitation for journalists, particularly when dealing with personal or collective decisions to engage in self-censorship. Few newsrooms and media organizations have their own code of ethics, and while the professional journalists' associations in these countries have a journalists' code of ethics, there are several challenges in its effective implementation. Ethical guidelines and professional support are essential for journalists' decision making as it relates to their engagement in practices of self-censorship.

Journalists' sociopsychological characteristics

Journalists' individual and sociopsychological characteristics also have a role in the motivation and decision making to engage in self-censorship, particularly factors such a gender, age, political views and educational levels. For instance, Bar-Tal (2017) underlines that there is some evidence that "individuals with more conservative views practice and support more self-censorship" (p. 60). Likewise, research conducted in Mexico found that more women journalists admitted having engaged in self-censorship as a protective measure in comparison with male journalists (Hughes and Márquez-Ramírez, 2017). Similarly, it is important to evaluate journalists' level of education and professional experience, and how these aspects influence the decisions to engage in self-censorship. In short, it is crucial to enrich the research on these structural constraints for journalists and news media organizations and emphasize a gender perspective to understand the intricacies of self-censorship, issues of sexual harassment and aggression against women journalists (UNESCO, 2018) and the challenges to improve the conditions for freedom of the press and freedom of expression in these insecure democracies of Central America.

Context of violence and press freedom in Central America

Central America is considered the "most dangerous region to live" according to the United Nations Office on Drugs and Crime (UNODC), because the numbers of homicides or unlawful killings are the highest in the world (UN News, 2019). UNODC data from 2017 reveals that El Salvador had 61.8 homicides per 100,000 people; Honduras had 41.7 homicides per 100,000 people; and Guatemala had 26.1 homicides per 100,000 people. The majority of the victims of this violence are male and young people who live in marginalized communities; some of them are members of youth gangs, and others are victims of the violence perpetrated by gangs and other criminal groups. In this violent context, journalists and media organizations have also been victims of aggressions, intimidations, threats and, in some cases, murders in these Central American countries (Benítez, 2017).

Conditions of press freedom in El Salvador

The World Press Freedom Index by Reporters Without Borders (RSF), which evaluates press freedom conditions in 180 countries, estimates that press freedom in El Salvador has deteriorated in the last decade. In 2010, El Salvador was in the 51st position, but by 2019 it was in the 81st position out of 180 nations evaluated. The Committee to Protect Journalists (CPJ) reports that six journalists have been killed in El Salvador since 1992, and these journalists were covering topics such as delinquency, gangs and politics. The main suspected perpetrators of these killings are youth gangs and other criminal organizations, but most of these cases remain in impunity. In this respect, El Salvador does not have a national protection mechanism for journalists and media workers; however, in 2018 the

Association of Journalists of El Salvador (APES) presented to the Salvadoran National Assembly a legislative proposal for the creation and implementation of protection mechanisms in cases of aggression and threats against journalists. More recently, some journalists and news media organizations have been victims of threats and intimidation in retaliation for publishing reports that reveal the participation of police forces in extrajudicial killings and other human rights abuses (Benítez, 2017). Other journalists and communicators have denounced the existence of political and economic pressure on media owners to end certain broadcast media news and opinion programmes (IACHR, 2017). In 2018, the Office of the Ombudsman for the Defence of Human Rights published a study on the working conditions of female journalists in El Salvador. This investigation found that most women journalists received a lower salary compared with their male colleagues, the existence of discriminatory practices against female journalists within the media organizations, and the fact that all the journalists participating in this assessment recognized that they were victims of sexual harassment and abuse within the newsroom and in their field work (IACHR, 2018). Thus, it is evident the need for more research and advocacy for tackling the phenomenon of gender-based violence against women journalists, and understand how these hostile conditions influence female journalists to engage in self-censorship not only about the topics they are reporting on, but also about their own experiences of being victims of sexual violence and harassment.

Conditions of press freedom in Guatemala

Guatemala, based on the 2019 World Press Freedom Index by Reporters Without Borders (RSF), is in 116th place. According to the Committee to Protect Journalists (CPJ), 24 journalists have been killed in Guatemala since 1992, but most of these murders have not been investigated and the authorities have not determined whether these killings were related to the journalistic work of the victims (IACHR, 2018). The Office of Special Rapporteur for Freedom of Expression of the Inter-American Commission on Human Rights (IACHR) has documented several cases of self-censorship among Guatemalan journalists, and cases of intimidation perpetrated predominantly by local politicians, members of the National Police and organized crime, particularly in areas outside the capital. Hence, the IACHR (2017) has described how in Guatemala "under the difficult working conditions, some journalists have reportedly continued to engage in self-censorship to protect themselves from attacks and threats" (p. 224). Some of these threats are perpetrated by drug trafficking cartels operating in the region, particularly in rural communities, border departments and small cities outside the capital (UNESCO, 2013). In 2005, the Guatemalan government established the Public Ministry Unit for Crimes against Journalists; however, most journalists consider that this unit has been inefficient in responding to the complexity of violence, aggression and the levels of impunity for killing of journalists (Rafsky, 2014). In 2012 the United Nations Universal Periodic Review of Guatemala recommended the establishment of a national protection mechanism for journalists, but until now the government has been ineffective in implementing this recommendation, which is an urgent demand from several Guatemalan media outlets and journalists' professional organizations (UNESCO, 2013). In 2019, Reporters Without Borders expressed its concern because Guatemalan president Jimmy Morales promoted a climate of attacks against journalists, which generated tensions with the press and further promoted practices of self-censorship (RSF, 2019).

Conditions of press freedom in Honduras

Undoubtedly, Honduras is the country with the worst conditions regarding press freedom and violence against journalists in Central America. Indeed, the Special Rapporteur for Freedom of Expression of the Inter-American Commission on Human Rights recognizes that Honduras is one of the most dangerous countries in the region to practise journalism (IACHR, 2017). In the 2019 World Press Freedom Index by RSF, Honduras is in 146th position out 180 countries. Honduran journalists face a variety of types of aggression, stigmatization through social media and attacks perpetrated predominantly by the military police and the army (RSF, 2019). Furthermore, the Honduran president Hernández has implemented several actions to control and silence outspoken journalists and critical media organizations, especially community media and independent media organizations (IACHR, 2017). News media organizations, particularly those located in areas outside the capital, recognize that they do not cover or investigate certain sensitive topics. Journalists have admitted engaging in self-censorship, especially when covering topics such as drug trafficking, money laundering, organized crime, gangs, abuses perpetrated by the police or the army, and high levels of government corruption (Rafsky, 2014). Many Honduran journalists recognize that the failure of the State to investigate the killing of journalists provokes the engagement of self-censorship. Hence, some journalists "self-censor as a result of violence and repression" (Owens, 2014, p. 52). In 2015, Honduras approved a protection mechanism for human rights defenders, journalists and justice system workers; however, this mechanism has encountered several limitations resulting in an ineffective implementation (Rafsky, 2014). In this respect, the Special Rapporteur for Freedom of Expression of the Inter-American Commission on Human Rights has demanded to the Honduran State that this protection mechanism needs to adopt "all the necessary measures to generate trust among journalists and prevent attacks" (IACHR, 2017, p. 254).

Violence against journalists and its impact on self-censorship

In summary, these three Central American countries share at least seven common aspects that constrain press freedom and generate conditions for journalists' engagement in self-censorship, especially for "fear of reprisal by those who feel their criminal or special interests are being threatened by the press" (Estévez, 2010, p. 13).

The following are the factors that have the greatest impact on practices of self-censorship among journalists and media organizations:

(1) State authorities in these insecure democracies of Central America do not comply with their responsibility to prevent, investigate, prosecute and punish crimes and attacks against journalists and media organizations (IACHR, 2017). In fact, some journalists recognize that sometimes they engage in self-censorship as a mechanism for self-protection and their sources (Sánchez, 2017).

(2) Some journalists acknowledge that they avoid covering or self-censor regarding certain sensitive topics and stories, especially those related to organized crime and drug trafficking; instead they base their reporting on official sources, press releases and information from think tanks and foreign embassies (Rafsky, 2014).

(3) Some journalists avoid covering the issue of youth gangs, especially the large youth gangs with territorial presence in these three countries (Rafsky, 2014). In fact, members of these gangs have been sentenced for killing journalists in the region; for instance in 2009 the photojournalist Christian Poveda was killed after he produced the documentary "*La vida loca*", an ethnographic film about the everyday life in one of these youth gangs.

(4) Some journalists in these countries, especially those reporting on public insecurity, violence and human rights abuses, confess that they do not trust police officers (Sánchez, 2017). Thus, some journalists do not report cases of aggression or attacks on public authorities, or in cases of threat and implementation of protective measures, some journalists refuse to be escorted by police officers, because journalists do not have confidence in the police or believe they might be in fact the perpetrators of some of these threats or attacks (Sánchez, 2017).

(5) Journalists working in local and community media in Central America are more vulnerable to several forms of violence and aggressions (UNESCO, 2013). Indeed, from a global perspective there is evidence that "nearly nine out of ten journalists killed worldwide are journalists reporting in their own community" (Smyth, 2012, p. 30). Moreover, a study with Guatemalan journalists found that "journalists outside Guatemala City regularly reported engaging in self-censorship" (UNESCO, 2013, p. 26). Thus, the risk and the fear of becoming a victim of violence influence the conditions for journalists' engagement in self-censorship.

(6) There is an increasing concern about the level of violence, sexual aggression and online harassment against women journalists in these countries, and the practices of self-censorship about these abuses within the newsroom and media organizations. Moreover, there is evidence that online harassment of female journalists can have a chilling effect on women working in the media (UNESCO, 2018).

(7) Journalists in these Central American countries are facing new digital threats, online harassment and intimidations, especially through social media platforms such as Facebook and Twitter. Some of these digital attacks

include doxxing, disinformation and smear campaigns, hacker attacks on news media organizations' web sites, and implementation of sophisticated forms of government surveillance. Consequently, these digital attacks and new forms of aggression and gender-based violence are motivating some journalists to engage in self-censorship and to abstain from using social media as a public platform for expressing their opinions and arguments in the complex and fluid cyberspace.

Conclusion

When journalists engage in personal or collective practices of self-censorship as a consequence of external pressures, violent threats and intimidation, citizens' right to get quality information and partake in informed decision-making processes are significantly undermined. The "watchdog" role of journalism for promoting transparency and accountability is weakened through practices of self-censorship. The prevalence of private media and the absence of strong public and community media configure media systems that lacks diversity and plurality in its news agenda and inclusion of all the political and social sectors of these three Central American countries. Thus, media concentration and the influence of political and economic elites also affect the levels of independence and freedom for the work of journalists and news media organizations.

I have argued that these Central American countries of Guatemala, El Salvador and Honduras can be analysed using the concept of "insecure democracies", because in these nations features of formal democratic regimes coexist with high levels of economic inequality, violence and organized crime. These countries also face critical challenges to overcome institutionalized corruption, an ineffective judicial system and high levels of impunity, especially related to the investigation and prosecution of murders and aggressions against journalists in the region.

The practice of journalism in Central America encounters a variety of structural legal, political, economic, professional and organizational constraints, as well as journalists' sociopsychological characteristics that influence the decision-making process to engage in self-censorship. There is a need for more research to understand the intricacies of self-censorship and to identify the possibilities to strengthen freedom of the press and investigative journalism. In this violent context, the prevalence of attacks and intimidation generates conditions and the inclination for journalists' and news media organizations' to engage in practices of self-censorship. Certainly, journalists from small cities and communities controlled by criminal organizations are the most vulnerable to becoming victims of aggression, and so engage in self-censorship. Nonetheless, many of these journalists in these countries continue with their work with the conviction that journalism is fundamental for the public interest and strengthening democracy.

I believe that it is vital that social, academic, political actors and journalists' associations contribute to improving the conditions for a free flow of information,

26 José Luis Benítez

freedom of the press and freedom of information in Central America. State authorities need to assume their responsibility to prevent, investigate and punish aggression towards and killings of journalists, and effectively support the implementation of national protection mechanisms for journalists and media workers. These mechanisms for the safety and security of journalists should be designed with a gender perspective and implemented according to the fundamental principles established by the United Nations Plan of Action on the Safety of Journalists and the Issue of Impunity. Likewise, the States need to report about the advance on the issue of safety of journalists and access to public information according to the Sustainable Development Goals established by the United Nations.

Ultimately, I think that it is crucial that universities promote more research about self-censorship and training opportunities on safety and security of journalists. Moreover, the active participation of journalists and media workers in associations and organizations is important new forms of professional solidarity, the creation and implementation of code of ethics in the media organizations, and improving the overall conditions of press freedom. Similarly, citizens and civil society organizations should engage in public debates and request support for public policies in order to promote diverse and plural media systems, and the essential exercise of online and offline freedom of expression in these insecure democracies of Central America.

References

Bar-Tal, D. (2017). Self-censorship as a socio-political-psychological phenomenon: Conception and research. *Advances in Political Psychology*, 38 (SI), 35–65.

Benítez, J.L. (2017). Violence against journalists in the Northern Triangle of Central America. *Media Asia,* 44 (1), 61–65.

Benítez, J.L. (2014a). Pluralism, digitalization and the contemporary challenges of media policy in El Salvador. In M.A. Guerrero & M. Márquez-Ramírez (Eds.), *Media systems and communication policies in Latin America* (pp. 122–138). New York: Palgrave Macmillan.

Benítez, J.L. (2014b). El derecho a la comunicación: una mirada desde Centroamérica. *Temas de Comunicación*, 29, 24–48.

Committee to Protect Journalists (CPJ) (2016). *Criminal defamation laws in Central America.* Retrieved July 29, 2019 from https://cpj.org/reports/2016/03/central-america.php

Committee to Protect Journalists (CPJ) (2019). CPJ's database on attack on the press. Retrieved from https://cpj.org/data/

Coronel, S.S. (2002). The role of the media in deepening democracy. Retrieved from http://unpan1.un.org/intradoc/groups/public/documents/un/*unpan010194*.pdf

Estévez, D. (2010). Protecting press freedom in an environment of violence and impunity. *Working papers series on U.S.–Mexico security cooperation.* Woodrow Wilson Center for International Scholars. Retrieved August 3, 2009 from www.casede.org/BibliotecaCasede/Protecting_Press_Freedom%20_Estevez.pdf

Guerrero, M. (2014). The 'captured liberal' model of media systems in Latin America. In M.A. Guerrero & M. Márquez-Ramírez (Eds.), *Media systems and communication policies in Latin America* (pp. 43–65). New York: Palgrave Macmillan.

Hughes, S. & M. Márquez-Ramírez (2017). Examining the practices that Mexican journalists employ to reduce risk in a context of violence. *International Journal of Communication*, 11, 499–521.

Hughes, S., Mellado, C., Arroyave, J., Benítez, J.L., de Beer, A., Garcés, M. & M. Márquez-Ramírez (2017). Expanding influences research to insecure democracies: How violence, public insecurity, economic inequality and uneven democratic performance shape journalists' perceived work environments. *Journalism Studies*, 18, 645–665.

Inter-American Commission on Human Rights (IACHR) (2012). *Principles on the regulation of government advertising and freedom of expression*. Retrieved August 25, 2019 from www.oas.org/en/iachr/expression/docs/publications/ADVERTISING%20PRINCIPLES%202012%2005%2007%20reduce.pdf

Inter-American Commission on Human Rights (IACHR) (2017). *Annual report of the Inter-American Commission on Human Rights. Volume II. Annual report of the Office of the Special Rapporteur for Freedom of Expression*. Retrieved May 10, 2019 from www.oas.org/en/iachr/docs/annual/2017/docs/AnnexRELE.pdf

Inter-American Commission on Human Rights (IACHR) (2018). *Annual report of the Inter-American Commission on Human Rights. Volume II. Annual report of the Office of the Special Rapporteur for Freedom of Expression*. Retrieved May 10, 2019 from http://oas.org/en/iachr/expression/docs/reports/annual/IA2018RELE-en.pdf

Márquez-Ramírez, M. & M.A. Guerrero (2014). Introduction: media systems in the age of (anti) neoliberal politics. In M.A. Guerrero & M. Márquez-Ramírez (Eds.), *Media systems and communication policies in Latin America*. (pp. 1–23). New York: Palgrave Macmillan.

Mastrini, G. & M. Becerra (2009). *Los monopolios de la verdad. Descifrando la estructura y concentración de medios en Centroamérica y República Dominicana*. Buenos Aires: Prometeo Libros.

McChesney, R.W. (2004). *The problem of the media. U.S. communication politics in the 21st century*. New York: Monthly Review Press.

Murat Yesil, M. (2014) The invisible threat for the future of journalism: self-censorship and conflicting interests in an increasingly competitive media environment. *International Journal of Business and Social Science*, 5 (3), 71–78.

Owens, K. (2014). *Honduras. Journalism in the shadow of impunity*. Toronto, Canada, and London, UK: PEN Canada; PEN International. Retrieved August 1, 2019 from https://pen-international.org/app/uploads/Honduras-Journalism-in-the-Shadow-of-Impunity1.pdf

Pew Research Center (2000). Journalists avoiding the news. Self-censorship: How often and why. Retrieved May 7, 2019 from www.pewresearch.org/wp-content/uploads/sites/4/legacy-pdf/39.pdf

Rafsky, S. (2014). *Who is killing Central America's journalists?* Committee to Protect Journalists (CPJ). Retrieved May 7, 2019 from https://cpj.org/reports/2014/09/who-is-killing-central-americas-journalists-impunity-violence-murders-unsolved.php

Reporters Without Borders (RSF). (2019). 2019 World press freedom index. Retrieved May 3, 2019 from https://rsf.org/en/ranking

Sánchez Reyes, M.I. (2017). Periodismo bajo fuego: La nueva guerra del crimen organizado en Centroamérica. *Anuario de Estudios Centroamericanos, Universidad de Costa Rica*, 43, 259–285.

Smyth, F. (2012). Journalist security guide. Covering the news in a dangerous and changing world. Committee to Protect Journalists (CPJ). Retrieved June 21, 2019 from https://cpj.org/reports/2012/04/journalist-security-guide.php

Thompson, J. (1995). *The media and modernity. A social theory of the media*. Stanford: Stanford University Press.

UN News (2019, July 8). Homicide kills far more people than armed conflict, new UN study shows. Retrieved from https://news.un.org/en/story/2019/07/1041981

UNESCO (2008). *Media development indicators: A framework for assessing media development*. Paris: Communication and Information Sector.

UNESCO (2013). Assessment of journalists' safety in Guatemala – Based on UNESCO's journalists' safety indicators (JSIs). Retrieved August 2, 2019 from https://en.unesco.org/sites/default/files/guatemala_jsi_pilot_study_english_july2016_0.pdf

UNESCO (2018). *Global trends in freedom of expression and media development. Global report 2017/2018.* France: UNESCO and University of Oxford.

Waisbord, S. (2002). The challenges of investigative journalism. *University of Miami Law,* (56) 2, 377–395.

Waisbord, S. (2012). Political communication in Latin America. In H. Semetko & M. Scammell (Eds.), *The SAGE handbook of political communication* (pp. 437–449). London: SAGE Publications.

3

RED LINES OF JOURNALISM

Digital surveillance, safety risks and journalists' self-censorship in Pakistan

Sadia Jamil

Introduction

The practice of self-censorship is increasingly considered as a serious threat for the future of journalism (Yesil, 2014). Journalists, in many countries of the world, self-censor due to pressure from governments, media owners and various societal pressure groups (Yesil, 2014, p. 71). The case of Pakistan is complex because the government's and military's intimidations, safety risks and digital surveillance all together have emerged as key factors forcing journalists to exercise self-censorship (Media Matters for Democracy, 2018). Especially, journalists reporting from the north-western tribal areas, the south-western province of Baluchistan and the southern seaport city of Karachi are under direct threat from both militant groups and intelligence agencies (Jamil, 2017a).

Reports by international organizations suggests that violent attacks on Pakistani journalists by extremist groups have considerably declined over the past few years, mainly because of the country's military operations in conflict areas and the expulsion of diverse militant groups from the tribal areas bordering Afghanistan (Reporters Without Borders, 2018). However, journalists feel more intimidated by state surveillance, threatening emails or telephone calls, beating and physical harassment on the streets, or kidnapping by unidentified people. Journalists are more concerned about their own physical safety and that of their families than ever before (Tohid, 2019). Consequently, they are compelled to compromise on their right to freedom of expression and as a precaution they have to practise self-censorship. For example, according to a latest report *Surrendering to Silence: An Account of Self-censorship among Pakistani Journalists* released by Media Matters for Democracy (2018, p. 19), 88 percent of Pakistani journalists exercise self-censorship in their reporting. The report suggests that journalists mostly practise self-censorship due to their news organizational policy (80 percent), sensitive nature of information (80 percent), to protect national interest (65 percent), to protect Pakistan's image (63 percent), fear of legal actions (57 percent) and threat of physical harm to self and family (52 percent) (Media Matters for Democracy, 2018, p. 22). Journalists, in Pakistan, are well aware that the most possible outcome of open and negative coverage of the army and its intelligence agencies would result in their being branded as anti-state or a rebel or a foreign agent.

More recently, there is a growing trend of digital surveillance under the Prevention of Electronic Crimes Act (2016) and the Investigation for Fair Trial Act (2013). Concerns have been raised on the legal provisions of Prevention of Electronic Crimes Act (PECA). A report by the Digital Rights Foundation (2018b, p. 3) suggests:

> The PECA was drafted in light of the counter-terrorism narrative and the National Action Plan aiming to eliminate hate speech and propaganda online by terrorists. Its passage has given even more unchecked power to authorities to regulate online content. Prior to the enactment of the law, requesting the blocking of a website, would require complainants to go through an inter-ministerial committee which would then direct the PTA [Pakistan Telecommunication Authority] to in turn tell internet service providers (ISPs) to block the relevant website. With the passage of the PECA, however, the PTA now has complete authority to directly block whatever it considers to be 'objectionable content'.

On the whole, the language of PECA is vague and so makes the law susceptible to misuse against any individual journalist or media organization. Also, the Act empowers PTA to impose restrictions on access to information. Section 37 of the PECA, for instance, mentions a list of restrictions permitting the PTA to block, take out and censor online content, which is against the integrity of Islam and morality, and which constitutes contempt of court and so forth; many of these aims are not legitimate and are contrary to Article 19 of the International Covenant on Civil and Political Rights (ICCPR).

Thus, the PECA law permits Pakistani state institutions to carry out an uninformed and disproportionate interception of communications by journalists. Now not only journalists' and their sources' privacy is at risk in Pakistan, but journalists are more prone to intimidation and physical risks that also compel them to hold back important information (Media Matters for Democracy, 2018). These facts help us understand that self-censorship has become a noticeable issue in Pakistan's news media. Yet, the details of the issue have largely been unexplored. This study attempts to fill this gap by addressing four research questions, namely: (i) Do Pakistani journalists self-censor due to safety risks and digital surveillance? (ii) What are the key areas of journalists' self-censorship due to safety risks and digital surveillance in Pakistan? (iii) Are Pakistan's journalists aware of safe(er) digital and encrypted communication? (iv) How does journalists' self-censorship affect their right to freedom of expression? To investigate these questions, data has been collected using survey, in-depth interviews (face-to-face) and a document review.

To shed light on these issues the chapter first articulates Reese's hierarchy of influences model and reviews literature on the concepts of censorship and self-censorship in Pakistan. The chapter goes on to explain the methodology of the study. Subsequently, the chapter presents and discusses the findings before concluding.

Literature review

Reese's hierarchy of influence model

Journalism scholars widely recognize that factors affecting news content can be categorized at different levels of analysis (Reese & Shoemaker, 2016). The *hierarchy of influences model* provides five levels of influence on news from the micro to macro levels, namely: (i) individual, (ii) routine, (iii) media organizational, (iv) extra-media, (v) and ideological levels.

At an *individual level*, news content is influenced by an individual journalist's attitude, training and background. The individual level of analysis recognizes the "personal traits of journalists, news values they adhere to, professional roles they take on, and other demographic features (e.g., gender, race, class)" (Reese & Shoemaker, 2016, p. 398), which are considered as affecting their work and their practice of self-censorship. It is largely viewed that journalists do share similar characteristics, values, roles and work routines worldwide despite cultural differences (Deuze, 2005, p. 19; Himelboim & Limor, 2011). In this study, individual journalists are considered as those who are full-time employees of Pakistan's mainstream news media organizations in order to explore how their individual attitudes, traits and demographic features influence the practice of self-censorship.

At a *routine level*, organizational policies, rules and orientations shape an individual journalist's work and news content. These organizational policies and rules enable and constrain the work journalists perform in their day-to-day routine and can also result in their self-censorship (Yesil, 2014). Reese and Shoemaker (2016, p. 400) in the re-assessment of their hierarchy of influences model suggest that "in the past we have thought of news values and occupational norms as a routines-level phenomenon". However, digital technology has transformed newsrooms and journalistic landscapes in many countries of the world by importing new values. A new class of actors including amateur journalists, bloggers, micro-bloggers, programmers and web analysts have emerged who have introduced innovative ways of producing news and distributing and sharing information (Eldridge, 2018). In constrained societies (like Pakistan), it is imperative to evaluate whether these transformations, including fast information distribution and sharing, help to report the truth in the public's interest and whether news organizations' policies force journalists to censor facts.

At an *organizational level*, a journalist operates in a "larger formal structure" of the organization within which they work. This level helps to understand "the influence of power that is exercised within the organizational boundaries, how decisions are made and implemented", and whether these decisions influence journalists to censor facts (Reese, 2001, p. 182).

32 Sadia Jamil

At an *extra-media level*, journalists and news content can be affected by macro-level influences from outside the media organization. This means that an individual journalist or media organization does not have power alone to shape news content, but that other institutions within society (such as government, military, advertisers, etc.) also influence news content. Consequently, fearing possible risks, journalists can be influenced to self-censor their stories.

At an *ideological level*,

> content is a function of ideological positions and maintains the status quo. The so-called hegemony approach locates the major influence on media content as the pressures to support the status quo, to support the interests of those in power in society.
>
> *(Reese, 2007, p. 35)*

This chapter argues that journalists in Pakistan can be influenced by dominant ideologies (i.e. religious ideology) in which pressure from religious organizations and militant groups might lead to the practice self-censorship (see also Jamil, 2017a).

In this study, the rationale for using Reese's hierarchy of influences model is to provide a five-level analysis of journalists' self-censorship in Pakistan. While Reese's hierarchy of influences model focuses on how different forces at different levels shape journalism practice and news content, the model also helps to illuminate the following: (i) the impact of individual journalists' attitudes and other demographic traits on their decisions and routine work, and how this may shape practices of self-censorship by Pakistani journalists operating in a constrained and risky environment, (ii) how organizational rules and policies and the power exercised by organizations' executives may shape practices of self-censorship, and (iii) how forces outside the media organizations (i.e. the influence of the broader environment and dominant ideology in the society) force journalists to censor their news stories. The model contributes to the examination of the levels at which Pakistani journalists exercise self-censorship and what factors at each level contribute to that self-censorship.

The concepts of censorship and journalists' self-censorship

Censorship has a long history and has been used in various ways in different countries of the world. It is generally considered as a tool for curbing truth and manipulating facts (Wilkes, 2013). In the past decade, concerns have been raised regarding the issue of self-censorship among journalists. It is largely viewed that self-censorship is posing more serious threats to journalism practice than censorship by state authorities (Yesil, 2014, pp. 71–75). The literature distinguishes between censorship and self-censorship as two different concepts. Mužíková et al. (2013) suggests:

> In general, there are two forms of censorship in the media: the first is enforced by the state, political, religious or private party while the second stems from the very same party that is publishing the idea or media message. The latter

form is known as self-censorship and is practiced in order to avoid trouble or sanctions from state officials, striking controversy, offending an audience, initiating lawsuits or other problematic consequences.

(Cited in Yesil, 2014, p. 73).

Censorship mostly is exercised directly and provides a clear framework to journalists for do's and don'ts in their routine work by forces including government, military and even the media organizations. *Self-censorship*, on the other hand, is exercised by individual journalists as a "precaution" or a "personal defence" (Tay, 2013). Tapsell (2012, p. 229) suggests that "self –censorship appears, when journalists limit or ignore aspects of a story because they fear repercussions from those with vested interests who are cited in their report".

There can be many factors that cause journalists to ignore or censor facts such as the government's restrictions, political pressure, political or corporate interests of media owners, cultural and religious norms; but also their own attitudes, their personal political and religious affiliations (Mužíková et. al., 2013; Wilke, 2013; Tapsell, 2012; Skjerdal, 2010; Riva-Palacio, 2006; Hayes, Scheufele, & Huge, 2006). Noticeably, the most common reason for journalists to self-censor facts deliberately remains fear, or pressure that forces them to hold back information in any context (Mužíková et. al., 2013).

Journalists' practices of self-censorship arguably vary from country to country. Contextual and cultural differences not only shape journalistic practices, but also the nature of censored issues may vary in different countries. Therefore, the following section reviews the literature on journalists' self-censorship in Pakistan.

Journalists' self-censorship in Pakistan

Pakistani journalists are recognized as the most vocal ones in South Asia, but they are increasingly exercising self-censorship due to pressure being exerted by the military, extremist groups, government, intelligence agencies and increasing security risks (Jamil, 2017a, 2017b; Siraj, 2009; Media Matters for Democracy, 2018; Nadadur, 2007). As stated in the introduction, in a recent study conducted by Media Matters for Democracy (2018, p. 22), 88 percent journalists in Pakistan say they self-censor their work – 63 percent stated that they do it to protect Pakistan's image and 65 percent said that they do it to protect the national interest. The report also highlights that Pakistani journalists are compelled to practise self-censorship in religious and state affairs because of the country's Official Secrecy Act (1923) and harsh blasphemy laws (i.e. Pakistan Penal Code, 1860). For instance, the study conducted by Media for Democracy highlights that surveyed respondents practice self-censorship when sharing information and opinion about military and religion in Pakistan. The report reveals that:

> Respondents admitted they were most likely to self-censor information and opinions about the military and religion in their professional work and

personal conversations. Pakistan's powerful security establishment has historically kept a strong check on the flow of news and information in the country. Religious groups in the country are quick to label dissenting voices un-Islamic and often invoke anti-blasphemy law clauses against any form of expression that goes against their interpretation of religious beliefs. Security-related matters and religion appear to be two main areas where journalists seem unwilling to take many risks.

(Media Matters for Democracy, 2018, p. 8)

Widespread surveillance of journalists' digital communications by government and intelligence agencies has raised concerns among journalists and media workers in many countries. When analysing the case of Pakistan, online threats are also one of the major factors fostering journalists' self-censorship in the country. For example, according to a recent report by the Digital Rights Foundation (2018a), 78 percent male and female journalists experience online threats and harassment (p. 6) and 45 percent of them exercise self-censorship due to digital insecurity (p. 9). Considering these facts, this study addresses the challenges to Pakistani journalists in relation to digital surveillance, safety risks and self-censorship, in order to make recommendations that may mitigate these challenges.

Methodology

This study uses the quantitative method of survey and the qualitative method of in-depth interviews (face-to-face). Using *purposive sampling*,[1] a total of 100 male and female journalists (in a ratio of 70 to 30 percent respectively), who are full-time employee of Pakistan's mainstream media organizations, participated in the survey. The closed-ended questions for research questions one and three in this study seek to explore journalists' responses as straightforward "yes" or "no". For research question two, the multiple-choice question seeks to investigate the key areas of their self-censorship. Almost all journalists, in the survey, have provided their feedback comfortably. However, five male journalists did not provided their feedback comfortably and expressed their fear of participation in a research project that focuses on digital surveillance in Pakistan.

In addition, using purposive sampling, 25 working journalists from Pakistan's mainstream news media organizations have also been interviewed, 17 male and 8 female, ranging in age from 30 to 60 years old. Each was interviewed for approximately 45 minutes. All interviews were conducted in Urdu (i.e. the journalists' mother tongue) and later interview transcripts have been translated into English verbatim. All the journalists who participated in the study, surveys and interviews, were full-time employees of 23 mainstream media organizations of Pakistan.[2] The main location of data collection was Karachi, which is the media hub of the country. In order to ensure the privacy and safety of interviewees, their names have been replaced by letters (between A and W). Moreover, the study uses *relative frequency statistics*[3] to present the survey results in the form of percentages and *thematic analysis*[4] to analyse the gathered data under five key themes that have emerged from the research questions of the study.

Findings

Journalists' self-censorship, safety risks and digital surveillance in Pakistan

The study's survey results show that 93 percent of the respondents say they self-censor news stories due to physical, financial, legal, topic-specific and the public risks.[5] Journalists' survey responses reveal that 85 percent of them self-censor sensitive information by virtue of digital surveillance of their mobile phone and online communications. The interview data validate the finding that the journalists exercise self-censorship because of offline and online safety threats. According to one of the interviewees from a local television news channel:

> Pakistani journalists are not physically safe because of target killing, kidnapping and mob lynching. Journalists are financially threatened by unnotified job terminations and they are forced to censor facts that affect the vested interests of media owners, government and army. Online threats and harassment have increased in recent years. Male and female journalists both face the risks of email hacking, verbal abuse on social media, threatening mobile calls and messages through SMS and WhatsApp. Female journalists are more vulnerable to online sexual harassment. So, it is not only the risks of kidnapping or murder, but digital risks have rather increased the chances of physical threats to journalists [...] Journalists have two options: either to censor their professional and personal communications or to use clues, code language and hints to communicate with their sources.
>
> *(Interviewee O)*

The interview data reveal that the journalists who self-censor because of digital surveillance are not only concerned about their own safety and privacy of communication, but also that of their sources. For instance, a male television news producer states:

> I know a couple of incidents in which my colleagues' sources were attacked and physically harmed. Surveillance of mobile phone communication is risky for journalists and their sources both because it is very easy for intelligence agencies to locate the source.
>
> *(Interviewee B)*

Similarly, another male journalist from an Urdu-language newspaper talks about digital surveillance and self-censorship in Pakistan and states:

36 Sadia Jamil

> Journalists' online and mobile communications are constantly monitored and I have faced online harassment through threatening WhatsApp messages and emails many times. So, my editor is quite careful and he usually prefers not to report any story that may result in any sort of harm to me and my colleagues. We exercise caution.
>
> *(Interviewee I)*

In this study, some interviewed journalists explicitly highlight that self-censorship occurs at various levels. For example, a male interviewee from an English-language newspaper suggests:

> Self-censorship is occurring at various levels. Individual journalists practice self-censorship not only because of any sort of threat and pressure, but also because of their demographic features – especially ethnicity. I am a Balochi. At times I have censored my news stories related to missing people of Balochistan and army because of safety risks. Ideologically, journalists' religious and political school of thoughts also motivate them to construct the news story to reflect particular religious or political perspectives, which turns news story into an opinion piece lacking truth or facts. Some of my colleagues censor actual facts related to news stories of political parties that they do not like. At a routine level, media organizations have different policies that defines a journalist's level of freedom and his/her practice of self-censorship. Pakistan's media has always been fragmented in right and left wings. Therefore, news content is censored according to the organization's policies that reflect its religious and political affiliations. Media organizations have their political and corporate interests too, which decide the level of journalists' self-censorship in most of the media organizations.
>
> *(Interviewee J)*

Moreover, the interview data also highlight that self-censorship occurs at the extra-media level, which means the impact of structural (contextual) factors within which journalists and media organizations operate in Pakistan. For example, a majority of interviewed journalists (17 out of 25) mentioned the government's pressure, military and intelligence agencies' interventions in journalists' work, political pressure, cultural barriers, religious restrictions, growing violent extremism and crimes as the key factors in their self-censorship.

Key areas of journalists' self-censorship due to safety risks and digital surveillance

The survey findings show that 93 percent of the respondents say they self-censor information related to military/or intelligence agencies and 74 percent say they self-censor information related to government's policies and actions. Moreover, due to safety threats, 98 percent of the respondents say they censor stories related to religion, and 61 percent say they censor stories related to politics. Moreover, a number of the respondents (37 percent) say that they exercise self-censorship when reporting on social issues, such as stories about homosexuals and sex. The interview data substantiate these findings and reveal three main implications of journalists' self-censorship:

- Journalists are unable to cover sensitive stories especially related to national security, military/or intelligence agencies and religious affairs because of safety risks and digital and physical surveillance.
- Journalists are unable to report on details of corruption cases at government and other institutional levels due to threats and digital and physical surveillance.
- Journalists feel abuse of their right to freedom of expression when they "mould a news story" or "manipulate or censor actual facts" due to pressure from various groups (including the government, military/or intelligence agencies, political parties, religious groups and media owners) or due to safety risks and digital surveillance.

In addition, some interviewed journalists highlight that self-censorship occurs in business reporting as well. For instance, according to a male reporter from an English-language newspaper, "I have censored corruption cases in corporate sectors a couple of times only because of my editor's and owner's policy of not reporting misdeeds of those with whom the organizations share corporate interests" (Interviewee D). This implies that government and military are not the sole players making journalists self-censor, but that media owners' policies (i.e. organizational influence) may also lead to self-censorship.

Figure 3.1 explains the key areas of journalists' self-censorship in Pakistan. The figure illustrates the percentage of surveyed journalists who say they exercise

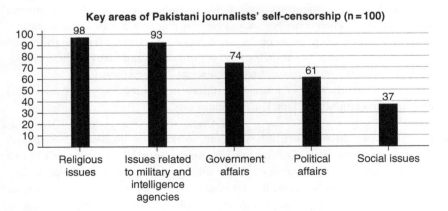

FIGURE 3.1 Key areas of journalists' self-censorship due to safety risks and digital surveillance

self-censorship when reporting on affairs related to government, military or intelligence agencies, politics, religion and society/or culture (RQ2: what are the key areas of journalists' self-censorship due to safety risks and digital surveillance in Pakistan?)

In addition, in response to the survey's closed-ended questions about whether journalists self-censor news stories at routine level and whether they censor their personal communication on mobile phone, email, WhatsApp and other social media, including Facebook and Twitter, the data show that 65 percent say they self-censor their news stories at routine level and 20 percent of them censor their personal communication due to digital surveillance and risks related to it. Interviewees' feedback also suggests that the promulgations of the Prevention of Electronic Crimes Act (2016) and the Investigation for Fair Trial Act (2013) have enabled government and intelligence agencies to monitor communication between journalists and their sources. One serious implication of this surveillance is an increased level of physical risk to journalists and their sources, apart from affecting the privacy of communication between the two parties.

Journalists' level of awareness for safe digital and encrypted communication

The survey results indicate that while 17 percent (49 out of 70) of the male respondents are aware of safe digital and encrypted communication, 6 percent of the female respondents (2 out of total 30) are familiar with the concept of encrypted communication. Interview data reveal that no proper training is given to journalists to make them aware of possible digital risks, even in big media organizations.

The interviewees' responses also highlight that many journalists do not pay attention to individual safety measures such as the use of VPN, password protection for communication devices, use of protected Wi-Fi access and customized privacy settings on social media. A few interviewed journalists (4 out of 25) suggest that there should be courses at university and media organization level that teach journalism students and professionals safe digital communication and how to protect themselves from cybercrime. For example, according to a female reporter from a television news channel: "most of the journalists do not receive training for digital safety either at university or at their media organizations, and many of them are not aware of internet-related risks and technical terms" (Interviewee Q).

Talking about the role of journalists' unions in training journalists for digital safety and laws around it, a female news editor says:

> Trust me! Many journalists who are working in small-scale newspapers and television news channels are not even aware of the concept of VPN or encrypted communication or simply how to be a safe user of digital devices. Then many journalists do not know about the concepts of cyber and digital crimes. How can you expect them to apply safety tools in digital communication? Neither universities nor journalists' unions pay attention to train journalists for digital safety and legislation related to it. Big media organizations

do organize in-house training sessions but that does not reflect the situation of entire Pakistan. [...] Rural journalists across Pakistan are in such a miserable condition that they even do not know how they are being monitored digitally and what can be consequences of digital risks for their physical safety.

(Interviewee L)

Hence, this study reveals the necessity of journalists' digital safety training, which is imperative to improve their physical security while at work and in their personal lives.

The implications of journalists' self-censorship for their right to freedom of expression

Survey findings suggest that all of the participating journalists agree that they have to compromise on their right to freedom of expression due to self-censorship. The interview data substantiate these findings and reveal that Pakistani journalists are unable to exercise their right to freedom of expression, particularly in their professional lives, because of threats to their physical safety, and surveillance of their mobile and online communications. For instance, according to the editor of an Urdu-language newspaper:

Censorship has a long history in Pakistan. Earlier, there used to be an open state censorship through promulgation of laws and suspension of newspapers' licences. Now, government and army use indirect means to exercise control that forces journalists to self-censor the news content. Then there are different types of safety threats. People think that it is the threat of murder or kidnapping that fears a journalist. No! Journalists do mould and manipulate facts to safe their jobs and quite often they do so to avoid mob attack and lynching especially if the news story is related to any religious issue.

(Interviewee R)

Despite being unable to exercise their right to freedom of expression, interviewed journalists' responses highlight some other implications of their self-censorship as well. For example, an interviewed journalist states:

Many journalists have left their profession because of government's and owner's pressure of censoring facts. They are not comfortable with the frequent use of hints, clues and code language in their professional and personal lives. Journalists' self-censorship is not only affecting their right to freedom of expression, but also people are not receiving the information they ought to receive.

(Interviewee H)

40 Sadia Jamil

What role are journalists' unions playing in discouraging the trend of self-censorship that is silencing journalists in Pakistan? To answer this follow-up question, this study suggests that a majority of interviewed journalists are not satisfied with the role of journalists' unions in discouraging the practice of self-censorship in the country. Interviewees' responses show that journalists' unions rather tend to persuade journalists to exercise caution, even if that means self-censoring their reports. With regard to this, a senior journalist from a television news channel says:

> Journalists' unions are divided into groups in Pakistan. Just take the example of Karachi Press Club. One can find two to three journalists' groups operating there. Therefore, it is tough to have a collective action or policy to combat safety risks and self-censorship. Yes, there is one point upon which most of the journalists' unions agree and that is to exercise 'caution' and to be careful.
>
> *(Interviewee M)*

Despite being segregated in different groups, the Pakistani journalists need to have mutual efforts to combat threats to their safety at all levels (i.e. individual, routine, organizational and institutional). Merely exercising caution in the form of self-censorship is not enough to ensure their safety; rather it shall continue to create a chilling effect on their right to freedom of expression.

Discussion and conclusion

Journalism is a risky profession in Pakistan. A decade ago, the risks and challenges journalists confronted were limited to their physical security across the country. Some recent studies have revealed that the Pakistani journalists do face other types of risk including psychological, financial, legal, topic- and gender-specific, public and digital risks (Jamil, 2017a). In particular, Pakistani journalists face digital or online threats in various forms which include, but are not limited to, being hacked, threatened, blackmailed, harassed over a sustained period of time, sexually harassed, having their data stolen, being cyber-stalked, receiving malware or phishing emails.

While some attention has been paid by Pakistan's government to improve the physical security of journalists, there has been a delay in understanding the intertwining of journalists' digital and physical safeties and the implications for their work and practice of self-censorship. With regard to this, in a UNESCO report, Henrichsen, Michelle and Joanne (2015) underline that "a large proportion of journalists killed in recent years were easy targets because they were exposed by the digital tools they use" (Digital Rights Foundation, 2018a, p. 2; see also Henrichsen et al., 2015). Interviewees' feedback, in this study, also reveals that journalists' physical safety has been severely threatened due to digital risks and surveillance and that this is the key reason for their practice of self-censorship. As illustrated by this statement from a senior journalist in a local English-language newspaper, "journalists' kidnapping, unlawful detention, forced disappearances and murders are some serious forms of physical risks that are fostering self-censorship in Pakistan's news media" (Interviewee C).

The Investigation for Fair Trial Act (2013) permits the government and intelligence agencies to monitor journalists' and citizens' online data (such as emails and WhatsApp messages), telephone calls, and any form of computer or mobile phone-based communication, subject to a judicial warrant.[6] The Prevention of Electronic Crimes Act (PECA, 2016) was passed by Pakistan's National Assembly after the 2014 Peshawar school attack by a terrorist group. The law was passed under the National Action Plan by Pakistan's government to combat terrorism. PECA was formulated to deal with the digital risks of cyber-stalking, online harassment, forgery, blasphemy and forms of cyber-terrorism. However, the PECA law suffer from lacunae because of vague legal language that affects the public's right to privacy and criminalizes their right to freedom of expression. For example, the law has certain provisions that do affect the journalists' and their sources' privacy and criminalizes their right to freedom of expression and more broadly put them at risk of surveillance

The journalists' interview responses suggest that the growing trend of journalists' self-censorship is due to safety risks and digital surveillance in Pakistan. For example, 93 and 85 percent of journalists surveyed in this study say they self-censor due to safety risks and digital surveillance respectively. The study shows that journalists self-censor their personal communication, both to protect themselves and their sources from any physical harm and to ensure privacy of their communication. This is illustrated in the following statement: "No one would like to die or be kidnapped just because of being a journalist's source. We often use hints and clues to censor our professional and personal communications to ensure safety and privacy both" (Interview H).

Interestingly, it is not always safety risks and the pressure of surveillance that causes journalists to self-censor. The study reveals that some Pakistani journalists also self-censor because of their demographic features (especially ethnicity) and personal religious school of thought and political affiliations. For example, one interviewee states: "I know many journalists who censor facts just to support their particular religious sect and political party. Their reporting reflects biases towards people of other ethnicities in Pakistan. This is unethical" (Interviewee F).

Moreover, the findings show that self-censorship also occurs due to policies of media organizations. The following statement from a senior male television news reporter sums up this point:

> Every media organization has its own policies, rules and vested interests that largely define the religious and political ideology of owners. Journalists have to follow these policies in their routine and at times news stories are censored accordingly.
>
> *(Interviewee K)*

The study furthermore highlights that a majority of interviewed journalists (17 out of 25) say they self-censor news stories because of government's pressure, military's and intelligence agencies' interventions in their work, political pressure, cultural barriers, religious restrictions, and growing violent extremism and crimes. In particular, journalists say they often self-censor issues related to military/or intelligence agencies, government, religion, politics and some social matters (such as sex, homosexuals, adultery etc.) (see Figure 3.1). Some interviewed journalists note that avoiding writing on certain matters is also caused by the policy of media owners. For instance, according to a bureau chief of television news channel, "None of my stories can be on-aired without the permission of owner, especially if it is related to the army or some political parties. Many times, the content of my stories are changed" (Interviewee L).

A point of concern is that the journalists are neither aware of tools for digitally safe and encrypted communication, nor are they trained to protect themselves from digital risks. The survey results indicate that journalists rather censor their professional work and personal communication instead of adopting tools that can provide them with better and safer ways of digital communication. This chapter suggests the need to introduce comprehensive courses at university level that teach journalism students how to communicate safely using digital technologies.

To sum up, this study clearly indicates that Pakistani journalists face various kinds of insecurities and that they are prone to massive digital surveillance. These issues should be evaluated and addressed legally by state authorities. If ignored, the online threats and harassment against journalists and risks associated with their digital surveillance will arguably keep growing, thus maintaining or evening strengthening practices of self-censorship, affecting the public's right to know and the journalists' right to freedom of expression.

The right of journalists to carry out their work under safe conditions, without fear of being monitored, harassed, attacked, beaten and killed is of paramount importance for freedom of the press and freedom of expression. Past studies have highlighted a number of multi-faceted factors that cause journalists to self-censor facts such as government restrictions, political pressure, political or corporate interests of media owners, cultural and religious norms; but also their attitudes, personal political and religious affiliations (Mužíková et. al., 2013; Wilke, 2013; Tapsell, 2012; Skjerdal, 2010; Riva-Palacio, 2006; Hayes, Scheufele, & Huge, 2006). These past studies into self-censorship have mostly revealed causes of journalists' self-censorship with a lesser clarity about how different factors result in their self-censorship at micro (i.e. individual journalists' attitudes and ideologies), meso (i.e. routine and organizational levels) and macro (i.e. broader institutional) levels. This study uses Reese's hierarchy of influence model, which has helped to underline explicitly diverse constraints/or factors that cause the Pakistani journalists to censor information at various levels. Drawing on Reese's hierarchy of influences model, this study shows that Pakistani journalists are compromising on their right to freedom of expression and are compelled to practice self-censorship at individual, routine, media organizational and extra-media levels. Consequently, they are not only prone to psychological stress, but also they feel less empowered to perform their journalistic roles and to exercise their right to freedom of expression.

Freedom of expression is a fundamental human right. It also underpins most other rights and permits them to flourish. The right to express ideas and opinions freely on important issues and have access to information play a crucial role in the healthy development process of any society. A lack of freedom of expression and any limitation on it, either through laws and regulation, any sort of pressure or threat that results in journalists' self-censorship, is a problem that particularly can affect the marginalized communities in Pakistan such as non-Muslims (i.e. Hindu, Christian, Parsis and Ahmedis). Moreover, this study shows that the challenges of widespread surveillance and the digital risks associated with it cannot be viewed as something "less important" than physical security and both need to be considered as equally important for the creation of a secure atmosphere for journalists to work in.

When it comes to recommendations to combat self-censorship, the author urges the Pakistani government to carry out an independent review of laws protecting journalists' online and offline safety, thereby to ensure that the right to freedom of expression is robust and effective. More importantly, there is a need to introduce reforms to Prevention for Electronic Crimes Act (2016) and the Fair Investigation Trial Act (2013), which have become a legal tool for mass surveillance in the country.

In addition, the author urges the introduction of comprehensive courses at university level that teach journalism students how to communicate safely (either in professional or personal lives) using digital technologies. There should be training programmes by media organizations and journalists' unions for promoting awareness of digital risks and safety among journalists. The author also stresses that any training programme must differentiate between cyber and digital safety because these are two different notions. For instance, cyber security refers to the technologies, processes, and practices that are designed to protect networks, devices, programs, and data from attack, damage, or unauthorized access (Carlson, 2019). On the other hand, digital security is a comprehensive term, which incorporates diverse tools that a journalist can use to secure their identity, assets and technology in the online and mobile world (Mitra, 2010). The tools that a journalist can use to protect his or her identity include: anti-virus software, web services, biometrics and secure personal devices he or she carries with him or herself in routine. While, there is no big difference between the two, making journalists aware of both notions is imperative for discouraging the growing culture of self-censorship in Pakistan.

Notes

1 Purposive sampling refers to the "selection of certain groups or individuals for their relevance to the issue being studied" (Gray et al., 2007, p. 105). The purposive sampling has been chosen so as to ensure the representation of journalists from the selected mainstream media organizations that have nationwide coverage in Pakistan.

2 This study includes journalists from 25 media organizations in Pakistan including: Ten television news channels (i.e., SAMA News, Geo News, ARY News, Express News, Dunya News, Ab Tak News, AAJ News, JAAG News, Channel 92 and Pakistan Television Corporation); seven English-languages' newspapers (Daily Dawn, The News International, Express Tribune, The Nation, Daily Times, Business Recorder and Pakistan Today); six Urdu-languages' newspapers (Daily Jang, Daily Express, Nawa-e-Waqt, Daily Ummat, Khabrain and Daily Jurat)

3 "A relative frequency is the fraction of times an answer occurs. To find the relative frequencies, the researcher are required to divide each frequency by the total number of students in the sample. Relative frequencies can be written as fractions, per cents or decimals". (Dean and Illowsky, 2010, p. 1)

4 Thematic analysis helps to classify data under relevant themes in order to interpret the various aspects of research topic (Boyatzis, 1998; Braun & Clarke, 2008).

5 "Physical risks here refer to the risks of killing, kidnapping, detention, imprisonment, physical or sexual assault, rape, injury and any sort of physical attack that may lead to physical disability and harm. Financial risks mean the threats of job insecurity, pay-scale disparity and forced job terminations. Legal risks include the existence of impunity for crimes against journalists; unfair trial against journalists; manipulation and abuse of laws against journalists and the existence of stringent media laws. Public risks refer to the threats that are caused because of violent, unethical and abusive attitudes of the local public towards journalists, such as verbal abuse and physical harm or attack" (Jamil, 2017b, p. 10).

6 "Under Chapter 2 (Section 5), a warrant can be requested wherever an official has "reasons to believe that any person is likely to be associated with or is beginning to get associated with, any act leading to a scheduled office, or is in the process of beginning to plan such an act, or is indulging in such a conduct or activity that arises suspicion that he is likely to plan or attempt to commit any scheduled offence". This weak threshold ("reasons to believe") fall short of the standard of "reasonable suspicion" set by human rights law and it provides too broad a discretion to allow for the request of a warrant" (Digital Rights Foundation, 2018b).

References

Boyatzis, R.E. (1998). *Transforming qualitative information: Thematic analysis & code development.* Thousand Oaks, CA: Sage.

Braun, V. & Clarke, V. (2008). Using thematic analysis in psychology. *Qualitative Research in Psychology,* 3 (2), 77–101. Retrieved from: www.tandfonline.com/doi/pdf/10.1191/1478088706qp063oa.

Carlson, C. (2019). *How to manage cyber security risk: a security leader's roadmap with Open Fair.* Irvine: Brown Walker Press.

Dean, S. & Illowsky, B. (2010). *Sampling and data: frequency, relative frequency and cumulative frequency.* Retrieved from: www.saylor.org/site/wp-content/uploads/2011/06/MA121-1.1.3-3rd.pdf.

Deuze, M. (2005). What is journalism? Professional identity and ideology of journalists reconsidered. *Journalism,* 6, 442 – 464. Retrieved from: http://jou.sagepub.com/content/6/4/442.full.pdf+html.

Digital Rights Foundation (2018a). *Digital insecurity of journalists in Pakistan.* Retrieved from: https://digitalrightsfoundation.pk/wp-content/uploads/2018/01/Report-Digi-Insecurity-of-Journos.pdf.

Digital Rights Foundation (2018b). *Content regulation in Pakistan's digital space: June 2018 Human Rights Council Report.* Retrieved from: https://digitalrightsfoundation.pk/wp-content/uploads/2017/12/DigitalRightsFoundationSubmissionSpecialRapporteurFreedomofExpression.pdf.

Eldridge, Scott II. (2018). *Online journalism from the periphery: Interloper media and the journalistic field*. London: Routledge.

Gray, P.S., Williamson, J.B., Karp, D.A. & Dalphin, J.R. (2007). *The research imagination: An Introduction to qualitative and quantitative methods*. New York: Cambridge University Press.

Hayes, A.F., Scheufele, D.A. & Huge, M.E. (2006). Nonparticipation as self-censorship: Publicly observable political activity in a polarized opinion climate. *Political Behaviour*, 28 (3), 259–283.

Henrichsen, J., Michelle, B. & Joanne, L. (2015). *Building digital safety for journalism. A survey of selected issues: UNESCO report by the Division for Freedom of Expression and Media Development*. Retrieved from: unesdoc.unesco.org/images/0023/002323/232358e.pdf.

Himelboim, I. & Limor, Y. (2011). Media institutions, news organisations, and the journalistic social role worldwide: A cross-national and cross-organisational study of codes of ethics. *Mass Communication & Society*, 14 (1), 71–92. Retrieved from: http://dx.org/10.1080/15205430903359719

The Gazette of Pakistan. (2013). Investigation for Fair Trial Act. Retrieved from: www.na.gov.pk/uploads/documents/1361943916_947.pdf

Jamil, S. (2017a). Freedom under pressure? Threats to journalists' safety in Pakistan. In: Carlsson, U. and Poyhtari, R. (Eds.), *Assault on Journalism*. Gothenburg: NORDICOM.

Jamil, S. (2017b). Freedom of expression and threats to journalists' safety: an analysis of peace journalism education in Pakistan. *Journal of Association of Journalism Education*, 6 (2), 7–16.

Media Matters for Democracy (2018). *Surrendering to silence: An account of self-censorship among Pakistani journalists*. Retrieved from: http://digitalrightsmonitor.pk/wp-content/uploads/2018/05/report-1.pdf.

Mitra, A. (2010). *Digital security: cyber terror and cyber security*. New York: Chelsea House.

Mužíková, D., Chaaban, T., Salomon, J. & Lee, J.C.Y. (2013). *Global self-censorship struggles: Lebanon, Mexico, China, Hong Kong and Slovakia*. Retrieved from: www.salzburg.umd.edu/media-innovation/journalism-self-censorship.

Nadadur, R. (2007). Self-censorship in Pakistani Print Media. *South Asian Survey*, 14 (1), 45–63. https://doi.org/10.1177%2F097152310701400105.

Prevention for Electronic Crimes Act. (2016). PECA Bill. Retrieved from: www.na.gov.pk/uploads/documents/1470910659_707.pdf

Reese, S. (2001). Understanding the global journalist: A hierarchy-of-influences approach. *Journalism Studies*, 2 (2), 173–187

Reese, S. (2007). Journalism research and the hierarchy of influences model: A global perspective. Retrieved from: https://bjr.sbpjor.org.br/bjr/article/viewFile/116/115.

Reese, S. & Shoemaker, P. (2016). A media sociology for the networked public sphere: the hierarchy of influences model. *Mass Communication and Society*, 19, 389–410.

Reporters Without Borders (2018). *World Press Freedom Index*. Retrieved from: https://rsf.org/en/ranking.

Riva-Palacio, R. (2006). *Self–censorship as a reaction to murders by drug cartels*. Nieman Reports. The Americas. Summer 2006.

Shoemaker, P. & Reese, S. (1996). *Mediating the message: Theories of influence on mass media content*. New York: Longman.

Siraj, A. (2009). *Critical Analysis of press Freedom in Pakistan*. Retrieved from: https://aiou.edu.pk/SAB/gmj/GMJ%20Fall%202008/Article_1.pdf.

Skjerdal, T. (2010). *Justifying self-censorship: A perspective from Ethiopia*. Retrieved from: www.westminsterpapers.org/articles/abstract/10.16997/wpcc.149/.

Tapsell, R. (2012). Old tricks in a new era: Self-censorship in Indonesian journalism. *Asian Studies Review*, 36, 227–245.

Tay, S.J. (2013, September 17). Self-censor. Thoughts. Retrieved from: http://tayshaojie. com/self-censorship/.

Tohid, O. (2019, May 16). The resistence of Pakistani journalism is dying – and it frightens me. Retrieved from: www.dawn.com/news/1482657.

Wilke, J. (2013, May 08). Censorship and freedom of the press, In: *European History Online* (EGO), published by the Leibniz Institute of European History (IEG), Mainz 2013-05-08. Retrieved from: www.ieg-ego.eu/wilkej-2013a-en.

Yesil, M. (2014). The invisible threat for the future of journalism: Self-censorship and conflicting interests in an increasingly competitive media environment. *International Journal of Business and Social Science*, 5 (3), 71–78

4

CHILLING OR COSY EFFECTS?

Zimbabwean journalists' experiences and the struggle for definition of self-censorship

Nhamo Anthony Mhiripiri

Introduction

Censorship and self-censorship are global phenomena for good or for bad, and Zimbabwe is no exception. This chapter uses experiences and examples of Zimbabwean journalists to investigate the complexity of the phenomenon of self-censorship. It approaches self-censorship – the process whereby a journalist decides not to write or speak about essential issues of public interest – as influenced by structural (economic and political) issues as well as personal ones. Studies of the constrictive practices of censorship and self-censorship are numerous, emphasizing how they inhibit the media from performing their ideal roles of serving the public interest, promoting democracy, protecting human rights and exposing graft and malfeasance (Forster and Fackler 2011; Schroeder 2019). The chapter explores and evaluates how and why Zimbabwean journalists reach decisions to self-silence particularly on matters of public interest. The state, powerful social institutions, economic forces and individuals have historically interfered with or exercised direct control on the media (Williams 2010). According to Kevin Williams (2010), journalists always report to the public a small fraction of what they know, but not because of external pressure alone. Fear of offending authorities and powerful interests makes them self-censor. Self-censorship may now be increasingly prevalent, with the knowledge amongst journalists that they are likely to be under constant surveillance from state authorities (Williams 2018). It is this chapter's major concern to investigate what causes censorship and self-censorship amongst Zimbabwean journalists, and how Zimbabwean journalists understand and relate to self-censorship. This study thus problematizes the blaming of external sources, especially when journalists appear complicit in self-censorship in order to further their group or personal interests. When journalists self-censor not because of fear of violence or threats or other safety concerns, it is a much more insidious and devious act since firstly, such an act can pass without an outcry from the concerned journalists, and secondly, such wilful concealment of vital information undermines the public's right to know.

The chapter first presents a critical methodology for the study, followed by a brief explanation of the Zimbabwe socio-politico-economic and legal environment in which media practitioners operate. Journalism is theorized as a public service that must not be curtailed through censorship or self-censorship. Then the analysis is presented, focusing on how journalists explain factors leading to self-censorship and how they practise or experience it. Zimbabwean journalists' enunciations are critiqued against the backdrop of journalism as public service serving the public interest. The penultimate sections of the chapter discuss the role of donors or funders and the influence of restrictive media laws on self-censorship. Newer studies are showing that donor funding imposes self-censorship tendencies in journalists in specific instances (Wasserman et al. 2019). Ironically, when the Zimbabwean government was the darling of international donors in the early years of independence, it was not stringent in its muzzling of the media (see Chuma 2005), but when the same government went out of favour it systematically repressed the media.

The Zimbabwe Crisis and a restrictive media environment

Zimbabwe is a country of paradoxes, complexities and ambiguities. The dominant media image is often negative, and observers would believe it is a country at war, which is not the case. In the post-Mugabe period international watchdogs for freedom of the media and freedom of speech like Index on Censorship and Reporters without Borders continue to put Zimbabwe under the spotlight, with condemnations of shutdown of the internet or arrests/abductions of leaders of social movements, such as Pastor Evan Mawarire or Dr Peter Magombeyi. The Zimbabwe Crisis has received wide coverage, especially during the rule of former President Robert Mugabe. The USA and the EU imposed sanctions on the country, ostensibly to force the government to respect human rights and the rule of law. Critics noted abuses of freedom of expression and freedom of the media; hence, media reforms are always part of negotiations for a return to normalcy. Over the years, there have been abuses of journalists, notably, the arrest under the colonial Law and Order Maintenance Act (LOMA) and the detention and torture of journalists Ray Choto and Mark Chavhunduka at Cranborne Barracks in 1999, the abduction and torture of Jestina Mukoko in 2008, and the disappearance of journalist and activist Itai Dzamara in 2015. Choto and Chavhunduka had written and published in the *Standard* the story about 23 disgruntled soldiers who allegedly tried to wage a coup. Besides these abuses, there are also recorded cases of bombings of a printing press, closures of newspapers, harassment, beatings and murder of journalists, confiscation of equipment and forced deletion of photos. Media civil society organizations have systematically recorded these abuses of media freedoms and the Media Institute of

Southern Africa (MISA-Zimbabwe) publishes cases annually in the journal *So this is democracy*.

Although, since the ouster of President Robert Mugabe, there have been efforts to reform media law, several statutes remain that are inconsistent with the constitutional provisions on free expression and media freedoms. Media civil society and activists have campaigned against some laws that they condemn as draconian and stifling free expression. These laws include Access to Information and Protection of Privacy Act, Criminal Law Codification Reform Act, Interception of Communication Act and Broadcasting Services Act. Since these laws were used against many journalists over the years (Petras 2003, p. 168–172), there is a general view that their presence makes journalists self-censor for fear of costly and traumatizing arrest and prosecution. These laws are condemned as constituting strict national security laws, overly protecting the reputations of the President, Police and Defence forces. Whilst criminal defamation was ruled unconstitutional in 2014, journalists are convinced politicians and prominent persons use defamation suits to harass and intimidate the media.

Censorship/self-censorship and journalism as public service

At their idealized best, journalism and all forms of public media and communication serve the public interest. Good citizenship requires an astute informative journalist practice (Dahlgren and Sparks 1993). Regardless of whether the media are privately or community or publicly owned, the loftiest ideals of journalism locate the practice within public service (Coleman 2017, p. 334).

There are certain conditions that promote or "inhibit the realization of such a high-minded aspiration", according to Coleman. Such inhibitions include serving the narrow interests of personal advancement, class privilege and institutionalized loyalty at the expense of a universal public. While cases of direct censorship are measurable due to their overt nature and a media watchdog can take stock of them, self-censorship is rather difficult to establish unless journalists account for it. Moreover, there may be different reasons for self-censorship, including self-enhancement and self-aggrandizement, and these may be more or less institutionalized (Mabweazara 2010; Chuma 2013). This chapter argues that in fragile economies, such as Zimbabwe's, economic and financial imperatives can subordinate expected virtuous professional norms, standards and practices such as serving the public interest and promoting social justice. Amongst other challenges, political interference, polarized and partisan journalism and corruption are rife in Zimbabwe's legacy journalism (Chuma 2013: Shava 2013). The political interference and partisan journalism within Zimbabwean media practices are compounded by what Mabweazara (2010, p. 105) describes as "everyday newsroom practices and professional cultures" that are "rooted in occupational and organizational demands". The political and economic environment is not exempted from exerting pressures that manifest themselves in editorial policies and proprietary demands, hence affecting the sociological routines of news production such as source cultivation, selection and deployment (Mabweazara 2010, p. 105).

Notwithstanding Zimbabwe's structural problems and constrictive legal environment, journalists do self-censor for both personal gains and fear of repercussions, and it is worrisome when their testimonies considerably attest to the influence of personal gain in particular. This is often to enable them to cope in an adverse economic and political environment. Admittedly, it is difficult to neatly separate the influence of structural conditions on personal professional decisions. The contra-distinction of an ethical journalism calls upon journalists to reject base instincts as both professionals and individual citizens in a broader public community where their actions are determined by the best values enshrined in their inner consciences (Holt, 2012). They should be driven by the righteousness of their convictions instead of external pressures or inner selfish pursuits. All decent journalism and media codes of standards are clear about such values.

Definitions and theorization of self-censorship

Definitions of censorship and self-censorship are closely related although there are liminal differences between the two concepts. According to Ramadan Çipuri, "Ordinary censorship typically provides us with a duality: a censoring authority and the censored communicator" (2015, p. 76). Self-censorship, however, internalizes and operationalizes that duality within the same person, in that one impulse or desire moves the person in the direction of expressing something, but some other impulse or desire prevents the person from expressing it.

Media scholars tend to agree that censorship and self-censorship are usually intricately interrelated. Thus, Ramadan Çipuri (2015) regards censorship and self-censorship as "parts of the same vicious circle". Ironically, in spite of the perceived viciousness, Çipuri acknowledges that the effects of self-censorship are either "good" or "bad". Depending on contexts and situations, "good" self-censorship is motivated by lofty ideals such as promotion and protection of the national interest for public security concerns, protection of confidential information concerning victims of sexual assault, minors, amongst other considerations. "Bad" self-censorship has depraved motives such as protection of sectarian interests, or promotion of group or personal gain at the expense of the public interest. What is important is to unravel the two critical questions: (1) what causes censorship and self-censorship? and (2) how do Zimbabwean journalists understand and relate to self-censorship? Using Randal Marlin's classification of censorship, Ramadan Çipuri (2015) notes there are economic, political and personal *motives* for censorship/self-censorship. There are also personal and institutional *levels* at which censorship occurs. Self-censorship takes different *forms* induced by different *pressures* (Çipuri 2015, p. 79)

When writers self-censor, there is no record, they just stop writing or avoid certain topics and these decisions are lost to time. Without being able to record and document isolated cases the way we can with explicit government censorship, the only thing we can do is identify potential drivers to self-censorship. Media and communications scholar Terje S. Skjerdal (2010) emphasizes the "external pressures" and limitations imposed on self-censoring journalists. He posits:

> I define self-censorship as the withholding of journalistic material due to felt external pressure. Importantly, this definition involves not only limitations caused by government interference, but also those provoked by other actors and conditions, including cultural expectations and in-house procedures.
>
> *(2010, p. 99)*

Indeed, it might be difficult to extricate external origins from that which first evolves within the person. Of course, there is an interplay, but my argument is that journalists should also take responsibility and to some extent their decisions not to write or say are a personal choice that subordinates or undermines serving the public interest and social justice. The sense of self permits the person to engage with *one's* self and with external others. I am more comfortable with the definition which assigns both external and internal/personal motives for self-censorship. This definition does not over-emphasize the coercive factors behind self-censorship at the expense of personal volition.

In a previous study with Ethiopian journalists Skjerdal (2010, p. 99) discovered his informants identified four justifications for self-censorship, namely, relegation of ethical responsibility; elasticity of journalistic editing; confidence in critical audiences; and adherence to social responsibility. Whilst exploring the conflict between self-censorship and journalistic professionalism, Skjerdal (2010) distinguishes between acceptable and unacceptable self-censorship practices as experienced by Ethiopian journalists. He discovers the journalists rationalize why they restrain themselves from publishing critical information. Relegation of ethical responsibility is when the news organization for which the journalist works imposes editorial censorship on their behalf, thereby removing ethical responsibility from the journalist. Elasticity of journalistic editing entails soft censorship that involves hiding facts with the connivance of the editorial desk. Where journalists, especially in state affiliated entities, realize that audiences see through their lies and concealment of facts, they persist with their devious methods with the consolation that the audiences know the facts. Adherence to social responsibility is when journalists comply with notions of rulers' perception of the media's duty to practise development journalism in line with the government's official policies.

"Voluntary" self-censorship and the Zimbabwean context

The definition of censorship denotes direct or overt restriction on free expression or freedom of the media. The popular understanding of self-censorship involves a person's involuntary self-silencing (Skjerdal 2010; Miller 2006; Williams 2010). A journalist's *intentional* but non-virtuous act of self-censorship is often overlooked, especially when there is complicit acceptance of perspective, or normalization/

52 Nhamo Anthony Mhiripiri

naturalization of the ordinarily unacceptable. Systems and ideologies can condition individuals to self-censor using what Louis Althusser has termed Ideological State Apparatuses and Repressive State Apparatuses. The Zimbabwean Crisis that has resulted in the polarization of Zimbabwean media along political lines demands a re-evaluation of the notion of self-censorship. Instead of merely focusing on the involuntary nature of self-censorship, there is a need to reconsider instances when journalists self-censor and voluntarily comply with political and commercial interests at the expense of serving the lofty ideals of the public good and public interest.

Harassment, intimidation, arrests and other forms of restriction of free expression against journalists lead to chilling effects. Numerous examples exist where Zimbabwean journalists were abused (Mukundu 2008: Mhiripiri 2015; see also MISA annual reports) and their rights violated, leading to the adoption of self-preservation by such journalists and others when faced with the choice of whether to write or not to write, to tell or not tell. The chilling effect is almost always obvious in such instances.

However, in addition, journalists are systematically recruited into party and commercial systems, collaborating with powerful interest groups and formations. Some Zimbabwean journalists blatantly promote particular political interests, or are active party members. Several journalists contested as political candidates for both the ruling ZANU-PF and the opposition party Movement for Democratic Change.

The transitional period after the fall of President Robert Mugabe brought optimism with it, but given that political tensions often escalate during electoral years such as 2018, it is important to ascertain the incidence of forced or voluntary self-censorship. This is especially important given the role of Zimbabwe's military and secret police in imposing restrictions on journalists, some of them extrajudicial, since the late 1990s. There is a systematic record of the interference of these state apparatuses in the operations of journalists. Evaluating self-censorship in the Zimbabwean context is important especially when journalists voluntarily self-censor in collusion with the hegemonic economic or political authorities. This is dangerous because the public interest is sacrificed through political and economic expedience or personal aggrandizement. My research findings and analysis starting immediately below after my section on critical methodology on self-censorship partly reveal that self-censorship becomes a suspect scheme in which the journalist is embroiled.

A critical methodology of self-censorship and the public interest

Using the Zimbabwean experiences, this chapter calls for the exploration and evaluation of the concept of self-censorship in a realm where journalists are expected to both make ethical decisions and exercise freewill, including when making job-related decisions that impinge on the public's right to know. The study is based on systematic archival research and media monitoring of cases concerning Zimbabwean journalists' brushes with the law and authorities since the late 1990s up to now when MISA Zimbabwe and Media Monitoring Project of Zimbabwe[1] recorded important cases. It also makes use of journalists' own discussions on private social media groups on *Facebook* and *WhatsApp* on censorship and collusions of journalists with political and economic powers. I am friends with numerous journalists on *Facebook* and *WhatsApp* and often receive their posts and conversations which gave me insights into their attitudes on journalistic ethics. I conveniently selected the revealing posts that confirm the prevalence of self-censorship, although in most instances their authors presented themselves as ethical and upright. Interviews on the subjects of censorship and self-censorship were conducted with selected journalists using a snowball approach. Sixteen practising journalists were interviewed in 2019 using emailed questionnaires; nine of them having attained senior levels in the profession, and five were editors. All collected materials were subjected to critical discourse analysis (CDA) in order to ascertain their thematic and ethical slants, and what implications the statements contain pertaining to the furtherance of the public interest, democratic principles and promotion of social justice. The interviewed journalists were evenly selected, three each from privately owned and publicly owned newspapers and broadcasting stations, including the Zimpapers, Associated Newspapers of Zimbabwe, Alpha Media Holding, AB Communications and Zimbabwe Broadcasting Corporations. One interviewee has worked for a state security magazine. Due to the sensitivity of the information that was required of them, all of the journalists, except for two in the privately owned media, requested confidential protection of their identities. I have therefore opted to extend confidentiality also to those who were prepared to have their names published in order to create uniformity of presentation. I have also deliberately mentioned the names of the media companies that own various titles under their name so that the informants are not traceable to a particular title. All the interviewed journalists are university graduates holding a journalism or media studies degree, and 14 of them had a master's degree as their highest academic qualification, or they were studying towards such a degree. These journalists are amongst Zimbabwe's most educated and are conversant with the critical ethical requirements of their profession.

The journalists were directly asked to state which of the following types of story were likely to be affected by self-censorship: political stories, sports and entertainment, and business stories. Gender and LGBTI, climate and environment, and donor-based stories, amongst possible other categories, were implicitly addressed in a section on "any other" influences of self-censorship. A previous study conducted on the incidence of self-censorship pertaining to reporting homophobia in Zimbabwe's newsrooms is also used to augment the findings for the current chapter (Mhiripiri 2014). In this earlier study, journalists were explicitly interviewed on whether their news organizations had policies on reporting homosexual and queer sexualities, and whether the journalists were comfortable reporting on such issues.

54 Nhamo Anthony Mhiripiri

Forty journalists responded to the questionnaire. The journalists were drawn from a cross-section of newspaper companies, radio stations and electronic media houses. Among them were three editors, one director and six freelancers not attached to any specific media house.

Some of the submissions in this chapter emanate from critical discussions or publications on *Facebook* and *WhatsApp*. I conveniently chose relevant topics that journalists discussed on news production practices. Journalists have discussed their own operations in social media platforms in which I am a member.

Zimbabwe's prolonged economic and political crisis starting from the late 1990s certainly has traceable influences on how journalists operate. The questionnaires administered to journalists did not specifically mention the crisis in order for the journalists to mention it for themselves. The assumption was that asking a question on the Zimbabwean crisis and the related sanctions imposed by Western governments on the ZANU-PF government could easily make respondents focus on that at the expense of other possible pertinent influences over self-censorship. As such, the focus on the "purposive" actions of journalists beyond the structural causes is a deliberate methodological approach with its own limitations. The limitations of this research include the failure to gather specific responses from female journalists, although questionnaires were circulated to the media houses mentioned above.

It is unarguable that Zimbabwe's restrictive media laws influence journalists to self-censor as a precautionary measure. However, in the specially administered questionnaires that provide the bulk of my findings below, Zimbabwean journalists did not specifically cite the media laws and their potential to influence self-censorship. Of course, observation of the laws and ethics on protection of reputation, for instance, makes journalists practise cautionary self-censorship lest they are penalized for breach of law. Several other laws have been criticized as "draconian" and their amendment or repulsion are part of the reforms that are demanded to improve Zimbabwe's democratic climate. In the questionnaire responses, the journalists paradoxically did not specifically pinpoint any law as a cause for self-censorship. Constantly living alongside the laws might have resulted in them taking them for granted and so much a matter of fact that they did not find a single mention in the questionnaires.

While there is the Interception of Communications Act which allows the state to snoop into the affairs of private citizens and other juristic persons, no journalist expressly mentioned that he or she is now restrained in the manner they write due to fear of state surveillance. The state's use of new digital technologies was not directly mentioned as an inducer of self-censorship, notwithstanding the journalists' consistent condemnation of repressive laws that have hindered free expression over the years. The absence of condemnation of the laws in the formally administered questionnaire, however, is contrary to the scathing criticism of the same laws I have heard journalists articulate at local gatherings such as workshops, or when some of them discussed with me in confidence and informally.

Below, the findings on the phenomena of Zimbabwean journalists' self-censorship and the analysis of journalists' opinions and actions are presented.

Zimbabwean journalists' understanding of self-censorship

The interviewed journalists' definitions of self-censorship tended to concur with the preceding academic conceptualizations that emphasize how external powerful forces compel journalists or any others communicator to curtail what type of information they can publish. Understated or not stated at all is the journalist's voluntary, intentional or self-willed/personal choice of self-censoring. Where they confirm or attest to the act of self-censorship journalists often adopt the identity of victims, thereby absolving themselves of responsibility in the act of self-censoring (Skjerdal 2010: Mabweazara 2010). They rather point to external factors that push them to self-censor. In the case of state-affiliated media journalists, they blame the editorial management and ruling party politicians for the silencing of certain perspectives, and those working in the privately owned media often blame proprietary powers and newsroom/editorial culture. The will to hold onto a job and survive in an adverse socio-economic environment is not left far off behind absolving self-blame or blaming powerful external other forces. In the following definitions on self-censorship, the first three directly or implicitly blame an outside other for the decision to self-censor. Only Journalist C defines without blaming either an external other or the internal self.

Editor 1

> Self-censorship *is* the act of censoring oneself because you fear governments, politicians etc. It is the exercising of control over what one says and does, especially to avoid criticism. It can also be as a result of interference by a company's leadership, politicians or a result of yellow journalism where the reporter is paid for killing stories. Thus self-censorship is characterized [by] fear, hypocrisy or otherwise.

Journalist A

> This is when a journalist controls what they say or publish in order to avoid annoying owners/shareholders of the media house they work for, the politically powerful, advertisers or in some instances audiences. This can be done without overt pressure from anyone but just the thinking of the consequences that will visit the journalist upon publishing of the story.

Journalist B

> Self-censorship is whereby journalists do not write or publish certain stories for fear of losing or jeopardizing their jobs or offending the authorities. It is a sort of self-preservation whereby the journalists look the other way to save their jobs.

Journalist C

> It is a decision made consciously by a journalist not to cause publication of a story or article in the newspaper, media house he or she works for. In short, not to write a story or stories even if all information has been availed to him or her and, by all measure, constitute a news article.

Fear is a key denominator in self-censorship especially where there is a culture of impunity on arrests, imprisonment, harassment and violence against journalists. A culture of violence against journalists is prevalent throughout the world (Cottle et al. 2016; Clark and Grech 2017, p. 221). During former President Robert Mugabe's rule, there were many documented cases of violence and abuse of journalists in Zimbabwe. Such cases linger in journalists' memories. The most frightening prospects are abductions, torture or elimination of journalists. The disappearance of journalist and activist Itai Dzamara in 2015 is still too recent for Zimbabwean journalists to forget.

The practice of self-censorship in Zimbabwean media: Which stories are likely to be affected by self-censorship?

From the information gathered through responses to questionnaires administered to Zimbabwean journalists, their discussions on *Facebook* and *WhatsApp*, and my informal discussions with them over the years, Zimbabwean journalists' accounts partly resemble the Ethiopian narratives Skjerdal (2010) cites, although there are variations in the justifications. Barely do the journalists mention "ethics". Newsroom routines and fear of losing a job for failure to adhere to employer expectations rank highest, with 12 out of 16 mentions. Political interventions attracted seven mentions. Audiences as controlling stakeholders are only mentioned when journalists self-censored stories on queer sexualities.[2]

Most Zimbabwean journalists implicate external causes or pressures for the incidence of self-censorship. Largely blamed are outside powerful forces that often induce fear, hence the cautious decision to practise restraint as a form of self-preservation. Rarely are personal volition and free will cited as the basis for the decision to self-censor. As noted above, self-censorship is not inherently bad. Nonetheless, self-censorship due to self-preservation or self-advancement is chilling.

The respondents were evenly divided on which story content was likely to elicit self-censorship. Fifty per cent indicated that all types of stories were malleable to self-censorship, and another 50 per cent cited political and business stories as the ones mostly to be affected. Of the first group, Editor 1 explicitly states, "In my view self-censorship applies to all news beats. It actually depends on where one's allegiances lie". Journalist B was more elaborate:

> All [story] categories [are likely to be affected by self-censorship]. Political stories for obvious reasons. Business stories, because the company being

written about can happen to be a big advertiser. Gender and LGBTI – given the homophobia culture in Zimbabwe journalists may end self-censoring themselves. Climate and environment – such stories can involve the politically powerful or big business. Sports and entertainment – the negative effect some stories can have on the sports or arts personalities' careers can lead to self-censorship. Some of these personalities are politically connected or sponsored by big business who are advertisers.

Editor 2 noted that seemingly innocuous news beats such as the entertainment and religious desks are seriously corrupted since top Zimbabwean pastors and musicians bribe journalists in order to bar their criminal or moral transgressions from publication. Journalists in lower ranks end up despairing and not writing about the shenanigans of the musicians and pastors/prophets when they realize their stories are killed/spiked. However, they suspect that newsroom gatekeepers conveniently use their investigative stories to further extract bribes and rent from the rogue musicians and pastors. A journalist with a tabloid newspaper said:

> We just stop writing about the pastors and musicians because we realize we are lining senior editors' pockets. Any new such story only gives corrupt editors bargaining power with the personalities that they protect from public exposure.

On ideology, editorial interference and newsroom routines

Adherence to a preferred ideology espoused by the media proprietors, or that supported by government and the ruling party, is intertwined into the newsroom routine regardless of whether one is working for the state-controlled media or the privately owned media. Editors act as gatekeepers and ensure news production routines are observed to the satisfaction of proprietors, advertisers, political actors and other significant stakeholders depending on the nature of the story. Journalists used terms such as "political correctness", "correct ideology", and so forth, to qualify this tendency. Once again external pressures are interlinked with a journalist's "choice" to self-censor which, however, is a matter of compliance and expedience due to vulnerability. For instance, Journalist B says self-censorship can be a result of a voluntary decision instead of coercion:

> It applies both ways where threats are hurled towards journalists instilling fear into the practitioners, while on the other side one may choose to self-censor for want of aligning with the powers that be or to be seen to be politically correct.

Toeing the ideology of the dominant class, especially the ruling party, is part of the newsroom routines inculcated into novices. A common concern is the powerful forces' purported capture of the journalism profession. Journalist C, with over ten years' experience working for the Zimpapers stable, writes:

> There is nowhere, for example, a journalist working for the state-controlled media in Zimbabwe would recklessly ignore the ideological interests of their paymaster. It is an unwritten rule – one that one is never told but learnt from veterans already in employment. At Zimpapers, protecting the interest of the ruling Zanu-PF party is cast in stone. The editorial direction points to supporting the government of the day, which government has been Zanu-PF since independence in 1980.

Journalists usually conform or they simply are not published, hence Journalist B below says:

> Fear of offending mainly those in political power, shareholders of media houses and advertisers although sometimes fear of backlash from readers can also cause self-censorship. Self-censorship can also be caused by newsroom regimes and cultures. When a journalist realizes their story was not published because they included sensitive information, next time they write similar stories they will practise self-censorship. Editorial policies of media houses can lead to self-censorship as well.

Some information is self-censored if a conformist journalist believes it protects the national interest, especially when the journalist is working for the publicly owned media. There is chilling evidence that some Zimbabwean journalists are embedded in party politics and that others within the media profession complain of the capture of the profession by powerful politicians. Indeed, several Zimbabwean journalists have left the newsroom and joined party politics across the polarized divide of MDC and ZANU-PF contestation. This partly explains the polarization in Zimbabwe's media, pitting publicly owned media versus privately owned media. In trickier instances the vicious ZANU-PF intra-party factionalism finds willing "journalist-operatives" such as Tinashe Farawo who was secretly recorded trying to convince a government official to spy on a Minister in order to advance the interests of a competing faction. After being discredited as a journalist, his faction handlers facilitated his move from Zimpapers to become spokesperson for the Zimbabwe National Parks and Wildlife Authority (ZimParks). Whereas journalists from the North are embedded within organizations and state structures for ease of access of news and footage (Nohrstedt and Ottosen 2017, p. 247; Yin 2011, p. 565), Zimbabwean journalists are also embedded on partisan lines largely for economic opportunity. For example, journalists from government-affiliated stables have received vehicles or were allocated farms during the controversial fast track land reform, and yet others get better paying jobs or are given the chance to enter national politics. Several young and middle-aged journalists are Members of Parliament in the ranks of MDC or ZANU-PF, and one wonders how professional and objective they were before openly joining politics. Quite frequently, the government-aligned journalists maintain a cosy relationship and value warm relations with government sources and so pose uncritical questions when conducting interviews. Among Zimbabweans who are under USA and EU sanctions and travel bans there are journalists such as Reuben Barwe of ZBC and Caesar Zvayi of Zimpapers. Such journalists will self-censor for political expedience.

Government-affiliated media stables are prone to conform to ruling ZANU-PF ideology, and are more cautious not to stray off official views. Government espouses a commandist approach to its relations with the media and journalists internalize ruling party expectations as part of a loosely defined social responsibility and national interest. Social responsibility and national interest are principles that narrowly conflate with the party's political and moral perspectives (Fackler 2011, p. 110–111). Even in the post-Mugabe era, notwithstanding government pronouncements that the (state) media are freer, evidence points to the contrary. Several editors and journalists were dismissed, forced to resign or transferred to less prestigious stations because they were considered not to be supportive of President Emerson Mnangagwa's new dispensation. For instance, in January 2019 Joram Nyathi lost his job as editor of *The Herald* after he placed a story about President Mnangagwa on an inside page instead of the front page.

The blunt realities of existing in a politically frictious Zimbabwe, on one hand, and adhering to the best principles of journalism, on the other, are perhaps best articulated by journalist Dumisani Muleya in a *Facebook* post:

> Practising journalists must not be involved in partisan politics as reporters or candidates. We must just stay out of political parties and their factional affairs. […] You cannot be a player, coach and referee at the same time; it's really a no-brainer. There is a world of a difference between being plugged into political and business networks for access to good and quality information and doing their bidding. We must not succumb to pressures.
>
> *(May 4, 2018)*

Voluntary Media Council of Zimbabwe boss Lofty Dube tried to shame without naming the partisan journalists in another *Facebook* post:

> After all the election hype is over am doing a compilation of all Zimbabwe mainstream journalists Facebook posts and Twitter posts before and during elections for publication in an international journal on the role of Pseudo-journalists and political commissars masquerading as journalists in elections, what I have so far is heart-breaking … a contender for embarrassment to the profession (of coz will not include names to protect tattered reputations).
>
> *(August 3, 2018)*

Muleya and Dube's musings indeed reveal the difficulty in defining self-censorship when journalists become partners in political and business contestations. When an acting editor at *The Herald* was recently relieved of his post, he announced the development on *Facebook*. Tichaona Zindoga's post of October 29, 2019 entitled "I am not for sale" read in part: "Some people will be quite keen to know what is my next step, who I will meet and what politics I will play … My political convictions are known publicly … and remain the same" (October 29, 2019). This attracted an avalanche of criticism from fellow journalists and readers. One reader, Mfundo Mlilo, retorted:

> You are rumbling and clearly don't know what hit you. The day of reckoning has come so fast. ZANU-PF *sinjonjo*.[3] I hope you have learnt your lesson. Some of the things you call politics it's actually people's lives, security and livelihoods at stake.

Another reader, Pride Mkono, concurred:

> Tichaona must know nothing lasts forever and by covering up murder, rape and violence by the State makes him complicit. He has blood on his hands … May you take this time to connect with your conscience. Find time to remember all the stories and victims whom you disregarded as less human because they differed with your paymasters.

Although the post-Mugabe era came with a lot of optimism and promises of respect for human rights, it unfortunately degenerated into the repression of old with the shootings of demonstrators on August 1, 2018, and abductions of civil society members. Tichaona Zindoga was editing the *Herald* during this difficult period and the paper did not report critically on the Mnangagwa administration. That readers constantly use different platforms to articulate their displeasure with the partisan reportage of the state-controlled media is not taken heed of, meaning that audience pressure is relatively less significant as compared to political and economic pressures. It is not that journalists are totally dismissive of audiences' disapproval as shown in a private *WhatsApp* group of ZBC journalists, where one of them ruefully discloses a neighbour refused to assist jump-start his car on an extremely cold morning in the winter of 2019. The neighbour retorted: "Get assistance from ZANU-PF on whose behalf you tell lies!"

The economic environment

The Zimbabwean economic environment potentially induces self-censorship in a considerable number of journalists, in more insidious ways than merely protecting one's job against all odds and the imposition of unpalatable news values and routines. Economic needs are implicated in the censoring of some sensitive stories. In fragile economies such as Zimbabwe's journalists are poorly remunerated, and freelancers receive a pittance; hence, journalists are tempted to solicit for bribes and receive the so-called brown envelopes in order to "kill" or sanitize stories which are not favourable to powerful people or organizations. Journalists sometimes practise chequebook or brown envelope journalism where they receive bribes and gifts to self-censor. Journalist C is quite scathing about this scourge:

> Reasons [for self-censorship] differ but many are largely rooted in the editorial policy for the newspapers or media house one works for. However in my 16 years' experience in the newspaper industry at different levels of management, I have noticed some reasons are quite personal, like relations between journalist and the persons they were probably going to write about. Assuming it's an investigative article that was going to negatively portray, say, a businessperson that a reporter enjoys cordial relations [with], they self-censor. Some reasons stretch to corrupt tendencies where reporters self-censor for monetary gain. They get information enough to write an "earth shattering story" but they choose rather not to and are financially or materially rewarded.

In these instances, the boundary between self-censorship and corruption is thus quite liminal or simply non-existent. Economic donors are also implicated in inducement of self-censorship in Zimbabwean journalists, especially when news involves the questionable activities of both local and international donors. In the questionnaire responses and on *Facebook* and *WhatsApp* discussions, Zimbabwean journalists did not mention the influence of donors on self-censorship. However, my informal discussions with journalists, most of whom are my former students or acquaintances, they mention how donors are influential to their news production routines. Some treasure the occasional donor-facilitated workshops, international conferences and per diems as motives for not saying or not writing anything adverse or critical about this particular community. Donor funding of the development of African media has ambiguous characteristics, some of them verging on subtle self-censorship imposed due to dependence. Writing on the impact of foreign development aid on media system in seven African countries, Wasserman et al. (2019) observe that journalists who participated in their research project worried that the foreign assistance could "limit the stories they can tell, or influence the way they tell them". This is an oblique admission that foreign funding conditioned the journalists to think and present stories in particular ways, and the likelihood of self-imposed restrictions to satisfy donor standards and expectations is not far-fetched.

Zimbabwean journalists' self-censorship over queer sexualities

Mhiripiri (2014) conducted a critical discourse analysis (CDA) of news reporting on queer sexuality as well as interviewed journalists on their perceptions over the writing of queer-sexuality related stories. The CDA of newspaper stories from January to March 2014 revealed that there was considerable sensitivity and understanding in the way Zimbabwean journalists wrote about homosexuality and queer identity. However, this did not translate to a wholesale accommodation of these alternative identities. When interviewed, journalists disclosed fear of

62 Nhamo Anthony Mhiripiri

stigmatization and alienation if they showed open tolerance and understanding of homosexuality. The Zimbabwean cultural context induced self-censorship. This was in response to heteronormative patriarchy, the so-called Zimbabwean "tradition", Christianity, and political pressure where the central political leadership typified by ZANU-PF is virulently homophobic (Mhiripiri 2014, p. 12). Sixty-one per cent of the journalists indicated their newspaper editorial policies are homophobic; hence, self-censorship arises from the journalist's awareness of the discriminatory expectations of political, social and editorial gatekeepers who restrict the production and circulation of certain types of message or representation. The majority of Zimbabweans perceive homosexuality as a "Western" eccentricity promoted by Western governments. Journalists are therefore not courageous enough to go against the grain lest they are stigmatized and ostracized. Heteronormativity is dominant, though no journalist was previously censored publicly for writing about queer sexualities. Incidentally, on all types of news story that Zimbabwean journalists self-censor, consideration of audiences' possible negative or homophobic reactions to reporting on queer sexualities induce journalists self-censorship on writing about the subject.

Conclusion

Many Zimbabwean newsrooms inculcate self-censorship amongst journalists through a routinized process of decision-making that increasingly is predicated on deference to the dictates of party politics, influential organizations and institutions including the market and donor agencies. The influence of perceived cultural traditions cannot be under-estimated. These composite forces reduce critical thinking or adherence to known journalistic ethical principles. What is learnt from participation in newsroom cultures and editorial routines is bolstered by discussions with peers and colleagues in the profession. The pragmatics of self-censorship thus manifest as techniques of personal and professional survival, self-preservation or an expedient response to environment and what is perceived as opportunity. Impediments of journalistic practice that result in self-censorship are intricately linked to media systems, types of news content, ownership, government control of information, deference for pro-market and donor-funders, culture and traditions, restrictive state the state's control of legacy media. However, a disturbing number of journalists self-censor for personal reasons such as self-aggrandizement and corruption. Fourteen out of the 16 Zimbabwean journalists who responded to the questionnaire for this study cited political and economic opportunity and material reward, including receiving brown envelopes, as inducers of self-censorship. This study reveals that journalists are not always innocent victims of self-censorship induced externally through institutional structures. Some journalists deliberately take the risk and are prepared to pay the highest prize for their ideals, principles and in furtherance of social justice. Judging from the findings, it is unfortunate to note that an increasing number of Zimbabwe's journalists prefer self-censorship for reasons that compromise the media as a genuinely functioning space for critical discussion and exposure of social ills. A combination of the hardships presented by the Zimbabwe crisis, journalists' need for job security and economic opportunity and cultural considerations, especially when reporting on sexualities alternative to heterosexuality, explain this development. In Zimbabwe's fragile economy, it is difficult to implicate structural conditions alone for journalists' culpability to insidious forms of self-censorship. Both a structural reconfiguration of Zimbabwe's local and international politics and a re-emphasis on journalistic normative values are necessary to return journalism to proper public service where journalists cease to self-censor. Indeed, there is undue external interference on journalists, which includes political and editorial influence; however, self-censorship is in some remarkable instances a highly individual experience, which requires further study of journalists' psychological motives.

Notes

1 MMPZ is a media watchdog affiliated to MISA. See https://nehandaradio.com/tag/media-monitoring-project-zimbabwe/ (accessed November 28, 2019)
2 The study on reporting homosexuality in the Zimbabwean media was conducted in an earlier research project (Mhiripiri 2014)
3 Translates as: "ZANU-PF is malevolent".

References

Çipuri, R. (2015). Reasons of self-censorship landscape for journalists, *Thesis International Research Review*, 1: 75–92.
Chuma, W. (2005). Zimbabwe: the media, market failure and political turbulence. *Ecquid Novi: South African Journal for Journalism Research*, 26(1): 46–62.
Chuma, W. (2013). *The state of journalism ethics in Zimbabwe*. Harare: Voluntary Media Council of Zimbabwe.
Clark, M and Grech, A. (2017). Unwarranted interference, fear and self-censorship among journalists in Council of Europe member states. In U. Carlsson and R. Pöyhtäri (Eds.), *The assault on journalism: building knowledge to protect freedom of expression*. Göteborg: Nordicom.
Coleman, S. (2017). Journalism and the public-service model: In search of an ideal. In K. Kenski and K.H Jamieson (Eds.), *The Oxford handbook of political communication*. New York: Oxford University Press.
Cottle, S., Sambrook, R. and Mosdell, N. (2016). *Reporting dangerously: journalists' killings, intimidation and security*. London: Palgrave McMillian.
Dahlgren, P. and Sparks, C. (1993). *Communication and citizenship: journalism and the public sphere*. London: Routledge.
Fackler, M.P (2011). Social responsibility theory and media monopolies. In S. Forster and M.P Fackler (Eds.) *The handbook of global communication and media ethics, Volumes 1 & 2*, West Sussex: Wiley-Blackwell.
Forster, S. and Fackler, M.P (2011). *The handbook of global communication and media ethics, Volumes 1 & 2*, West Sussex: Wiley-Blackwell.
Holt, K. (2012). Authentic journalism? A critical discussion about existential authenticity in journalism. *Journal of mass media ethics*, 27(1): 2–14.

Mabweazara, H.M. (2010). Newsmaking practices and professionalism in the Zimbabwean press. *Journalism Practice*, 5(1): 100–117.

Mhiripiri, N.A. (2014). Reporting homophobia in the Zimbabwean media. In IFJ Africa Office (Ed.), *Reporting homophobia in the Zimbabwean and Nigerian media*, Dakar: International Federation of Journalists.

Mhiripiri, N.A. (2015). Narratives of the Zimbabwe Crisis, national sovereignty and human and media rights violations. In Said Adejumobi (Ed.), *National Democratic Reforms in Africa: Changes and Challenges*. New York: Palgrave MacMillan.

Miller, D.T. (2006). *An invitation to social psychology: expressing and censoring the self*. Belmont, CA: Wadsworth-Thomson.

Mukundu, R. (2008). Zimbabwe journalists under assault. *Zimbabwe Independent*. www.theindependent.co.zw/2008/05/02/zimbabwe-journalists-under-assault/ (accessed October 5, 2019).

Nohrstedt, S.A and Ottosen, R. (2017). What's wrong with war journalism? Why and how legal aspects of conflicts need better reporting. In U. Carlsson and R. Pöyhtäri (Eds.), *The assault on journalism: building knowledge to protect freedom of expression*. Göteborg: Nordicom.

Petras, I. (2003). Zimbabwe. In *So this is democracy: report on the state of the media in Southern Africa 2002*. Windhoek: MISA.

Schroeder, R. (2019). Media, freedom of speech, and democracy: journalists under pressure in Europe. In A. Giannapooulos (Ed.) *Media, freedom of speech and democracy in the EU and beyond*. Tel Aviv: Tel Aviv University.

Shava, T. (2013). *Report: Zimbabwe journalists abandon ethics, embrace corruption*. VOA. www.voazimbabwe.com/a/journalism-in-zimbabwe-ethics-abandon-ethics-corruption/1737919.html, (accessed May 9, 2018).

Skjerdal, T.S. (2010). Justifying self-censorship: a perspective from Ethiopia. *Westminster Papers in Communication and Culture*, 7(2): 98–121.

Yin, J. (2011). Ancient roots and contemporary challenges: Asian journalists try to find the balance. In S. Forster and M.P Fackler (Eds.) *The handbook of global communication and media ethics, Volumes 1 & 2*, West Sussex: Wiley-Blackwell.

Wasserman, H., Gadzepko, A. and Paterson, C. (2019). How foreign aid shapes journalism in Africa, www.news.uct.ac.za/article/-2019-07-08-how-does-aid-influence-journalism-in-africaa (accessed August 22, 2019).

Williams, K. (2010). *Get me a murder a day: a history of media and communication in Britain*. London: Bloomsbury Academic.

Williams, N. (2018). Writers silenced by surveillance: self-censorship in the age of big data. OpenDemocracy, www.opendemocracy.net/en/opendemocracyuk/writers-silenced-by-surveillance-self-censorship-in-age-of-big-data/SSS (accessed April 10, 2019).

5

LÈSE-MAJESTÈ AND JOURNALISM IN TURKEY AND EUROPE

Aytekin Kaan Kurtul

Introduction

Ever since the genesis of the independent press in the 17th century, *lèse-majesté* crimes have been a thorn in the side of journalists in wider Europe. From John Trenchard and Thomas Gordon who felt the need to "disguise" themselves as Roman politician Marcus Porcius Cato Uticensis when opposing the monarchy (Trenchard & Gordon, 1995) to Gustave Flaubert who felt compelled to alter parts of his novel *Madame Bovary* due to his fear of violating Napoleon III's "Decree containing the Regulation on the Printing Press and Booksellers" which largely dealt with *lèse-majesté* (Balleix, 2012), journalists and contributors to their publications sought to avoid the Sword of Damocles by resorting to self-censorship. This was the case in what used to be the Ottoman Empire in the 19th century, when a regime of censorship imposed by a tyrannical sultan led to an aptly named "Era of Despotism" and trampled upon dissenting voices in the press, who had to cower behind pseudonyms, puns and metaphors so that they would never get to see the notorious dungeons of "Abdul the Damned".

Yet what were these *lèse-majesté* crimes and are they still around? From a linguistic point of view, as the reader will notice, it is a French term composed of two words: "*lèser*" or "to injure" and "*majesté*" or "majesty". Historically, its inception as a crime of defaming the head of state (*laesa maiestas*) dates back to the 1st century BC, when the Roman Republic was transformed into an absolute monarchy by Octavian, whose deified status made him "flawless" and immune to criticism (Vervaet, 2010). In modern times, while some constitutional monarchies still attribute "sanctity" to their monarchs, the legal justification of *lèse-majesté* laws is more "secular": the head of state's quality as the ultimate representative of the state itself. The crime of insulting the head of state, therefore, isn't merely the defamation of a person but an offence against the state; hence the envisioned penalties are harsher, and, in most civil law systems, prosecution doesn't require a complaint by the "offended" person.

The question is, then, how do *lèse-majesté* regimes affect the practice of journalism today? NGOs such as International PEN often express their concerns about the application of *lèse-majesté* laws and actively campaign for their abolition (English PEN & Index on Censorship, 2009). However, despite the fact that such laws exist in other European countries such as Belgium, Spain, Greece, Italy, Denmark, Sweden and Poland (Griffen, 2017) and that the European human rights mechanism has addressed the matter in key judgments, there are cases in which prosecution acts as an extension of the executive, thereby effectively outlawing political dissent. The case of Turkey is a prime example of such a situation: with a record number of *lèse-majesté* trials since the election of President Recep Tayyip Erdoğan, Turkish journalism is jeopardized with the constant threat of detention and arrest, which prompts journalists to emulate their forebears in trying to circumvent this threat by applying self-censorship.

In assessing the reasoning behind this extremity, this chapter starts out with the history of *lèse-majesté* in Turkey: from the blacklists and arbitrariness of the "Era of Despotism" to the rule of law introduced with the Republican Revolution, this study underscores that while Turkey has had the notion of *lèse-majesté* for centuries, its application as a means to silence journalists and other dissidents is only relevant to periods of autocracy. On that basis, parallels are drawn between the current situation which, in theory, benefits from a modern civil law system, and the tradition of *lèse-majesté* in Turkey, in order to further stress that the mere presence of a criminal provision on insulting the head of state can be exploited at the hands of a prosecutor in bad faith. Last but not least, in contextualizing the example of Turkey within international human rights law and a wider European context, the chapter underscores that *lèse-majesté* laws can be exploited anywhere. This task is undertaken by assessing the relevant case law of the European Court of Human Rights (ECtHR) which not only reveals the excesses that in other Member States of the Council of Europe (CoE) have affected the lives of journalists and other citizens, but also sets the legal standards that the members of the Council (including Turkey) have to abide by in guaranteeing freedom of political expression.

To that end, through historical and modern examples of *lèse-majesté* laws in light of international human rights law, the chapter makes use of comparative legal analysis as its main method, supplemented by historical analysis and legal case study. In the final analysis, it is emphasized that *lèse-majesté* laws can, *per se*, generate a legal regime that can be exploited by an executive branch that seeks to silence dissent, thereby compelling journalists to resort to various forms of self-censorship.

Ottoman *lèse-majesté* and the tyranny of Sultan Abdülhamid II

Prior to the reform edicts of the 19th century, crimes against the State in the Ottoman Empire were governed by Sharia law: more specifically, within the context of "بَغَى" which corresponded to "defying the boundaries set by God, rebelling against authority", in legal terminology. Therefore, although defaming the monarch *per se* wasn't mentioned in Sharia, any act of opposition to the Monarch would be a violation of "divine boundaries", whose punishment would be left to the discretion of the sitting judge (*tazir*) who would initially issue a warning to the offender. If the warning weren't heeded by the offender, the penalty would be death (Okka, 1997).

This structure changed to an extent when the Ottomans began to codify in mid-19th century. The Ottoman Penal Code of 1858 "secularized" *lèse-majesté* by dedicating a specific provision to the crime of "defaming the Sultan via the press" which was defined under Article 138 of the Code. The codification of *lèse-majesté* also replaced the discretionary element in the proceedings with a definite penalty; thus, any publisher responsible for publications that offended the Sultan or the government would be fined while their publications would be temporarily or permanently banned. The Code was supplemented in that regard with Article 15 of the Publishing House Act of 1858, which envisioned a penalty of imprisonment for a term of from six months to three years (Kudret, 1977). Nevertheless, this setback was counterbalanced with the Ottoman Basic Law (1876) – the proto-constitution of the Ottoman Empire which enshrined freedom of the press in Article 12. As a result, the press flourished and the first Turkish newspapers were printed under the protection of the Basic Law (Topuz, 2003).

The reigning sultan at the time was Abdülhamid II: a seemingly reformist monarch who had risen to the throne after his uncle had been overthrown in a soft revolution by Ottoman reformists (Kızıltan, 2014) and his older brother had been deemed mentally unfit to rule. Surrounded by reformist ministers, he initially granted their wishes of a liberal society, only to stage his counter-revolution within two years, dissolving the young Ottoman Parliament and suspending the Ottoman Basic Law.

With the re-establishment of absolute monarchy, Abdülhamid II set his sights on the press. His first step was to further the Printing Act of 1864 enacted by his uncle who had sought to emulate Napoleon III's Decree (Kudret, 1977) and, indeed, in 1878 Abdülhamid II enacted the Martial Law Decree, which allowed the High Imperial Chamber of Printing to censor every publication including (after 1881) textbooks and journals (Topuz, 2003). In practice, imperial censorship consisted of an "in-depth" search for "blacklisted" words such as "nose" (Abdülhamid II had a large nose) and "republic" (Topuz, 2003). The result was a society under constant pressure, living in fear of being targeted by the Sultan's spies (*jurnal*) and lacking a voice due to the lack of a free press.

Under such dire circumstances, early Turkish journalists had to resort to a form of self-censorship that would be emulated by their successors in the 21st century: use of pseudonyms. Among such journalists were notable political figures and poets, such as the prominent Turkish nationalist Ziya Gökalp (who used, *inter alia*, the pseudonym Tevfik Sedat) (Altın, 2010) and "the Turkish suffragette" Halide Edip (who began to use a pseudonym towards the end of Abdülhamid's reign) (Adıvar, 2015). In addition to such figures, there were those who were bold enough to use their real names but still had to publish clandestinely. The most prominent

68 Aytekin Kaan Kurtul

of these individuals was Captain Mustafa Kemal (Atatürk) who, after being released from prison, published a newspaper with his comrades from the *Vatan ve Hürriyet Cemiyeti* ("Motherland and Liberty Committee"), an organization which aimed to restore the constitutional monarchy (Duman, 2006). The attempt was initially unsuccessful; however, the organization later joined the larger Committee of Union and Progress (*İttihat ve Terakki Cemiyeti*) (Dayı, 2001) which spearheaded the struggle against Abdülhamid II and effectively restored the constitutional monarchy in 1908, in an event that would be dubbed "the Young Turk Revolution".

The Young Turk Revolution brought about several changes that improved the exercise of press freedom. Firstly, censorship and pre-publication authorisation were lifted, and more than 200 newspapers were registered (that number was four before the Revolution) (Topuz, 2003). Secondly, even though offending the Sultan was still a crime, it was seldom applied as he became a figurehead and executive power rested in the hands of his Young Turk ministers. On the other hand, the Committee of Unity and Progress wasn't entirely tolerant of open criticism as some historians attribute the murder of journalists Hasan Fehmi, Ahmet Samim, Zeki Bey and Hasan Tahsin to Young Turk militants (Topuz, 2003).

Nonetheless, the reforms enacted by the Committee of Unity and Progress became the precursor to an even more substantial revolution, namely the Republican Revolution, that radically changed the constitutional structure, criminal law and culture of journalism in the country.

Republican era: insulting the President in the "Old Republic"

After a three-year-long War of Independence and months of negotiations with Allied powers, the Republic of Turkey was founded in 1923. Under the guidance of the founding father of the State, Mustafa Kemal Atatürk and his close advisor, the renowned jurist Mahmut Esat Bozkurt, the country adopted a new legal system, effectively replacing Ottoman law with a Continental European civil law model. Within the context of criminal law, the example that was followed was the Italian *Codice Zanardelli* or the Zanardelli Code, which, in turn, was influenced by the French Penal Code of 1810 (Musio, 1999). While adopting the principles of Italian criminal law was not a big technical issue, there was a constitutional matter that had to be addressed with regard to the interpretation of *lèse-majesté* crimes: in 1926, when the new Turkish Penal Code entered into force, Italy was a constitutional monarchy while Turkey was a young republic. Hence, the penalty envisaged in Article 122 of the Zanardelli Code had to be adapted to the fact that the head of state in the Republic of Turkey was a political figure elected by parliament and did not possess the "sacred" title of the Italian king. Thus, Article 158 of the Turkish Penal Code provided a *relatively* lenient penalty of a term of imprisonment of at least three years. Furthermore, the Turkish provision, unlike the one in the Zanardelli Code, provided a two-level approach: if the offence were committed in the absence of the president, the *maximum* penalty would be a term of imprisonment of three years. Nonetheless, both the Italian provision and the Turkish provision were collocated in the category of "crimes against the State" and under both systems, the crime of defaming the head of state was distinguished from the crime of defamation in terms of procedure. In other words, unlike a normal defamation case which would require a complaint by the victim, in the case of defaming the president, the prosecutor could act on his/her own volition – albeit with the permission of the minister of justice.

In doctrine, there was some agreement among Turkish and Italian jurists regarding the objective elements of the crime, especially in terms of offences committed by persons immune to prosecution for "doing their job", that is, members of parliament. Indeed, though more than half a century apart, both Alberto Borciani (1924) and Faruk Erem (1991) agreed that the immunity of deputies should expand to accusations of "defaming the President of the Republic". Correlatively, there was also an agreement on the two-fold nature of defaming the head of state; that is, on the fact that a criminal provision that penalized such conduct would be protecting the integrity of both the president as a person as well as that of the state (Manzini, 1934; Olgaç, 2016).

In terms of jurisprudence, before the current Turkish Penal Code entered into force in 2004, the high courts in Turkey had already established (*Turkish Court of Cassation judgment no. 989/1*, 1989) that the subjective element of the crime was not required, as it was logically impossible to "involuntarily" offend the president. Therefore, the debate (not to mention confusion) related to the means and content: How could the crime be committed in the absence of the president and, more critically, what kind of expressions would amount to an offence?

As regards the former question, the courts were unanimous in supporting the idea that all means of private communication would trigger the mitigating factor, that is defaming the president "behind his back". Alas, there had been no such unity among the courts in addressing the contents of the crime, which left much discretion to judges and the political climate (Mumcu, 1986).

"Fortunately" for politicians, most former presidents of the Republic of Turkey did not pursue criminal proceedings, preferring to resort to civil lawsuits instead. Alas, despite the linguistic modernisation and the influence of the European Convention for the Protection of Human Rights and Fundamental Freedoms (ECHR) in the current Turkish Penal Code, praxis has proven to be much more restrictive – especially for journalists.

"Insulting the President" in the current Turkish Penal Code and its application in the Erdoğan era

After several years of drafting, the current Turkish Penal Code entered into force in 2004, roughly a couple of years after current President Erdoğan's Justice and Development Party won the parliamentary elections for the first time. The most visible difference between the new text and the old one was the language, since the former code had many obsolete terms of Arabic origin that were not used in modern Turkish. More importantly, in terms of content, the new Code incorporated some constructs of international criminal law, substituted the death penalty with life imprisonment, abolished the "Italian" distinction between felonies and misdemeanours (*cürüm ve kabahatler; delitti e contravvenzioni*) and greatly increased the overall number of offences.

Despite the modernisation, however, "insulting the President" was among the many crimes that were carried over from the former criminal code, albeit with structural differences. Indeed, in the current code, Article 299 states:

(1) Whoever insults the President of the Republic is sentenced to a term of imprisonment of from one year to four years.
(2) If the crime is committed publicly, the penalty is increased by a sixth of the provided term.
(3) The prosecution on grounds of this crime is dependent on the permission of the Ministry of Justice.

Given that the condition provided in paragraph 3 was also present in the former provision, there is but one major difference between the two in terms of structure: in the current one, committing the crime publicly would trigger an aggravating circumstance. In practice, the current provision has proven to be more draconian as any means of committing the crime, save a private conversation, could potentially be a public act and, indeed, it has been established as such in case law. Thus, it has been especially difficult for journalists to effectively criticize the President of the Republic, as a "harsh" criticism of whoever was in office could potentially result in a maximum penalty of four years and eight months in prison.

Notwithstanding, the turning point for the application of the provision has been the presidential election in 2015, which was won by the current President Recep Tayyip Erdoğan. Up until he took office, Article 299 was a provision that prosecutors seldom referred to; although he was known for filing civil lawsuits against journalists, artists and cartoonists for their harsh criticism, "offensive" lyrics or humorous depiction of his image (Önderoğlu, 2006). As a matter of fact, even though there had been 848 indictments on grounds of "insulting the President of the Republic" during his predecessor, President Gül's eight years in office (which was about four times more than the indictments that were made during Gül's predecessor, President Sezer's term), that number pales before the 12,305 (and counting) indictments made since President Erdoğan took office (Akdeniz & Altıparmak, 2018). Indeed, only in 2017, there had been 20,539 inquiries on grounds of Article 299, 6,033 of which were deemed to have grounds for an indictment (Karakaş, 2018).

A close look at case law further reveals that most inquiries were based on online articles and posts on social media, which automatically trigger the aggravating circumstance as per paragraph 2 of Article 299. The scope of such inquiries was vast, including children who commented on an opposition party's post on Facebook ("13 yaşındaki çocuğa 'Cumhurbaşkanına hakaret' suçlamasıyla hapis cezası", 2017), users who shared a Gollum meme (Molloy & Akkoç, 2015) and political leaders who shared their views in online newspapers ("TKP, Communist Party of Turkey General Secretary Kemal Okuyan sentenced to 11 months in jail for 'insulting Erdoğan'", 2018) – all of whom have been prosecuted on grounds of Article 299, paragraph 2, thereby prompting many internet users to apply measures of self-censorship in order to avoid prosecution.

One of the main methods used by such internet users and online journalists has been akin to the one used by their ancestors who lived under the tyranny of Abdülhamid II: the use of pseudonyms. However, as public prosecutors could discover the identity of the users with relative ease by detecting the IP address, this method has since become almost exclusive to the printed press (Akkurt, 2014). Thus, internet users have complemented this method with a new tool: Virtual Private Network (VPN), which provides users with an encrypted connection to the internet, making it difficult for third parties to identify the user by designing complex security protocols and allowing the user to connect to the internet as if he/she were in another country. Notwithstanding, according to the "Censorship and Self-Censorship Report" released by the *Susma Platformu* in 2018, many internet users and journalists are still afraid to express themselves freely, feeling compelled to apply self-censorship even as they respond to questions from third parties as they "cannot be sure that this is a set-up by the government" (Susma Platformu, 2019).

Aside from the grim developments strictly within the framework of criminal law, the constitutionality of Article 299 has also been called into question after the Constitutional Referendum of 2017. The referendum, which allowed the formerly impartial president of the republic to join a political party and granted him (among other things) the executive powers of the prime minister, effectively abolishing the latter office. Some jurists have therefore underscored the formerly symbolic office of the president, pointing out that the will of the lawmaker depended on the nonpartisan nature of the office, which was deemed to be symbol of national unity. Therefore, they argued that Article 299 had to be reviewed in light of the new circumstances (Şen, 2018). Moreover, in late 2017, judges from İzmir lodged an application to the Constitutional Court, arguing that, as an elected public official, the president's person is already under paragraph 3(a) of the general provision on defamation (Article 125) and that defendants accused of insulting the president are effectively deprived of the right to prove their claims as per Article 39 of the Constitution of 1982. The judges then affirmed that the application of the ECHR, as an international treaty signed and ratified by the Republic of Turkey, is a matter of constitutional law and, as such, any incompatible provisions of "lower rank" would have to be annulled (*Constitutional Court of the Republic of Turkey judgment no. 2016/186, Section IV*, 2016).

Having established the impact of *lèse-majesté* laws on the daily lives of journalists, it is therefore imperative to review the relevant case law of the European Court of Human Rights (ECtHR) and observe whether the example of Turkey is compatible with international human rights law and, by extension, comparable with other examples from the continent prior to examining the landmark judgment of the Constitutional Court.

72 Aytekin Kaan Kurtul

Lèse-majesté before the ECtHR and recent developments in Europe

Among the courts of various regional human rights systems, the ECtHR is not known for its consistency in addressing questions related to freedom of expression. Indeed, there is a blatant lack of continuity in cases involving blasphemy, historical revisionism and so-called "religious practices", which has drawn criticism from the human rights community over the years (Zucca, 2013). Nonetheless, this hasn't been the case with *lèse-majesté* as, the Court has been fairly consistent in upholding the right to freedom of political expression in face of excessive restrictions based on *lèse-majesté* laws. Unsurprisingly, ECtHR case law on *lèse-majesté* laws largely stemmed from applications by persecuted journalists, yet even those cases that involved politicians and activists shed light upon what the Court considers an excessive intervention with freedom of expression. Given that the Court's case law determines how freedom of expression, as enshrined in Article 10 of the European Convention of Human Rights, ought to be practised across the continent (with the exception of Belarus), being informed of related judgments is fundamental for both the practice of journalism and free speech advocacy:

- In the very first case about insulting a chief executive, *Lingens v. Austria* (1986), which involved a journalist who had accused the Austrian chancellor of collaborating with a former Nazi and got convicted on grounds of "regular" defamation, the Court asserted that

  > Whilst the press must not overstep the bounds set, *inter alia*, for the " protection of the reputation of others", it is nevertheless incumbent on it to impart information and ideas on political issues just as on those in other areas of public interest. Not only does the press have the task of imparting such information and ideas: the public also has a right to receive them.
  >
  > *(paragraph 41)*

  And ruled that

  > the limits of acceptable criticism are accordingly wider as regards a politician as such than as regards a private individual. Unlike the latter, the former inevitably and knowingly lays himself open to close scrutiny of his every word and deed by both journalists and the public at large, and he must consequently display a greater degree of tolerance.
  >
  > *(paragraph 42)*

- In the first case about defaming a government, *Castells v. Spain* (1992), the applicant was a Basque nationalist senator who had harshly criticized the Spanish government by stating that the crimes committed against the Basque community were wilfully neglected and claiming that the government was "increasingly going to use the ruthless hunting down of Basque dissidents as a political instrument". The senator was therefore charged with "falsely accusing the Government" as per Article 161.1 of the Spanish Penal Code and eventually sentenced to a term of imprisonment of one year and a day, thereby compelling *Castells* to address the ECtHR. For its part, the Court reaffirmed (*Handyside v. United Kingdom*, 1976) the principle that freedom of expression "is applicable not only to 'information' or 'ideas' that are favourably received or regarded as inoffensive or as a matter of indifference, but also to those that offend, shock or disturb" (paragraph 42), and ruled that

> the limits of permissible criticism are wider with regard to the Government than in relation to a private citizen, or even a politician [...] the dominant position which the Government occupies makes it necessary for it to display restraint in resorting to criminal proceedings, particularly where other means are available for replying to the unjustified attacks and criticisms of its adversaries or the media.
>
> *(paragraph 46)*

Thereby establishing that both politicians and journalists have the freedom to use "offensive language" when referring to individuals like heads of state and chief executives.

- In *Colombani and others v. France* (2002) the Court addressed the crime of "defaming a foreign head of state". The applicants were a group of journalists working for the famous *Le Monde* newspaper and, in the matter at hand, had published an article claiming that Morocco would become the prime exporter of hashish in the world and the chief provider of the substance in Europe thanks to the contribution of the entourage of King Hassan II. The king then conveyed an official demand for criminal proceedings to the French Foreign Ministry, which obliged and conveyed the matter to the Ministry of Justice – thus began the proceedings. Although the first-degree court acquitted the journalists, the Paris Court of Appeals found them guilty of "defaming a foreign head of state" and sentenced them to pay a fine of 5000 francs in addition to 10,000 francs of damages to King Hassan II. The applicants then appealed the case to the Court of Cassation, only to be rejected. Thus, they brought the case before the ECtHR, which ruled in the journalists' favour, citing the fact that the provision of the French Freedom of the Press Act on grounds of which the applicants had been sentenced didn't effectively guarantee the right to prove one's claims (*exceptio veritatis*) and that crimes of "defaming heads of state" constituted an exorbitant limitation of freedom of expression in view of "today's political practice and conceptions".
- In *Pakdemirli v. Turkey* (2005) the case involved a centre-right MP, Ekrem Pakdemirli, who had harshly criticized the then president of the republic, Süleyman Demirel, calling him (among other things) a "liar", a "slanderer"

and "politically handicapped". In response, President Demirel had filed a civil lawsuit, claiming moral damages. Losing the lawsuit, Pakdemirli brought the case before the ECtHR, arguing that there had been a disproportionate limitation of his freedom of expression. In its judgment, the Court pointed out that the fact that the lawsuit in question was a civil one wouldn't, *per se*, mean that it wouldn't constitute a violation of Article 10 and, perhaps more boldly, established that a special law of defamation would be in any case "against the spirit" of the European Convention on Human Rights. Thus, the Court underlined that the civil nature of the lawsuit on the national level didn't alter the "scales of justice" between freedom of political expression and the "integrity" of the politician and affirmed that *lèse-majesté* laws were, *per se*, incoherent with the Convention.

- In *Otegi Mondragon v. Spain* (2011) the Court dealt with the crime of defaming a monarchic head of state for the first time. Much like *Castells*, the case involved a Basque nationalist who, during a press conference in Bilbao, said

> How is it possible for them to have their picture taken today in Bilbao with the King of Spain, when the King is the Commander-in-Chief of the Spanish army, in other words the person who is in charge of the torturers, who defends torture and imposes his monarchical regime on our people through torture and violence?

He was therefore charged with "injuring the Crown" and eventually sentenced to imprisonment for a term of one year by the Supreme Court. Although the execution of the sentence was stayed for three years, he was in pre-trial detention related to other criminal proceedings at the time the court delivered its judgment. The judgment was, once again, in favour of the applicant and, despite the fact that the "offended" person was a monarch and not a political figure like the president of a republic, the court emphasized that "freedom of expression is all the more important when it comes to conveying ideas which offend, shock or challenge the established order" and that

> the fact that the King is "not liable" under the Spanish Constitution, particularly with regard to criminal law, should not in itself act as a bar to free debate concerning possible institutional or even symbolic responsibility on his part in his position at the helm of the State, subject to respect for his personal reputation.

> *(paragraph 56)*

- The current president of the Republic of Turkey was personally involved in another case before the ECtHR, namely *Tuşalp v. Turkey* (2012) The applicant was Erbil Tuşalp who, at the time, was a columnist for the libertarian socialist daily *BirGün*. The subject matter of the application consisted of two civil lawsuits filed by the then Prime Minister Erdoğan on grounds of a couple of articles that Tuşalp had written on 24 December 2005 and 6 May 2006. In said articles, Tuşalp had referred to the then prime minister (PM) as a "civil servant of the United States of America", claimed that the PM suffered from a "psychopathic aggressive illness" and accused him of corruption. In response, PM Erdoğan filed two civil lawsuits against him, claiming moral damages, and won both of them. In assessing Tuşalp's application, the Court considered that "journalistic freedom also covers possible recourse to a degree of exaggeration, or even provocation" (paragraph 44) and that the statements of the applicant consisted of "value judgments based on particular facts, events or incidents which were already known to the general public" (paragraph 47). The Court then went on to rule that

> the use of vulgar phrases in itself is not decisive in the assessment of an offensive expression as it may well serve merely stylistic purposes [...] style constitutes part of communication as a form of expression and is as such protected together with the content of the expression.
>
> *(paragraph 48)*

And that, since Turkish courts had failed to establish that the articles had any concrete influence on PM Erdoğan's personal life and political career, there had been a violation of Article 10.

- Last but not least, the Court addressed a case of defaming a republican head of state in *Eon v. France* (2013). The applicant, Hervé Eon was a 49-year-old socialist from Laval who had felt offended when the then President Nicholas Sarkozy said, "Get lost you poor prick!" (*"casse-toi pauvre con!"*) to a farmer from his hometown. He therefore decided to put that same phrase on a placard the next time President Sarkozy visited his town. Unfortunately, he was charged under Article 26 of the Act on the Freedom of the Press for "offending the President of the Republic" and, after the Court of Cassation finalized the proceedings, Eon got sentenced to pay a meagre, suspended fine of 30 euros. Deeming it a matter of principle, Mr Eon made an application to the ECtHR arguing that the fine in question constituted an excessive intervention in his right to free speech, despite the minimal amount. The Court agreed and affirmed that, although the expression itself was undoubtedly offensive, the applicant had made a political statement by expressing his dissatisfaction with the language used by the President during his previous visit to his town.

Although national lawmakers don't tend to change legislation due to ECtHR judgments, this has been the case with France where Article 36 of the Act on the Freedom of the Press was abrogated following the *Colombani and others* case (*Act no. 2004–204 of 9 March*, 2004). Also, coinciding with the final judgment on the *Eon* case, the crime of "offending the President of the Republic" was "demoted" (*Act no. 2013–711 of 5 August*, 2013) to a crime of offending a public official as per

Article 48, paragraph 2 of the same Act. The example of France thus demonstrates how the case law of the ECtHR could potentially become an effective tool in amending national legislations.

In addition to France, there have been several states in Europe that have abolished the crime of a head of state or government independently from ECtHR case law. The United Kingdom, for instance, abolished the crime of seditious libel in 2009 (*Coroners & Justice Act*, 2009), formally recognising that it had already become redundant. In Norway, the 2005 Penal Code didn't include Article 101, paragraph 2 of the 1902 Penal Code which penalized "the defamation of the King or the Regent", effectively abolishing the crime. The Netherlands, on the other hand, came up with a solution similar to that of France and "demoted" the crime of insulting the King to the "status" of the crime of insulting public officials (Schuetze, 2018).

Even though the current trend both in the regional human rights mechanism in Europe and national legislatures of the continent points at abolition, there are countries in Europe where *lèse-majesté* laws are still applied vigorously. The example of Spain, which continues to maintain similar provisions despite losing a couple of directly related cases before the ECtHR, and that of Poland where Article 135.2 of the *Kodeks Karny* is widely deemed to be used to silence the opposition (Tilles, 2019), represent an obstacle to a continent-wide consensus.

Conclusion: judgment of the Constitutional Court and perspectives for the future

As expressed by the judges who made the aforementioned application to the Turkish Constitutional Court, Turkey is a party to the ECHR and the ECtHR has jurisdiction over individual complaints filed by Turkish citizens. Furthermore, the Committee of Ministers of the Council of Europe has a very clear stance on freedom of the press online, as stated in a recent Recommendation to Member States, underscoring that journalists in the countries should not be subjected to threats or harassment by the state:

> Journalists and other media actors using the Internet are not subject to threats or harassment by the State. They do not practise self-censorship because of fear of punishment, harassment or attack.
>
> *(Committee of Ministers Recommendation CM/Rec (2016)*
> *5 to Member States on Internet Freedom, 2016)*

Nonetheless, the Turkish Constitutional Court upheld Article 299 of the Turkish Penal Code, on the grounds that:

> Differently from the generic crime of defamation and the crime of offending a public official, the legal interest sought in the application of the crime of

offending the President of the Republic is the protection of the integrity of the State as well as the person of the President.

(Constitutional Court of the Republic of Turkey judgment no. 2016/186, Section IV, 2016)

It is a missed opportunity, as the Court could have set a precedent in view of the current transformation in Turkish constitutional law and ECtHR case law, yet it opted for a "traditional" justification for rendering the head of state immune to criticism. In a more general context, the judgment isn't simply a failure to comply with the standards set by the regional human rights mechanism: It's a demonstration of how the freedom of the press and freedom of political expression in general are severely threatened in the presence of *lèse-majesté* laws.

In other words, the mere existence of *lèse-majesté* laws begets the legal grounds for arbitrary measures against journalists. A country may indeed be considered a safe haven for journalists, with little to no prosecutions on grounds of *lèse-majesté* laws, yet a government with ever so slightly autocratic tendencies can potentially turn that around by raising the tension in the country's political climate and influencing the judiciary. The example of Turkey, in that regard, serves as an example of how a "dormant" provision can be revitalized, which, in turn, can compel journalists to resort to self-censorship.

It is unjust to expect journalists to depend on the benevolence of the prosecution or the executive branch of the state to exercise their profession. We no longer live in an era of absolute monarchies: It is therefore the duty of all democratic lawmakers to remove such archaic obstacles to the exercise of freedom of political expression and, if they aren't willing to act, it is the duty of every citizen to use the legal tools provided by the European human rights mechanism and raise awareness on the issue so as to generate public pressure on those who legislate as our representatives.

References

Adıvar, H. E. (2015). *Türkün Ateşle İmtihanı* ["The Turk's Trial by Fire"]. Atlas Kitabevi.

Akdeniz, Y. & Altıparmak, K. (2018). Turkey: Freedom of Expression in Jeopardy. Violations of the Rights of Authors, Publishers and Academics under the State of Emergency. Retrieved June 09, 2019, from www.englishpen.org/wp-content/uploads/2018/03/Turkey_Freedom_of_Expression_in_Jeopardy_ENG.pdf

Akkurt B. (2014, March 26). 'Özünlü ile söyleşi: "Fanzini buruşturup atabilirsiniz ama ruhunu asla". ["Interview with Özünlü: You can crease a fanzine and throw it away but you can never take away its spirit"]. Retrieved June 09, 2019 from www.sabitfikir.com/soylesi/faruk-emre-ozunlu-ile-soylesi-fanzini-burusturup-atabilirsiniz-ama-ruhunu-asla

Altın, H. (2010). Ziya Gökalp'in Eğitim Tarihimiz Açısından Önemi ["The Importance of Ziya Gökalp for our Educational History"]. *History*, 2, 2.

Balleix, C. (2012) *Les censures de Madame Bovary de Gustave Flaubert* ["The Censorship of Madame Bovary by Gustave Flaubert"]. Université de Nantes.

Borciani, A. (1924). *Le offese all'onore: Studio giuridico riassuntivo sui reati di ingiuria e diffamazione nel diritto italiano* ["Offences against Honour: Summarized Legal Study on Crimes of Insult and Defamation in Italian Law"] (12th ed.). Unione Tip. Editrice.

78 Aytekin Kaan Kurtul

Constitutional Court of the Republic of Turkey judgment no. 2016/186, Section IV (2016).

Council of Europe (2016). Committee of Ministers Recommendation CM/Rec(2016)5 to Member States on Internet Freedom.

Dayı, S. E. (2001). Mustafa Kemal Atatürk'te Cumhuriyet Fikri ve Gerçekleştirilme Safhaları ["Mustafa Kemal's Idea of a Republic and the Phases in Its Realisation"]. *Atatürk Dergisi*, 3(1).

Duman, S. (2006). Mustafa Kemal'de cumhuriyet düşüncesinin doğuşu ve Cumhuriyet'in nitelikleri ["The Birth of the Republican Ideal in Mustafa Kemal and the Characteristics of His Republic"]. *Kastamonu Eğitim Dergisi*, 14(1), 245–264.

English PEN & Index on Censorship (2009). *A Briefing on the Abolition of Seditious Libel and Criminal Libel*. Retrieved October 25, 2019 from www.englishpen.org/wp-content/uploads/2015/09/seditious_libel_july09.pdf

Erem, F. (1991). Cumhurbaşkanına Hakaret ["Insulting the President of the Republic"]. *Türkiye Barolar Birliği Dergisi*, 1, 13.

European Court of Human Rights (ECtHR) (1976). Handyside v. United Kingdom App. no. 5493/72.

European Court of Human Rights (ECtHR) (1986). Lingens v. Austria App. no. 9815/82.

European Court of Human Rights (ECtHR) (1992). Castells v. Spain App no. 11798/85.

European Court of Human Rights (ECtHR) (2002). Colombani v. France App no. 51279/99.

European Court of Human Rights (ECtHR) (2011). Otegi Mondragon v. Spain App. no. 2034/07.

European Court of Human Rights (ECtHR) (2013). Eon v. France App. no. 26118/10.

Griffen, S. (2017). Defamation and insult laws in the OSCE region: A comparative study. Vienna: Organization for Security and Co-operation in Europe.

Judgment no. 1989/1 of the Turkish Court of Cassation (1989).

Judgment no. 2008/1624 of the Ankara Enforcement Court (2008).

Judgment no. 2015/3066 of the 16th Criminal Section of the Turkish Court of Cassation (2015).

Karakaş, B. (2018, December 08). "Cumhurbaşkanına hakaret" davalarında rekor artış ["Record Increase in the Lawsuits on Grounds of 'Insulting the President of the Republic'"]. DW: 08.12.2018. Retrieved June 09, 2019, from www.dw.com/tr/cumhurbaşkanına-hakaret-davalarında-rekor-artış/a-46622702

Kızıltan, Y. (2014). I. Meşrutiyetin İlanı ve İlk Osmanlı Meclis-i Mebusan'ı ["Declaration of the First Constitutional Monarchy and the First Ottoman Assembly of Deputies"]. *Gazi Üniversitesi Gazi Eğitim Fakültesi Dergisi*, 26(1), 251–272.

Kolbüken A. B. (2015). "Cumhurbaşkanına Hakaret" Suçu Üzerine Bir Deneme ["An Essay on the Crime of Insulting the President of the Republic"]. *Ankara Barosu Dergisi*, (3).

Kudret, C. (1977). *Abdülhamit Devrinde Sansür* ["Censorship in the Era of Abdülhamit"]. Milliyet Yayın Limited Şirketi Yayınları.

Loi n° 2004–204 du 9 mars 2004 portant adaptation de la justice aux évolutions de la criminalité ["Act no. 2004–204 of 9 March 2004 introducing the adaptation of justice to the evolutions of criminality"] (2004).

Loi n° 2013–711 du 5 août 2013 portant diverses dispositions d'adaptation dans le domaine de la justice en application du droit de l'Union européenne et des engagements internationaux de la France ["Act no. 2013–711 of 5 August 2013 introducing various provisions of adaptation in the field of justice in applying EU law and laws deriving from the international engagements of France"] (2013).

Manzini, V. (1934). *Trattato di diritto penale italiano* ["Treatise of Italian Penal Law"] (Vol. 4). Torino: UTET.

Molloy, M. & Akkoç, R. (2015, December 03). Director Peter Jackson wades into Turkish debate over 'evil' Gollum. Retrieved June 9, 2019, from www.telegraph.co.uk/news/worldnews/europe/turkey/12030987/Lord-of-the-Rigns-director-Peter-Jackson-wades-into-Recep-Tayyip-Erdogan-Gollum-debate.html

Mumcu, U. (1986, March 06). TİP kurucuları Aybar'ın evini karakola sordular ["The founders of the TİP went to the police station to ask the address of Aybar's house"]. *Cumhuriyet*, pp. 6–9.

Musio, S. (1999). La vicenda del Codice Rocco nell'Italia repubblicana ["The Case of the Rocco Code in Republican Italy"]. *Centro Interuniversitario di Ricerca*. doi: ISSN 1827-0565

Okka, S. (1997). *İslam Hukuku ve Osmanlı Uygulamasında Bağy Suçu* ["Crimes against the State in Islamic Law and Ottoman Praxis"] (LLM dissertation) Konya: Selçuk Üniversitesi Sosyal Bilimler Enstitüsü.

Olgaç, S. C. (2016) Cumhurbaşkanına Hakaret Suçu ["The Crime of Insulting the President of the Republic"]. *Akademik Teklif*, 142.

Önderoğlu, E. (2006, November 02). Leman Dergisine Başbakan Davası Başladı ["The PM Lawsuit against Leman Mag has commenced"]. Retrieved June 09, 2019, from https://bianet.org/bianet/medya/87213-leman-dergisine-basbakan-davasi-basladi

Pakdemirli v. Turquie App. no. 35839/97 (ECtHR, 2005).

Schuetze, C. (2018, April 11). Dutch Parliament reduces penalties for insulting king. Retrieved June 13, 2019, from www.smh.com.au/world/europe/dutch-parliament-reduces-penalties-for-insulting-king-20180411-p4z8yx.html

Şen, E. (2018, April 27). Cumhurbaşkanına Hakaret Suçu ["The Crime of Insulting the President of Turkey"]. Retrieved June 09, 2019 from www.haber7.com/yazarlar/prof-dr-ersan-sen/2316249-cumhurbaskanina-hakaret-sucu

13 yaşındaki çocuğa 'Cumhurbaşkanına hakaret' suçlamasıyla hapis cezası. ["Prison sentence to 13-year-old child on charges of insulting the President"] (2017, October 07) *Gazete Karınca*. Retrieved June 09, 2019, from http://gazetekarinca.com/2017/10/13-yasindaki-cocuga-cumhurbaskanina-hakaret-suclamasiyla-hapis-cezasi/

Tilles, D. (2019, May 07). Poland's 'insult laws' and the threat to free speech. Retrieved June 13, 2019, from https://notesfrompoland.com/2018/08/21/polands-insult-laws-and-the-threat-to-free-speech/

TKP (Communist Party of Turkey) General Secretary Kemal Okuyan sentenced to 11 months in jail for 'insulting Erdoğan'. (2018, January 18). *soL International*. Retrieved June 09, 2019, from http://news.sol.org.tr/tkp-general-secretary-kemal-okuyan-sentenced-11-months-jail-insulting-erdogan

Topuz, H. (2003). *II. Mahmut'tan Holdinglere Türk Basın Tarihi* ["History of the Turkish Press from Mahmut II to Corporations"] (8th ed.). Remzi Kitabevi.

Trenchard, J. & Gordon, T. (1995). *Cato's Letters or Essays on Liberty, Civil, and Religious, and Other Important Subjects*. Indianapolis: Liberty Fund.

Türkiye'de Sansür ve Otosansür Raporu ["Report on Censorship and Self-Censorship in Turkey"] (February 11, 2019). Retrieved June 09, 2019 from http://susma24.com/wp-content/uploads/2019/02/mehtap-susma-turkce.pdf

Tuşalp v. Turkey App. nos. 32131/08 and 41617/08 (ECtHR, 2012).

Vervaet, J.V. (2010). The Secret History: The Official Position of Imperator Caesar Divi Filius from 31 to 27 BCE. *Ancient Society*, 40, 79–152.

Zucca, L. (2013, January 07). Lautsi: A Commentary on a decision by the ECtHR Grand Chamber. *International Journal of Constitutional Law*, 11(1), 218–229. https://doi.org/10.1093/icon/mos008

6

ONLINE SURVEILLANCE AND THE REPRESSIVE PRESS COUNCIL BILL 2018

A two-pronged approach to media self-censorship in Nigeria

Olunifesi Adekunle Suraj

Introduction

UNESCO's Global Report (2017/2018) on *World Trends in Freedom of Expression and Media Development* has observed increased incursions into citizens' privacy as a result of surveillance.

In Nigeria, since 1999, when the country's democratic institutions appeared stable, the state of press and Internet freedoms in the country has degenerated from lack of interest to sporadic clampdowns on press (Freedom House, 2016). Recently, Nigerian citizens have been met with extreme measures culminating in government online surveillance and repressive legislative bills aimed at subverting the free activity of citizens and journalists online (Reporters Without Borders, 2019). There have been concerted efforts from government ministries, particularly the Ministry of Information and Culture Ministry of Defence and State House of Assemblies, to legislate against, monitor, censor and restrict online freedom of expression (Amnesty International, 2019). These efforts have had a regressive effect on press freedom. The surveillance regime has a way of stifling press freedom and encouraging self-censorship as people become extremely careful of making statements considered critical of state officials and government policies due to fear of being arrested, detained or punished. It has been observed that this situation can create an atmosphere where citizens are intimidated to keep certain truths and facts to themselves, thereby creating a culture of "forced silence" (Penney, 2018).

In similar manner, a resurgence of governments' increasing resistance to press freedom and freedom of expression has also been reported in other parts of the world, even in countries with advanced democracies. For instance, the Spain's "gag law" and France's "snoopers' law" could be cited as repressive laws that tend to restrict press freedom and shield the ruling class from public scrutiny. Also, the arrest of Twitter users and shutdown of social media in some African countries such as Democratic Republic of Congo, Zimbabwe, Zambia, and Ethiopia are cases of government intolerance to online freedom of expression (Media Foundation for West Africa, 2018). As UN Special Rapporteur Frank La Rue once stated "communications surveillance should be regarded as a highly intrusive act that potentially interferes with the rights to freedom of expression and privacy and threatens the foundations of a democratic society" (La Rue, 2013).

Nigeria is currently facing security challenges and therefore has stressed the need for online surveillance as a means of ensuring public order and curtailing extremist expressions. However, it is expected that such considerations should be within pre-defined legal frameworks that are fair and reasonable to citizens and have the capacity to safeguard online freedom of expression and discourage self-censorship. Contrariwise, it is evident that there are not sufficient measures in place to protect journalists from intrusive and potentially chilling surveillance by security forces in Nigeria.

It is on this basis that this chapter examines Nigerian journalists' perceptions of the government's two-pronged approach – online surveillance and the Nigerian Press Council Act; and the extent to which this two-pronged approach restricts democratic discourse and freedom of expression in Nigeria. In the following, cases of assault and surveillance mechanisms in Nigeria are described and discussed, before the terms "self-censorship", "chilling effect" and "spiral of silence" are defined and explored. Then, the methodology adopted in the study is presented, followed by an analysis of the respondents' responses.

Cases of assault, monitoring and surveillance in Nigeria

Contrary to Section 39(1) of the 1999 Constitution, the Nigerian government through its Defence Ministry has directed the nation's security agencies to screen social media communications of notable Nigerians (ThisDayLive, July 5th, 2018). Furthermore, they are toying with the idea of having a council, whose duty will be to regulate the use of social media as recommended by the National Council on Information (NCI) (The Sun, July 25th, 2017). According to the newspaper report, the government is also planning to set up social media monitoring centres to be coordinated by the Ministry of Communication and the Office of National Security Adviser (ONSA) as part of the government's "chilling" strategy in stifling and curtailing online expression.

According to a Committee to Protect Journalist (CPJ) report (Witchel, 2018), Nigeria is listed among the 12 countries in the world where journalists are killed with impunity. In its 2018 Global Impunity Index, CPJ observed 13 unresolved murders of journalists within the reporting period. Based on data collection from the International Press Center (IPC) in Nigeria, it was also revealed that 14 journalists and other media organizations in the country have suffered various forms of assault including death threats from state actors in 2017 (Premium Times, November 3rd, 2017). Moreover, an Amnesty International Report (2019) equally observed that at least 19 media practitioners have suffered attack between January and September

2019. The Socio-Economic Rights and Accountability Project (SERAP) in its 2019 report also observed that at least 36 Nigerian journalists were attacked between January and July in 2019. The report further noted that 109 journalists were attacked between 2010 and 2015 and that in 2018, at least 45 broadcasting stations "...were sanctioned by the authorities on unfounded allegations of breaching some codes of conduct" (SERAP, 2019, p. 25–28). According to Media Matters for Democracy (2018), the assaults on journalists comprise issues such as: intrusion of social media accounts, detainment without trial, sentence to jail terms, physical assaults, threats by security agents, and closure and invasion of media houses. This level of unfettered interference has led to Nigeria being ranked among the countries with a very poor human rights record. In fact, Reporters Without Borders 2019 Press Freedom Index report rated Nigeria as "intolerant" for press and net freedom. In addition to online surveillance and digital assaults against journalists, press laws are also in existence. These repressive laws are meant to "gag" Nigerian journalists with the intention of making them toe the government's line. Hence, by creating a chilling effect, it appears as if the government intends to deter individuals from expressing themselves freely.

The Nigerian Press Council Bill 2018 (as amended)

Repressive anti-media laws are not new in Nigeria. For instance, in 2015, there was a sponsored anti-social media bill tagged "an Act to Prohibit Frivolous Petitions and other Matters Connected Therewith". The bill, also known as the "Social Media Bill", granted the Nigerian security authorities the power to spy on text messages, online conversations and other social media. The bill, judging by its content, was targeted at Nigerian bloggers, civil society advocates, and citizen journalists as it sought to penalize false statements made on social media platforms. The bill, similar to the Nigerian hate speech bill, spelt out jail terms and huge fines for individuals who shared "abusive content" about politicians and other public figures. The same can be observed with the Cybercrime Act and the 2013 Terrorism (Prevention) (Amendment) Act which spelt out death sentences for those found guilty, and it is now being used to target journalists that are critical of government.

The Nigerian Senate, in a renewed effort to curtail media freedom, considered another controversial anti-media bill titled "the Nigerian Press Council Amendment Bill" 2018 (as amended). The bill, proposed to replace the Nigerian Press Council Act 1992, seeks to regulate journalism practice by establishing a statutory body instead of the self-regulatory role of the press (as stipulated by Nigerian constitution). A critical assessment of the bill reveals it as a subtle hybrid of previous anti-media bills and decrees meant to gag the press and citizens journalists by creating a chilling effect through deterrence and self-censorship.

The Nigerian Press Council Bill 2018 (as amended), unduly interferes in the operations of the media as businesses registered under the relevant laws of the federation and seek to criminalize citizens journalism by not recognizing citizens and online journalists as journalists. For instance, the bill in its section 20 states that:

> Any person, not being a registered journalist who – (*b*) without reasonable cause takes or uses any name, title, addition or description implying that he is authorized by law to practice as a registered journalist, commits an offence.

In the Section 29 sub-sections (a) and (b), it further states that:

> A person shall be qualified for appointment as an editor if he – (*a*) is a registered member of the Nigerian union of Journalists; and (*b*) has, for a period of not less than 5 years served as a reporter or acquired working experience as a journalist in a reputable newspaper house, electronic news medium or news agency.

Besides, the bill gives extra-judicial powers to the Nigeria Press Council by usurping the powers of the courts, thereby seeking to incapacitate the media in exercising its role as the watchdog of society.

National security has always been used as a justification to enact measures that present a challenge to media freedom. As a result, a CIPESA (Collaboration on International ICT Policy in East and Southern Africa) report (2017) noted the possibility that journalists covering terrorism are more likely to be accused of granting attention and legitimacy to terrorists. However, this observation does not give government the liberty to restrict press freedom. Governments with authoritarian tendencies, have always tended to promote national security at the expense of freedom of expression. Hence, in order to curtail the government's anti-democratic activities, media stakeholders in Nigeria have taken actions to challenge government proposals in this respect. As a way of opposing the controversial Press Council Bill, concerned media stakeholders in Nigeria sponsored the Digital Rights Bill (later turned down by the President), challenged sections 24 and 38 of the Cybercrimes Act that have been repeatedly used to persecute online critics in the last few years, and took the government to court on its proposed Press Council Bill 2018 (as amended). These efforts are yet to yield any meaningful impact.

Conceptualizing self-censorship, chilling effect and spiral of silence

According to Schauer (1978, p. 689), "chilling effect" is at its core an "act of deterrence". The fear, risk and uncertainty built into laws, regulations and the legal system generally can deter people from exercising their rights. The issue of chilling effect is not new. Scholars have consistently observed that the perception of an intimidating climate can significantly chill one's willingness to publicly disclose political views (Scheufele & Moy, 2000; Shanahan, Glynn & Hayes, 2007). Recently the possibility of "chilling effects" online – the fact that laws, regulations, or state surveillance can deter people from exercising their freedoms or engaging in legal activities online – have been the concern of several scholars (Solove, 2006; Schneier, 2015). The concerns are attributed to growing Internet regulation, censorship, online surveillance and state cyber-policing, which appear to be gaining global prominence.

Judging by the open and dynamic design of the Internet, it was initially thought that online expression would offer opportunities for diversity of views without fear of conforming to existing narratives. However, Stoycheff, (2016) in his summation observed that there is insufficient evidence that online contexts can significantly liberate the expression of minority opinions or reduce conformist behaviour. Instead, he believes that the Internet's unique back door design allows government interception and surveillance of discordant political views that may be used to suppress the citizens even further. In other words, the ability of any government to covertly monitor the online activities of their citizens may make online opinion climates chilly. Stoycheff's (2016) observation confirms earlier studies by Liu and Fahmy (2011); and other studies, for instance, studies on chat rooms (Ho & McLeod, 2008), Facebook (Fox and Warber, 2015), Twitter (Miyata, Yamamoto, & Ogawa, 2015) and online review sites (Askay, 2015) indicate that people confronted with a climate hostile to participants' particular opinions have the tendency to self-censor both online and offline.

However, surveillance is not the only cause of chilling effect. According to Media Matters for Democracy (2018) and UNESCO (2017), threats and actions by government and non-government entities, extremists and terrorist groups may also cause deterrence and may indeed generate chilling effects. Spielberg (2017) and Kunelius et al. (2017) also observe that conventions of loyalty to authorities within news organizations might have a

> "...chilling effect" on journalists as many editors seem to disregard the journalistic principle of the people's right to know when it comes to national security and surveillance. In this case, a journalist becomes "the self who volunteers to be silent".
>
> *(Chueng, 2013, cited in Sun, 1997, p. 13).*

Self-censorship for journalists, according to Lee (1998), can occur both at individual and organizational level. At individual level, Lee (1998) observed that journalists may get involved in certain editorial actions such as omission, dilution and distortion to get favours from their employers or avoid receiving punishments from their superiors. However, when self-censorship is implemented by the editorial board of a media house, probably due to growing governmental pressure on the news agenda, journalists working in such an environment are automatically compelled to "continually absorb, internalize, and reinforce" (Lee, 1998, p.57) the mindset of their already censored working environment. In this context, journalists are either coerced or made to conform. This form of internalization, according to Lee (1998), has a strong link with Elisabeth Noelle-Neumann's "spiral of silence" theory, which observes that people are less willing to air their views publicly if they sense those views are contrary to a dominant majority position and could lead to their social isolation (Noelle-Neumann, 1984).

The advent of social media has brought about an expansion of media and civic space as groups and individuals once considered passive now use the new media to amplify their voices (Pereira, Rocha and Poplin, 2012). However, social media have also been found to be susceptible to "spiral of silence" effects (Hampton, Rainie, Lu, Dwyer, Shin & Purcell, 2014). According to Sohn and Geidner (2015) spiral of silence effects could facilitate a repression (coercion) of minority opinion on a global scale. Therefore, journalists who are critical of government and whose voices are in the minority are more likely to self-censor or keep silence, avoiding writing about or discussing certain topics, including discussion of political issues that seem not to favour popular government propaganda. It is obvious that if a government makes a practice of routinely monitoring online conversations, these chilling effects will be compounded, threatening the use of online platforms as a forum for self-expression.

Methodology

The research was conducted using survey and interview methods. The study employs a questionnaire with 217 respondents and interviews with ten key informants drawn from the Nigerian Union of Journalists, Nigerian Guild of Editors, Coalition of Nigerian Civil Society Organizations, Newspaper Proprietors' Association of Nigeria, the Online Publishers Association of Nigeria and the Guild of Professional Bloggers of Nigeria. These associations are the foremost recognized bodies through which the positions of media practitioners on any issue regarding journalism practice are communicated to the government and the public. For the interview session, two (key) persons in each of the organizations mentioned above were selected for the interview. Based on a snowball sampling technique, data were solicited from 350 Nigerian media practitioners selected from broadcast media (34 radio and 12 television stations), print (20 newspapers) and online media including independent writers, social media commentators/influencers and media scholars residing in Lagos (the media hub of Nigeria). With the aid of research assistants and Google Form, respondents answered the questionnaire either online or face to face. Most of the respondents were reached through their monthly media union stakeholder meetings. The respondents' anonymity and the confidentiality of their replies were guaranteed through the non-insistence of personal and organizational details in the questionnaire. The questionnaire was designed to examine Nigerian journalists' perceptions of the government's two-pronged approach of online surveillance and the repressive Press Council Bill 2018 and their likely chilling effect on democratic discourse and freedom of expression. The questionnaire (see Appendix A) is an adapted version of a validated questionnaire instrument used in earlier research conducted by FDR Group on behalf of PEN America Center to examine the issues of chilling effect and self-censorship in the United States of America in 2013 (PEN America Center, 2013).

Out of 350 targeted respondents, 217 responded, giving a response rate of 62%. The 10 key informants were interviewed individually and at different times. While

86 Olunifesi Adekunle Suraj

relevant statements and texts were extracted from the interviews for further discussion, responses from the other 217 survey respondents were analysed using the statistical software package SPSS. The analysis was descriptive in nature: simple frequency counts and percentages. The demographics of the respondents are summarized in Appendix B. Through the in-depth interviews, respondents were able to give more insight into the sensitive issues of self-censorship and surveillance that we are dealing with in this chapter.

Data analysis and findings

Government surveillance

In the questionnaire, journalists were asked (i) how closely – if at all – they follow news stories about the government's online surveillance of social media in Nigeria, and (ii) how worried they are about current levels of government surveillance of Nigerians. A majority (70%) of the respondents admitted that they had been following closely the news relating to government surveillance. However, while a majority of the respondents (72%) claimed that they were worried about the development, a large percentage (88%) expressed the concern that many Nigerians might not be aware of being monitored online.

From the interviews conducted, all of the respondents were worried about government surveillance using hate speech and fake news as a pretext. According to one respondent, who is a civil right activist, the present administration, he noted:

> ... through its policies and public statements by its functionaries, has successfully created an atmosphere that emboldens security agents as the arbiter of free speech online ... We are deeply concerned that free speech online continues to suffer sustained attacks from agents of government under the leadership of Mr President. The restriction of access to 21 news websites including Naij.com is just one of the several attempts by the government to curtail people's rights online.

In a related question, when asked about their concern about government surveillance activities, the percentage went up as majority of the respondents (83%) were not comfortable with government secret programmes of collecting and analysing metadata on citizens' online activities. A majority of the respondents (78%) equally frowned at government collaboration with technology providers in gathering personal information on Nigerians which a majority (74%) considered as government violation of personal privacy. However, opinion is evenly divided between those that approve (44%) and those that disapprove (43%) of government intrusion into privacy when "national security" becomes a major concern.

Nonetheless, the results from interviews revealed that government surveillance is widely perceived to be an infringement on the rights to privacy and freedom of expression. According to a spokesperson for one of the civil organizations:

The action is a violation of the rights of Nigerians to freedom of expression and the privacy of their communications guaranteed by the Constitution and international human rights instruments to which Nigeria is a party. Such a move provides enormous opportunities for abuse of power and the violation of the fundamental rights and freedoms of Nigerians.

Government surveillance and free speech

When asked about the concern for national security as a basis for government's efforts to compel journalists to reveal sources of classified information, the findings showed that a majority of the respondents (88%) are worried about government suppression of press freedom. In addition, 87% are equally worried about government harassment of journalists to disclose their sources of classified information in the name of national security. Expressing his objection to the government concern for security, one of the interviewees believed that:

> While we recognize the obligation to protect against hate speech that constitutes incitement to hostility, discrimination or violence, this should not be used as a pretext to clamp down on legitimate exercise of the right to freedom of expression that does not constitute incitement to discrimination, hostility or violence. Blanket clarification of expression that falls short of expression that constitutes incitement to violence, hatred or discrimination under international law can only limit media freedom and chill discourse deemed controversial or critical of government.

In a follow up question relating to national security, journalists were asked if government should be allowed to monitor activities of people and journalists online so as to fight terrorism. Around half of the respondents (54%) believed that government should be allowed to monitor activities of people and journalists online so as to fight terrorism. Simultaneously, however, a majority of the respondents (75%) believed government intention to monitor the identity and speech of social media commentators online on the basis of fighting terrorism is actually a subtle means of creating a chilling effect and achieving self-censorship. A majority of the respondents (79%) believed that self-motivated rather than national interest is the basis for government online surveillance. A majority (78%) were also of the opinion that this exercise is harmful to journalists because it impinges upon the privacy they need to work freely. The comments by those interviewed on this issue further revealed that journalists perceive government online surveillance as a means of instituting a culture of "forced silence" through coercion and conformity to self-censorship. According to one of the respondents in the interview session:

> This new development [referring to government online surveillance] follows a noticeable trend in Nigeria, where policies and legislation like the Cybercrime Law have been made by the ruling class to silence the voices of

88 Olunifesi Adekunle Suraj

ordinary Nigerians. Digital rights like privacy and freedom of expression are important features of modern societies and must not be allowed to be abused by people who are afraid of criticism.

The proposed Press Council Bill and media independence in Nigeria

Journalists' views were also sought on the proposed Press Council Bill 2018 and its likely effect on media independence and freedom of expression in Nigeria. A majority of the respondents were of the strong opinion that the proposed Press Council Bill would restrict media independence with almost three-quarters of the respondents (70%) affirming that the bill is another means of gagging the press in Nigeria. These findings were corroborated by some of the respondents in the interview sessions. Without any dissent, all the respondents interviewed believed that the proposed new press council bill would undermine media independence. One of the respondents who self-identified as a "media activist", noted that:

> The bill rarely intends to protect the people. It is about the government, government officials and public officers. The demand by the bill for an affidavit to be attached on a petition is in itself frivolous. Imprisoning someone for not submitting a petition with an affidavit is at best draconian. Nigerians need protection, too, but perhaps not of this type. If we must systemically regulate social media, it must be geared towards protecting the people, not the government.

Another respondent representing one of the unions of media practitioners in Nigeria believed that the: "… the proposed Nigerian Press Council Bill essentially seeks to criminalize journalists and the practice of journalism in the country".

Journalism under threat

Journalists confirmed that they are victims of government online surveillance and self-censorship. A majority of the respondents (89%) thought it was possible for metadata from their phone calls or emails to be collected and analysed by government. However, while 57% of the respondents were certain or suspected it had happened, 32% believed it was possible, but unlikely. A very high proportion of the journalists (76%) also believed that it was possible that the content of their phone calls, emails, internet searches and their organizational affiliation had been listened to, read or tracked.

As a means of validating the responses above, the respondents were invited to respond to certain cross-validating questions such as: suppose they were writing an email or making a phone call to someone abroad who is affiliated with an anti-government organization or known for their antipathy toward the government, what would be the chance that such a message would end up being read by government officials? The results showed no difference to the initial responses. In fact, a higher percentage of the respondents confirmed that their email to someone considered as anti-government would end up being read by government officials, in the same way a high percentage of the respondents (79%) believed their phone calls to someone known for their antipathy toward the government would be monitored and recorded by government officials. Furthermore, four out of five respondents (84%) confirmed that journalists and independent writers writing a story or poem that describes anti-government militants in a positive light would most likely be tracked and monitored by government security agencies.

Extent of practising self-censorship

In order to examine the extent to which Nigerian journalists practised self-censorship as a result of government online surveillance and the proposed government press council bill, the respondents were asked if they or any of their colleagues has over the past year or two avoided commenting on a particular topic, limited their activities on social media, declined opportunities to meet people government considered as security threats or refrained from making Internet searches or visiting websites on topics that appear anti-government. The results showed that Nigerian journalists do practise some level of self-censorship probably to escape the government's punitive measures. For instance, in order to avoid government surveillance, a majority of the respondents (75%) said they avoided writing or speaking on a particular topic that might be considered critical of government, avoided being too visible on social media (69%), declined opportunities to associate with people who appear as a security threat to the government (57%), deliberately steered clear of certain topics in personal phone conversations or email messages (66%) and refrained from conducting Internet searches or visiting websites on topics that may be considered controversial or suspicious (56%). Validating these findings, an interviewee acting on the basis of membership of a coalition comprising a group of civil right organizations in Nigeria believed that:

> Monitoring Nigerians on social media would criminalize their freedom and the activity of journalists that are critical of the government and censor the media from reporting on sensitive and critical information that is relevant to the public interest but controversial to the government. It would have a chilling effect on media activities in Nigeria, and pose a serious threat to the ability of Nigerians to meaningfully participate in their own government.

Journalists' safety measures against self-censorship

The findings of this study show that as a means of escaping government surveillance and guiding against self-censorship, most of the respondents (75%) appear to have resorted to taking extra precautions to protect the anonymity of their sources, while a considerable percentage of the respondents (57%) admitted to disguising their digital footprints. Some of the respondents interviewed are of the opinion that the

90 Olunifesi Adekunle Suraj

safety measures as advanced by journalists in the survey have become necessary in the light of the ambiguous constitutional stance on press freedom in Nigeria (which does not necessarily specify against censorship) and are also due to the unreliable, bureaucratic court processes in Nigeria (that does not dispense justice speedily). According to a programme manager in one of the civil rights organizations:

> What we have is the criminal defamation laws. Our laws are more or less negative and work against the media. In the world, the movement is towards civil defamation but in Nigeria, we still have criminal defamation which should not be. What we also found out is that the state goes ahead to prosecute cases that are meant to be handled by individuals.

He added that the court by delaying justice appears to be contributing to the culture of impunity. According to the respondent, "By the time you go for court case, you will be so shocked that your case might take up to 20 years. These are the kinds of thing that get people and journalists frustrated".

Enforcing a culture of silence

It is obvious from this research that Nigerian journalists are already practising self-censorship as a result of government online surveillance and the proposed Press Council Bill. Furthermore, the non-recognition of independent writers, social media commentators and citizen journalists in the proposed anti-media Press Council Bill 2018 (as amended) is giving credence to Nigerian government's determination to stifle free speech and the country's negative reputation of being tagged "difficult" for press freedom (Reporters Without Borders, 2019). Moreover, the fact that the government refused to assent to the Digital Rights Bill confirmed the fear that Nigerian government will likely continue its online surveillance. In fact, the findings in this study have confirmed that the majority of the respondents are already victims of government online surveillance and self-censorship. The proposed Press Council Bill has equally been adjudged an extension of military rule during which the state surveillance of Nigerians and promulgation of various anti-media repressive press laws and decrees were the norm. Hence, it is believed that the online surveillance and the proposed repressive Press Council Bill (2018) have the tendency to compromise personal rights and freedoms online including freedom of expression, the right to opinion, privacy and anonymity, which in the view of many respondents is already promoting a culture of silence.

Meanwhile, in this reign of totalitarianism, respondents are already internalizing the fear of being surveilled as they appear to be more cautious in their digital activities. Unsurprisingly, people who fear that the government is monitoring their messages are more likely to self-censor, avoiding writing about or discussing certain topics, including political and social issues that could contribute positively to the

Media self-censorship in Nigeria **91**

public discourse. Thus, the government monitoring of social media poses significant risks to users' privacy and can create a chilling effect on free speech online.

As a result, we envisage that, should these mechanisms continue, the chilling effect can snowball in creating an atmosphere of fear and culture of "forced silence" where the citizens' most fervently held opinions and dissenting views relevant to public interest are unlikely to be aired, while the government's propaganda holds sway. In line with this study, several scholars (Nye, 2011; Zittrain, 2008; Deibert, 2013; Schneier, 2015), have raised genuine concerns about the possibility of regulatory "chilling effects" online. There is a growing concern that laws, regulations, or state surveillance can deter people from exercising their freedoms or engaging in legal activities on the Internet. More importantly, scholars (Scheufele & Moy, 2000; Shanahan, Glynn & Hayes, 2007) have consistently observed that perception of online surveillance could significantly chill one's willingness to publicly disclose political views. In fact, according to Solove (2006, p. 487), state surveillance and data gathering can create an atmosphere of "risk" and self-censorship, a kind of society-wide chilling effect comparable to "environmental harms" or "pollution". As Askay (2015) rightly indicated, people whose opinions are monitored have the tendency to self-censor online in the same way as when they are offline. According to US academic Brendan McQuade, "You internalize the fear of being surveilled, so you self-censor or become more cautious" (Mic.com, January 19th, 2016).

Hence, monitoring Nigerians on social media threatens the safety of media professionals, especially the online journalists and those perceived of being critical of government. It is thus obvious that if a government makes a practice of routinely monitoring online conversations as found in this study, these chilling effects will become compounded, threatening the use of these platforms as a way to explore alternative narratives, constructive criticism and dialogue. It might also prevent the media from carrying out its obligation to monitor governance and hold the government accountable.

Conclusion

Therefore, based on journalists' perceptions as established in this paper, it is evident that government's online surveillance is set out to violate citizens' personal privacy and the liberty of journalists in Nigeria. With a lot of objectionable clauses that act as a deterrent, the proposed Press Council Bill 2018 (as amended) appears more of a political instrument designed to suppress citizens' freedom of expression in a country that appears to be operating a "democratic dictatorship" style of governance in an "authoritarian democracy". Obviously, Nigerian journalists and online commentators appear to have found themselves immersed in a chilling environment where self-censorship is promoted and normalized while measures allegedly meant to ensure national security continue to trample on press freedom and freedom of expression. Lee (1998) had already observed that journalists can either be physically coerced, or made to conform through institutional self-censorship as enforced by government legislation. While it is broadly recognized that privacy and the ability to communicate free from surveillance are necessary in democratic discourse, this study reveals that journalists are now very cautious in freely seeking and receiving information or expressing themselves online. While introducing a bill to fight disinformation or hate speech should not be a problem however, such bills or laws ought to follow the universally adopted United Nations declarations and must protect citizens' right to freedom of expression and privacy rather than instituting self-censorship.

References

Amnesty International (2019). *Endangered voices: attack on freedom of expression in Nigeria.* London: Amnesty International

Askay, D. A. (2015). Silence in the crowd: The spiral of silence contributing to the positive bias of opinions in an online review system. *New Media & Society*, 17, 1811–1829.

CIPESA (2017). The growing trend of African governments' requests for user information and content removal from internet and telecom companies. CIPESA Policy Brief, July, 2017

Deibert, R. J (2013). *Black Code: Surveillance, Privacy, and the Dark Side of the Internet. Signal.* Ontario, Canada: McClelland & Stewart Limited

Fox, J. & Warber, K. M. (2015). Queer identity management and political self-expression on social networking sites: A co-cultural approach to the spiral of silence. *Journal of Communication*, 65, 79–100.

Freedom House (2016). *Freedom on the Net, Report on Nigeria Internet Freedom: June 2015 – May 2016.* Washington, DC: Freedom House.

Hampton, K., Rainie, L., Lu, W., Dwyer, M., Shin, I. & Purcell, K. (2014). Social media and the 'spiral of silence'. Washington, DC: Pew Research Center Report.

Ho, S. S. & McLeod, D. M. (2008). Social-psychological influences on opinion expression in face-to-face and computer-mediated communication. *Communication Research*, 35, 190–207.

Kunelius, R., Heikkilä, H., Russell, A. &Yagodin, D. (Eds.) (2017). *Journalism and the NSA revelations. Privacy, security and the press.* London: I. B. Tauris.

La Rue, F. (2013). *Report of the Special Rapporteur on the promotion and protection of the right to freedom of opinion and expression.* New York: United Nations. Retrieved from: www.ohchr.org/ Documents/HRBodies/HRCouncil/RegularSession/Session23/A.HRC.23.40_EN.pdf

Lee, C-C (1998). Press self-censorship and political transition in Hong Kong. The Harvard International Journal of Press / Politics, 3(55), 57.

Liu, X. & Fahmy, S. (2011). Exploring the spiral of silence in the virtual world: Individuals' willingness to express personal opinions in online versus offline settings. *Journal of Media and Communication Studies*, 3(2), 45–57.

Media Foundation for West Africa (2018). West Africa freedom of expression monitor, April–June, 2018. Retrieved from: www.mfwa.org/wp-content/uploads/2018/08/ West-Africa-FOE-Monitor-April-June-2018-july-30.pdf.

Media Matters for Democracy (2018). *Surrendering to silence: An account of self-censorship among Pakistani journalists.* Islamabad, Pakistan: Media Matters for Democracy.

Mic.com (2016) Social media surveillance could have a devastating impact on free speech. Here's why. January 16th, 2016. Retrieved from: www.mic.com/articles/132756/ social-media-surveillance-could-have-a-devastating-impact-on-free-speech-here-s-why.

Miyata, K., Yamamoto, H. & Ogawa, Y. (2015). What affects the spiral of silence and the hard core on Twitter? An analysis of the nuclear power issue in Japan. *American Behavioral Scientist*, 59, 1129–1141.

Noelle-Neumann, E. (1984). *The spiral of silence. Public opinion – our social skin.* Chicago, IL: Chicago University Press.

Nye, J. S. (2011). *The future of power.* New York: PublicAffairs.

PEN America Center (2013). *Chilling effects: NSA surveillance drives US writers to self-censor.* New York: Pen America Center.

Penney, J. W. (2018). Internet surveillance, regulation, and chilling effects online: a comparative case study. *Internet Policy Review,* 6, 2.

Pereira, G. C., Rocha, M. C. & Poplin, A. (2012). E-participation: social media and the public space, Conference: Proceedings of the 12th international conference on Computational Science and Its Applications – Volume Part I.

Premium Times (2017). Attacks on Nigerian Media: Journalists, regulators, others brainstorm on solutions, November 3rd, 2017. Retrieved from: www.premiumtimesng.com/features-and-interviews/248248-attacks-nigerian-media-journalists-regulators-others-brainstorm-solutions.html.

Reporters Without Borders (2019). *Data of press freedom ranking 2019.* https://rsf.org/en/ranking_table

Schauer, F. (1978). Fear, risk, and the first amendment: Unraveling the 'chilling effect'. *Boston University Law Review,* 58, 685–732.

Scheufele, D. A., & Moy, P. (2000). Twenty-five years of the spiral of silence: A conceptual review and empirical outlook. *International Journal of Public Opinion Research,* 12, 3–28.

Schneier, B. (2015). *Data and Goliath: The hidden battles to collect your data and control your world.* New York: W.W Norton & Company.

SERAP Report (2019). *"A downward spiral": How federal & state authorities are tightening the screws on media freedom in Nigeria.* Lagos: SERAP

Shanahan, J., Glynn, C. & Hayes, A. (2007). The spiral of silence: A meta-analysis and its impact. In R. W. Preiss, B. M. Gayle, N. Burrell, M. Allen, & J. Bryant (Eds.), *Mass media effects: Advances through meta-analysis* (pp. 415–427). Mahwah, NJ: Lawrence Erlbaum.

Sohn, D. & Geidner, N. (2015). Collective dynamics of the spiral of silence: The role of ego-network size. *International Journal of Public Opinion Research.* Advance online publication.

Solove, D. J. (2006). A taxonomy of privacy. *University of Pennsylvania Law Review,* 154, 477–564.

Spielberg, S. (2017). *The Post.* A feature film.

Stoycheff, E. (2016). Under surveillance: Examining Facebook's spiral of silence effects in the wake of NSA internet monitoring, *Journalism & Mass Communication Quarterly,* 93(2), 296–311.

Sun, Y. (1997). *Effect of self-censorship on news credibility: public's perception of Hong Kong Newspapers after the 1997 handover.* Master's thesis, Iowa State University, 2014, 13.

The Sun Nigeria (2017). FG moves to regulate use of social media, July 25th, 2017. Retrieved from: www.sunnewsonline.com/fg-moves-to-regulate-use-of-social-media/.

THISDAYLIVE (2018). Again, Senate moves to regulate social media, July 5th, 2018. Retrieved from: www.thisdaylive.com/index.php/2018/07/05/again-senate-moves-to-regulate-social-media/.

UNESCO (2018). *World Trends in Freedom of Expression and Media Development. Global Report 2017/2018.* Paris: UNESCO.

94 Olunifesi Adekunle Suraj

Witchel, E. (2018). Getting Away with Murder. CPJ's 2018 Global Impunity Index spotlights countries where journalists are slain and their killers go free. https://cpj.org/ reports/ 2018/10/impunity-index-getting-away-with-murder-killed-justice.php (accessed 1 September 2019).

Zittrain, J. (2008). *The future of the Internet and how to stop it.* New Haven, CT: Yale University Press.

Zureik, E., Stalker, L. H., & Smith E. (2010). (Eds.) *Surveillance, privacy and the globalization of personal information.* Canada: McGill-Queen's University Press. Available at: www.mqup. ca/surveillance--privacy--and-the-globalization-of-personal-information-products-9780773537071.php.

Appendix A

Questionnaire

Dear Respondent,

Kindly answer the following questions as frankly and truthfully as humanly possible. The study is purely an academic exercise. Your responses shall be treated with utmost confidentiality. Thank you for your cooperation, understanding and time.

Please tick (√) the appropriate option provided against each of the following questions.

1. How closely – if at all – are you following news stories about government's online surveillance of social media in Nigeria?
    Very closely (   )   Somewhat closely (   )   Not too closely (   )
    Not closely at all (   )   Not sure (   )
2. In general, how worried are you about current levels of government surveillance of Nigerians?
    Very worried (   )   Somewhat worried (   )
    Not too worried (   )   Not worried at all (   )   Not sure (   )
3. Government efforts to compel journalists to reveal sources of classified information.
    Very worried (   )   Somewhat worried (   )
    Not too worried (   )   Not worried at all (   )   Not sure (   )
4. The government's secret programme to collect and analyse metadata (e.g., time and location) on phone calls, emails, browsing and other activity of Nigerians.
    Very worried (   )   Somewhat worried (   )
    Not too worried (   )   Not worried at all (   )   Not sure (   )
5. Suppression of free speech and press freedom in the name of National Security.
    Very worried (   )   Somewhat worried (   )
    Not too worried (   )   Not worried at all (   )   Not sure (   )

6. Technology companies collaborating with the government to provide vast amounts of personal information on Nigerians.
Very worried (   )   Somewhat worried (   )
Not too worried (   )   Not worried at all (   )   Not sure (   )
7. If you knew that the federal government had collected data about your telephone or Internet activity would you feel that your personal privacy had been violated, or not?
Yes, would feel that personal privacy had been violated (   )
No, would not (   )   Not sure/Not applicable (   )
8. Overall, do you approve or disapprove of the government's collection of telephone and Internet data as part of anti-terrorism efforts?
Approve (   )   Disapprove (   )   Not Sure (   )

SA = Strongly agree, A = Agree, UD = Undecided, D = Disagree, SD = Strongly Disagree

		SA	A	UD	D	SD
9.	Self motive and personal interest rather than national interest is the basis for government online surveillance of the citizens' expression online					
10.	Increased government surveillance on social media is especially harmful to journalists because it impinges upon the privacy they need to work freely					
11.	Most Nigerians are unconcerned and uninformed about government surveillance on social media					
12.	Personal data collected by the government will be vulnerable to abuse because it may be used to target citizens who appears critical of government					
13.	Government should be allowed to monitor activities of people and journalists online so as to fight terrorism					
14.	Monitoring the identity and speech of social media commentators online by government for hate speech and fake news is a subtle means of restricting freedom of speech online					

		SA	A	UD	D	SD
15.	The proposed Press Council Bill will definitely restrict media independence					
16.	The proposed Press Council Bill is another means of gagging the freedom of the press in Nigeria					

How likely is it that the following has happened to you or any of your colleagues in the past year or two?

17. Metadata from phone calls or emails has been collected and analysed by the government
    a. Certain it has happened   ( )
    b. Suspect it has happened   ( )
    c. Unlikely but possible   ( )
    d. Highly unlikely   ( )
    e. Not sure   ( )
18. The actual content of phone calls or emails has been listened to or read
    a. Very likely   ( )
    b. Realistically possible   ( )
    c. Very unlikely   ( )
    d. Not sure   ( )
19. Things like Internet searches, website visits, and book purchases have been   by the government
    a. Very likely   ( )
    b. Realistically possible   ( )
    c. Very unlikely   ( )
    d. Not sure   ( )

What is your view on the following?

20 Suppose you were writing an email to someone abroad who was affiliated with an anti-government organization. What would be the chance that the message would end up being read by government officials?
   a. Very likely   ( )
   b. Realistically possible   ( )
   c. Very unlikely   ( )
   d. Not sure   ( )

21. Suppose you were making a phone call to someone living in an area of the world known for its antipathy toward the government. What would be the chance that the call would be monitored and recorded by government officials?
    a. Very likely   ( )
    b. Realistically possible ( )
    c. Very unlikely   ( )
    d. Not sure   ( )
22. Suppose you published a story or poem that describes anti-government militants in a positive light. What would be the chance that you would be placed on a list of people to be tracked and monitored by government officials?
    a. Very likely   ( )
    b. Realistically possible ( )
    c. Very unlikely   ( )
    d. Not sure   ( )

Over the past year or two, have you or any of your colleague done or seriously considered doing any of the following because you thought your communications might be monitored in some way by the government?

23. Avoided writing or speaking on a particular topic
    a. Yes, have done   ( )
    b. No, have not   ( )
    c. Have seriously considered   ( )
    d. Yes/have seriously considered ( )
    e. Not sure   ( )
24. Curtailed or avoided activities on social media (e.g., Facebook, Twitter)
    a. Yes, have done   ( )
    b. No, have not   ( )
    c. Have seriously considered   ( )
    d. yes/have seriously considered ( )
    e. Not sure   ( )
25. Declined opportunities to meet – physically or electronically – people who might be deemed security threats by the government
    a. Yes, have done   ( )
    b. No, have not   ( )
    c. Have seriously considered   ( )
    d. yes/have seriously considered ( )
    e. Not sure   ( )

26. Refrained from conducting Internet searches or visiting websites on topics that may be considered controversial or suspicious
    a. Yes, have done   ( )
    b. No, have not   ( )
    c. Have seriously considered   ( )
    d. yes/have seriously considered ( )
    e. Not sure   ( )
27. Took extra precautions to protect the anonymity of sources
    a. Yes, have done   ( )
    b. No, have not   ( )
    c. Have seriously considered   ( )
    d. Yes/have seriously considered ( )
    e. Not sure   ( )
28. Took extra steps to cover or disguise digital footprints (e.g., used stronger encryption software, changed to more secure digital service provider)
    a. Yes, have done   ( )
    b. No, have not   ( )
    c. Have seriously considered   ( )
    d. Yes/have seriously considered ( )
    e. Not sure/Not applicable   ( )

Demographics

29. How old are you? 29 or under ( )   30–39( )   40–49( )   50–59( ) 60–69( )   70–79( )   80 or older ( )
30. **Are you:** Male ( ) Female ( )
31. Which of these best describes what you do? Check all that apply. Editor ( ) Writer ( ) Blogger ( ) Journalist ( ) Narrative Nonfiction/Essayist ( ) Novelist or Short Fiction Writer ( ) Playwright ( ) Poet ( ) Academics ( ) Broadcaster ( ) social media commentators ( ) independent journalist ( )
32. Classification of organization you work for: Television ( )   Radio ( )   Newspaper ( )   Online TV ( ) Online Radio ( )   Online newspaper ( ) others...
33. Type of organization: Public ( )   Private ( )   Independent ( )
34. Years of practice: (a) 0–5 years   (b) 6–10 years   (c) 11–15 years (d) 16–20 years   (e) above 20 years

Appendix B

TABLE 6.1 Demographics of respondents

Item	Categories	Frequency	Percentage
Gender	Male	143	66.0
	Female	74	34.1
	Total	217	100.0
Age	29 or under	35	16.1
	30–39	58	26.7
	40–49	60	27.6
	50–59	60	27.6
	60–69	3	1.4
	70–79	1	.5
	Total	182	100.0
Type of Organization	Independent	32	14.7
	Private	129	59.4
	Public	56	25.8
	Total	217	100.0
Years of Practice	0–5 years	51	23.5
	11–15 years	42	19.4
	16–20 years	30	13.8
	6–10 years	67	30.9
	Above 20 years	27	12.4
	Total	217	100.0
Media outlet	Newspaper		34.1
	Radio		20.3
	Television		15.2
	Online Newspaper		17.1
	Online Television		4.6
	Online Radio		0.9
	Independent Journalist		17.8
	Total		100.0

7

THE "TRIPLE EFFECT" SILENCING FEMALE JOURNALISTS ONLINE

A theoretical exploration

Marte Høiby

Introduction

According to the Organization for Security and Co-operation in Europe (OSCE), online attacks on female journalists have become a serious threat to women's participation in journalism and the media. The OSCE claims that media plurality is currently at risk due to the retreat of female journalists from the online public sphere.

> Threats of rape, physical violence and graphic imagery show up in their inboxes and on their social media platforms as they go about their workday. In extreme cases these attacks lead to self-censorship or worse: women retreating from the public sphere, leaving the male-dominated field of journalism with even fewer female voices.
>
> *(OSCE, 2019)*

Seeking to protect democracy and freedom of the media, OSCE has established a specific initiative to enhance safety for women journalists online. Their "Protect Female Journalists Online" initiative, addressed under the Representative on Freedom of the Media, encompasses a separate track on the Safety of Female Journalists Online (SOFJO).

OSCE uses the slogans "Protect plurality" and "It's our responsibility" and goes further to underpin the point that I have previously made in my own research (see Høiby, 2016) – that female journalists in the field face a double burden because they are attacked for (i) being journalists and (ii) for being women taking active part in society. When women are journalists and active online, I further suggest that a disfavouring online environment creates an effect, which amplifies this burden. Journalists are regularly targets of online attacks and in the course of doing their job, they are faced with (often sexist) intimidation online. According to the most recent World Trends Report by the United Nations Educational, Scientific and Cultural

Organization (UNESCO), "Female journalists are targeted more frequently and more viciously by online abuse and harassment than their male colleagues" (UNESCO, 2019a, p. 8). The report underscores that the abuse is often highly sexualized and formalized through a focus on the women's physical traits, cultural background, and private life. Although such harassment and violence often intersect with racism and other forms of discrimination, I will, in this article, focus on gender. The immediate question arising from this is how and why female journalists are more harassed online than their male counterparts. And, in which ways does gender play a specific role in online harassment against journalists?

In June this year, the UNESCO headquarters in Paris arranged a symposium to address and improve the safety of women journalists (UNESCO, 2019b). It is the violent physical and psychological, often sexual, attacks on women that sparked this initiative from UNESCO, underscoring that the virtual space is only one arena where such assaults take place.

> The increase in attacks against female journalists and the specific threats faced by women journalists, including sexual harassment and violence, both online and offline, is a growing concern. With countless victims of violence and intimidation, there is a pressing need to explore new ways to reinforce the safety of women journalists on the ground.
>
> *(ibid.)*

Critically examining online harassment against women journalists as a potential driver to self-censorship, I first look specifically at gendered harassment against women in general – whether or not they are journalists and whether or not online. Further, I look to the online sphere and ask what is possibly making it such fertile ground for attacks. The third part of this chapter explores the extent to which online harassment is being used to silence journalists regardless of their sex. Is this a form of antipress violence that offer better conditions to perpetrators than physical attacks? Could it be regarded as even more effective, and perhaps especially so in the case of women journalists? What is the nature of the harassment women face, and what makes it an effective tool for perpetrators? Here I include theory on antipress violence and pay attention to incidents where male journalists have also experienced harassment online in connection to covering particularly sensitive stories. From an antipress violence perspective I assume the motive of attacks to be less gender sensitive and predominantly rooted in a desire to control information (Høiby, 2019). Within this scope of theory, I search for the potential core drivers to self-censorship among women journalists. This chapter presents a theoretical exploration of a phenomenon.

The anonymous patriarchy

To investigate whether attempts to silence female journalists are rooted in patriarchal social and -institutional structures or a general upsurge in harassment online, I look to situate these ideas in theory. I do not set out to differentiate between sexual harassment and other harassment in this chapter. The variation in the nature of attacks is broad and the sexualization of it understood as mere "wrapping". The form the violence takes has little significance for what the perpetrators seek to accomplish, which is to control, subjugate – and silence an "enemy" (Høiby, 2016; Mardorossian, 2014). Still, sexualized content is frequent or even dominant in sexist and misogynistic attacks, and consequently much of the discussion will centre on that.

Already in 1998, at the early days of Internet and social media use, Ferganchick-Neufang pointed out that student aggression towards female teachers in higher education institutions more often took the form of online harassment as online teaching increased. As "women have not traditionally held positions of power within academic institutions, their ability to maintain authority is often challenged by students who are uncomfortable with female authority figures" (Ferganchick-Neufang, 1998, p. 1). Building on the idea that student-to-teacher harassment already was a problem long before the virtual classroom appeared (Benson, 1984), Ferganchick-Neufang took interest to understand the conditions of the Internet that seemed to make women particularly prone to harassment in the virtual space. The author suggests that male (student) aggression towards women (teachers) is situated in the same reasons as it was before, but that the anonymity online enhances the freedom to act without responsibility. Further, lack of administrative and collegial support when insults (in the nonvirtual classroom) are reported creates a free space for the aggression to take place without consequences, and the virtual reality of online communication exacerbates this problem. "After all, it's *only* email! And yet, anyone who has experienced online harassment knows that the anguish of online harassment is just as harsh as in real life" (Ferganchick-Neufang, 1998, p. 17). Society remains to fully accept and treat the virtual sphere as part of our nonvirtual reality.

Early scholars in the field of sexism and virtual spaces have suggested that the online reality is a mere reflection of the offline and as sexist as "real life". An assumption like that would imply that the virtual world is as male-dominant as the nonvirtual, which is not necessarily the case. Firstly, and as I have argued in previous research (see Høiby, 2016), forces of masculinity and femininity work beyond those of the sex and the social gender-construct, which obscures what "game" is played by whom (Høiby, 2016) – both in physical and virtual reality. Secondly, there is the question of whether we behave the same way online as we do offline? Are these two realities the same – or even comparable at all?

Online representation, participation, influence and behaviour

To attend to the issue of representation – presence and influence – first: women in fact outnumber men on many social media platforms (Duggan & Smith, 2013; Heil & Piskorski, 2009). But mere presence does not guarantee a just share of power in society. Presence does not necessarily indicate participation, and participation can take various forms and cannot guarantee influence on potentially patriarchal structures. Ausserhofer and Maireder found "an immense gender gap" in studying tweets in the Austrian political Twittersphere (2013, p. 299):

> As to why there is such an uneven allocation of influence between men and women within the political Twittersphere, we can only speculate: does this trend simply mirror men's stronger representation in traditional politics – only 28.4 per cent of Austrian MPs are female – or do other unique factors lead to this disparity?
>
> *(Ausserhofer and Maireder, 2013, p. 309)*

While several networks of men were identified in Ausserhofer and Maireder's study, no similar women's networks existed. "It appears that women only play more prominent roles in the subnetworks composed mainly of citizens and early Twitter adopters" (p. 303). In the same fashion, a study by Heil and Piskorski (2009) of a random sample of 300,000 Twitter users found that men were more regularly addressed on Twitter – both by men *and* women – despite a female majority representation of 55% compared to 45% men (2009).

> [A]n average man is almost twice more likely to follow another man than a woman. Similarly, an average woman is 25% more likely to follow a man than a woman. Finally, an average man is 40% more likely to be followed by another man than by a woman. These results cannot be explained by different tweeting activity – both men and women tweet at the same rate.
>
> *(ibid. no page)*

Under the subject of women's representation also belongs the issue of objectification. Already in the 1990s feminist scholarship suggested that the online "exclusion of women and femininity is as obvious as the inclusion of male imagery. And when women do appear, it is often as objects of desire" (Coyle, cited in Ferganchick-Neufang, 1998, p. 1). Scholars warn that the exclusion of women in online spaces (e.g. in computer games and programming) and objectification of women (in pornography and advertisement) contribute to this alienation of women and a culture in which they become easy targets for (sexual) harassment (Coyle, 1996; Ferganchick-Neufang, 1998). Taking it further, systematic anti-feminist activism is set up and driven forward by the assistance of algorithms allowed by a flawed policy and poor governance structure online. "Reddit's karma point system, aggregation of material across subreddits, ease of subreddit and user account creation, governance structure, and policies around offensive content serve to provide fertile ground for anti-feminist and misogynistic activism" (Massanari, 2017)

Now to the question about online social conduct, of which the ease of anonymity is an aspect of potentially prevailing effect. A study by Fox, Cruz and Lee (2015) investigated the roles of anonymity and interactivity in response to sexist content posted in social media. They found that "anonymous participants expressed significantly more sexist attitudes than identified participants [and that] interacting with sexist content anonymously promotes greater hostile sexism than interacting with it using an identified account" (p. 440).

Grappling with the seemingly altered behaviours displayed in virtual space, John Suler (2004) built a theory about what he calls "the online disinhibition effect". The effect comprises six aspects of the virtual space that to varying degrees affect the behaviour of internet users and may make them more likely to engage in trolling or other forms of online social misconduct. The six aspects are: (1) dissociative anonymity, which eliminates responsibility for conduct; (2) invisibility (no eye contact or body language, only text); (3) asynchronicity (time disconnect, optional response time); (4) solipsistic introjection (self-created versions of others/dehumanization); (5) dissociative imagination (it is not real, a "game"); and, (6) minimization of authority (all are peers, no punishment). Altogether, these aspects are assumed to untie social restrictions (inhibitions) normally present in nonvirtual face-to-face communication.

In light of this, it seems that online harassment against women is a result of at least two things combined; an ungoverned platform on which women become "easy bait" *and* the processes of deep-rooted patriarchal cultures aiming to discredit and exclude women from social participation and leadership. An added concern is whether/the extent to which the online space creates a more fertile ground for such intentions and attitudes to spread both within the virtual and further onto the nonvirtual world. What is the potential of influence by online communities and ideas fostered by these? Is the barrier for interaction lower when "everyone else comments"? To what extent do ideas expressed online transfer to offline reality – if we can at all make that division?

The virtual nonvirtual reality

Fox, Cruz and Lee (2015) found that sexist attitudes in online posts were reflected in the study objects' attitudes towards women in the nonvirtual life. "[W]riting one's own sexist tweets led to greater sexism and diminished perceptions of female job candidates' competence compared to retweeting someone else's sexist tweets" (p. 440). They concluded that, "interacting with sexist content online can indeed carry over to sexist attitudes offline" (ibid.). Their study supports the "online disinhibition effect" and demonstrates how online anonymity can aggravate hostility, an effect which the study further suggests is exacerbated when people start *engaging* in hostile online conduct (as opposed to sharing the content of others). Thus, the virtual sphere, due to its opportunity for anonymous participation, has the potential to create a far more hostile environment than what can develop in the same manner offline. In other words, online and offline realities appear to produce and reproduce hostility in a shared system, and it is difficult to draw a line between them.

Taking account also of the ways information is conveyed and absorbed online, such as within cultural, ideological and political echo chambers, we can assume that people are influenced both as result of their inherent beliefs and by increasing involuntary or unselected exposure to ideas. If we consider Fox et al.'s (2015) theory about correlation between (online) interaction and beliefs, the Internet provides fertile ground for conformity to these ideas. In line with this, recent research suggests that the rise of the Internet has merely contributed to further marginalization of women, with audience fragmentation and the echo chambers of political communication in social media (Tuchman, 2013). Tuchman addresses the niches in the new media and questions whether the proliferation of new media brings opportunities to women at all. The niches are "social location(s) occupied by a particular medium or media outlet and characterized by the demographic characteristics of those who occupy it" (ibid. preface xii), functioning much like today's social media echo chambers in the sense that they construct "walls" around certain ideas and interests that bounce back to self-confirm. Tuchman points out that the problem with audience-targeted "niching" is that it reinforces existing attitudes and enhances the neglect of alternative realities. Media broadcasting is becoming "narrowcasting", a process in which media target their audiences, and predict and mirror their ideas, values, concerns and interests (ibid. preface xiv). The niches and "narrowcasting" are relevant to the endurance of patriarchal systems because they target women in a way that discourages change and reinforces the status quo.

This relates to Georg Gerbner's theory about symbolic annihilation, a term he coined in 1976 to describe the lack of representation of some groups in the media, often based on sex, ethnicity, sexual orientation or other characteristic, that contributes to uphold unequal social structures (see Gerbner & Gross, 1976). Tuchman refers to Angela McRobbie (2008) on how contemporary society draws on a vocabulary of "empowerment" and "choice" (McRobbie, 2008, cited in Tuchman, 2013, preface xvi) and in general promoting individualism as "a substitute for feminism" (Tuchman, 2013, preface xvi). Tuchman argues that by focusing on individual women, female members of the elite, often educated and well paid, it is easier for scholars to ignore how much contemporary media continue to engage in a symbolic annihilation of women (ibid. preface xvii). After all, "Gender is an institution and gendering is a basic social process. As such, both gender and gendering are tied to the other basic institutions of contemporary societies" (ibid. preface, xvi).

In other words, the (to a large degree unregulated) online sphere cannot be expected to tackle issues that are manifest in the "real world" institutions, and the flow of reality across these two differently regulated and inhabited spaces makes it quite a complex task to transfer ideas from the one to the other. Still, as in the nonvirtual sphere there exist some spaces online that are more sexist than others, and these are more accessible to the general (online) population than are physical spaces of the same kind. The opportunity to "niche", predict, mirror and target a desired audience is now given to everyone who has access to online media. This is perhaps what is in process when sexism drifts effortlessly into online social media platforms at the cost of – in particular – female journalists. The ungoverned spaces in the virtual spheres give such violence the conditions and freedom to proliferate.

Silence and self-censorship

The next probing question is what happens when women who partake actively in political or otherwise conflictive social discussions online are met with threats and harassment. Which forms does the violent behaviour against them take and what are the arguments used?

The #mencallmethings hashtag on Twitter was started by feminist author and former journalist Sady Doyle in 2011, as an initiative to recognize and tackle sexist abuse women writers (herself included) experienced online. Under the hashtag, female Twitter users could show and openly discuss examples of the online harassment they received from men.

Megarry (2014) analysed the tweets responding to this hashtag, to see how women describe and discuss the online verbal abuse received from men (Megarry, 2014). The author argues that the harassment conveyed deserves stronger recognition as online sexual harassment and that the practice is rooted in a desire to reject women's voices from the digital public sphere (p. 46). While the attacks were meant to silence their voices, the nature of the aggression categorically built on conservative patriarchal arguments. "[A]ll the women involved were subjected to a particular kind of online abuse which can only be used against the female sex in patriarchal society" (Megarry, 2014, p. 50). The variety in sexist hashtags displayed different aspects of attempted alienation of women in that environment, but a prevailing similarity was the targeting of their identities as women, and throughout "stereotypical ideas of femininity are consistently utilized in a derogatory manner" (p. 49).

Megarry's analysis discards any assumption that the online public sphere can provide an equal and democratic social platform, and considers the issue of online social equality to be "broader than that of women simply achieving numerical parity with men in digital spaces" (ibid.). The author shows that a strong female representation among social media users fails to contribute to feminist transformation in digital technology and patriarchal structures remain.

Online harassment towards women journalists is receiving increasing recognition from academic scholars in several countries, showing that the problem is one that reaches across the wired parts of the world. Chen et al. (2018) recently presented a study based on in-depth interviews with 75 female journalists working or having worked in Germany, India, Taiwan, the United Kingdom, and the United States of America. The results show that women journalists "face rampant online gendered harassment that influences how they do their jobs" (Chen et al., 2018, pp. 1–2).

> Many of the women report that if they aim to engage with their audience online – which is a job requirement for many of them – they frequently face sexist comments that criticize, attack, marginalize, stereotype, or threaten them based on their gender or sexuality. Often, criticism of their work is framed as misogynistic attacks and, sometimes, even involves sexual violence'.
>
> *(ibid. pp. 1–2)*

Silencing female journalists online **107**

Perhaps the online social institutions cannot be expected to work significantly differently from those "on the ground". Whether female journalists are attacked because they are women or because they are women engaging outside their institutionally designated area is probably not always clear-cut. In the virtual sphere, however, this double threat is exacerbated by the lack of regulation and prosecution of attacks, causing female journalists on the virtual frontline to battle several different persisting processes at the same time.

Antipress sentiment and attacks on women journalists

That journalists and media workers face risks and threats when simply doing their job is not new. But whether the pressure of threats and harassment is increasing is a discussion that has just begun. In *Reporting Dangerously: Journalist Killings, Intimidation and Security*, Simon Cottle, Richard Sambrook and Nick Mosdell (2016) make a case for an ever more perilous and pressured environment for journalists in general, whether they be male or female. Their argument is founded in statistical analysis of numbers from the International News Safety Institute (INSI), interviews with journalists working in what the authors term "uncivil" places, and accounts of industry and political responses. Adding theoretical historical aspects on violence and global development, they build a convincing argument around the paradox that, while nation-state violence is in decline, journalists are threatened, harmed and killed at a higher rate than ever before (2016, p. 200).

> The increased dangers and risks confronted by today's journalists are in part accounted for by journalism's historically forged, deepening and geographically expanding commitment to report on the precarious lives of those inhabiting dangerous, violent places around the world. This "expanding reach" and "civic deepening" of journalism are part and parcel of contemporary globalising society, a world marked by expansive communication systems, increased interdependency and human insecurity.
>
> *(ibid. p. 62)*

Suggesting that expanding reach and deepening engagement have come with globalization and technology (exposure and access), the authors further support the notion that has dominated academic problematization of this issue over the last two decades, namely the journalists' loss of status as neutral observer (e.g. Tumber and Palmer, 2004; Allan and Zelizer, 2004), not only through the embedding and pooling practices of the west in past wars, but also in societies torn by intrastate conflict. To briefly address the issue of security in a historical frame, the loss of status may have started when foreign correspondents covering the wars of former Yugoslavia found themselves navigating a field of fragmented frontlines, where intervention, insurgency and growing suspicion also turned against the journalists (McLaughlin, 2002; Loyd, 1999). This was the moment many journalists refer to as a turning point in their experience of journalistic independence in war and conflict reporting (Armoudian, 2016; Høiby and Ottosen, 2018). Further, in the first and second Gulf wars, pooling systems and embedding practices were introduced to safeguard the press forcing a "crucial epistemological shift" (Keeble, 2004, p. 49) where embedded journalists played a central role in what the author describes a manufactured 'war' myth (ibid.). The pooling system that limited journalists' access to enter the field was rationalized through a safety discourse, while its real purpose was later claimed as to prevent the media's exposure to real events.

It is widely understood that state militaries depend on control over the media's coverage of the wars. From there, what some scholars have termed "the information war" (Tumber & Webster, 2006) – the battle for public trust and opinion – is a parallel trail to any conflict of size. Now that means to control the press have diminished owing to technological advancement and global development and engagement, these efforts to control, according to Cottle et al. (2016), have turned into "governments or agencies adopting an anti-media position" (p. 20), further leading to the more recent attacks on media houses by US forces in the Middle East (Paterson, 2014) and journalists' growing vulnerability to attacks by jihadi groups (Cottle et al. 2016).

In a similar way, societies challenged by crime, drug trafficking and street violence are also subject to attempts to control the narrative. According to Gonzales de Bustamante and Relly (2015), the representative from the United Nations Office for Drugs and Crime has noted that "the mounting violence against journalists at the hands of members of organized crime who sought to control both territory and media-driven messages about their respective organizations in such a direct and open way represented a new phenomenon" (p. 686).

Although journalism, and especially areas of the profession dealing with politics, war, conflict and human rights issues, is still a male-dominated field of work, more women are entering this area of the profession. They too suffer subsequent attacks and threats. Journalists who get involved with information on conflicts in general suffer targeting and attacks – and perhaps increasingly so. The more politically inflammatory the topic, the worse the harassment against them gets. Thus, it is necessary to see the online harassment of women journalists in the context of this development. Although the harassment may appear as personalized and/or sexualized, the rationale is to control and silence through imposed self-censorship.

Added to the threats that are not primarily gender specific, are the sexual assaults women face in the daily course of doing their job – often perpetrated by sources, male colleagues and supervisors (INSI, Barton & Storm, 2015). In a survey of 227 female news journalists, 60 percent reported a belief that sexual harassment is a problem for women journalists (Walsh-Childers, Chance & Herzog, 1996). Over one-third reported sexual harassment as having been a problem for them personally and two-thirds said they had endured nonphysical sexual harassment. About 17 percent reported having experienced physical sexual harassment (Walsh-Childers, Chance & Herzog, 1996).

Having discussed the lack of security for women in online spheres in the section above, it seems that the offline environment similarly lacks structures to promote the participation of women journalists in male-dominated journalistic beats. Again, as Fox, Cruz and Lee (2015) argue, sexism online goes offline with the attitudes that are fostered and/or nourished in the online environment. After all, perhaps the reflection between these realities is closer than first anticipated.

A second, but related, point is that female journalists are more prone to harassment because they are "always on trial"; especially in coverage related to politics, human rights, and corruption or otherwise male-dominated or "tough" news beats (Høiby, 2016). They are not expected to be there and must demonstrate that they are suited. As career-driven women wanting to participate and make a difference, they depend on social acceptance and physical and mental strength in order to advance their careers. The heroism and bravado in this field of journalism have no space for "whiners" (Høiby, 2016).

Sports journalism is another male-dominant field within journalism. A recent study of this area shows that sex discrimination and harassment drive young women to seek other fields of journalism , keeping sports media male-dominated (Everbach, 2018). Everbach recommends that social media companies and sports media employers take steps to curb gendered threats and aggression, which could help retain women in the industry (Everbach, 2018). The study shows that while women journalists face continuing discrimination, the arrival of social media has subjected them to new forms of abuse. In sports media, the women develop strategies to avoid harassment by bonding with other women colleagues.

Reporting incidents of sexual abuse in the workplace is normally not something that helps women in pursuing a career in a male-dominated field of work. Again, with reference to Ferganchick-Neufang's student-teacher-harassment study (1998) and my own more recent study (Høiby, 2016), women in male-dominated occupations do not profit (in the short term) from reporting attacks of harassment. This makes them easy targets for assault, and their choice is often to retreat – or continue suffering in silence. Continuing uphill takes a lot of courage and patience.

Conclusion: A "triple effect"

This chapter explores and deconstructs the phenomenon of online harassment of women journalists. To conclude, I suggest there are three main concepts comprising the evolving phenomenon of online harassment against women journalists. I argue that this issue is predominantly (but not exhaustively) dependent on (1) systematic antipress violence, (2) persisting patriarchal social structures and (3) that the conditions of online space allow harassment to thrive. I have previously argued that the combination of the two former factors (antipress violence and patriarchal structures) creates a double burden for female journalists to carry in the field (see Høiby, 2016). In this chapter, I add the perspectives of the online environment that seem to bring an amplified effect. In a simple model (Figure 7.1), I make my point by placing these perspectives in layers, illustrating the level of threat with density in colour. It is in the middle where the three circles overlap that the densest sphere of threat occurs, and where I argue that women journalists are set to navigate online.

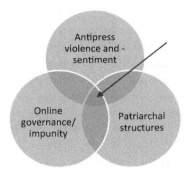

FIGURE 7.1 Level of threat towards female journalists

It is reasonable to suggest that this burdening climate may force many to exercise some level of self-censorship.

Online harassment of women journalists is a result of all its components; a combination of who they are (women), what they do (journalism), and the context they are operating within (online space/regulation). The effects of anonymity and otherwise lack of governance of the Internet (e.g. what Suler (2004) refers to as "minimization of authority") makes harassment an accessible and highly effective option that in addition offers impunity to perpetrators in exchange for a slight effort. Although the number of cases where individuals have faced prosecution for such crimes is increasing, these cases still represent the exception measured against the massive abuse that is taking place. This expectation of impunity similarly exists for harassment of women, since perpetrators go free every time a case of abuse goes unreported (which they often do). The idea that women are "whiners" if they file complaints about harassment and abuse in their workplace is widespread among both male and female journalists around the world (Høiby, 2016). That the online harassment is verbal and not based in physical action, further raises this expectation of perpetrators' impunity. Thus, it is twice as "easy to get away with" when the victim is a *woman* and she was "only" harassed *online*.

The accessible and collaborative features of new media technology that once prompted optimism about democratic participation in a more accessible and diverse public sphere is yet to accomplish what we had hoped for (Loader & Mercea, 2011). The idea that online networking provides platforms where "nothing and no one [can stop women] from creating [their] tribe and highlighting [their] cause" (Gautam, 2012, cited in Loader & Mercea, 2011, p. 757) now appears unrealistic. Instead of prompting historically marginalized groups to participate in public discussion, the absence of the traditional gatekeepers appears to have unchained several processes of marginalization.

What the result is for journalism remains to be shown. Chen et al. (2018) urge schools of journalism to increase their focus on such threats and provide students with the means to better tackle hostile online environments. "(T)he women in our sample overwhelmingly wanted more training to handle harassment and for their news organizations to protect them from abuse" (Chen et al, 2018, p. 15). Given the representation of women among students of journalism (which in many places is high), this is a suggestion that could potentially be very effective. Educating students about the threats of online abuse, the forms it can take and the consequences it may have for them, is vital. They must at least know that it is systematic, and that they are not to be blamed. Awareness of the institutions and tools that may help them can be a decisive factor as to whether we continue to have women in some parts of the profession in the future or not.

Although I emphasize the importance of preparing students for what they likely will encounter when they enter the field of work, this is all mitigation. Little is going to change unless the structures of the virtual spheres are reconsidered, and in terms of developing social resistance we treat reality as a whole with little distinction between on- and off- line. Institutions to support victims, and accessible systems to trace and find perpetrators so that they can be held accountable for actions, are as necessary online as in any other environment.

References

Allan, S. & Zelizer, B. (Eds.) (2004). *Reporting war: journalism in wartime*. London: Routledge.

Armoudian, M. (2016). *Reporting from the danger zone: Frontline journalists, their jobs, and an increasingly perilous future*. New York: Routledge.

Ausserhofer, J. & Maireder, A. (2013). National politics on Twitter. *Information,* Communication & Society, *16*(3), 291–314. https://doi.org/10.1080/1369118X.2012.756050

Barton, A. & Storm, H. (2015). Violence and harassment against women in the news media: A global picture (p. 40). Retrieved from International News Safety Institute (INSI) website: https://newssafety.org/uploads/IWMF.FINALA.PDF

Beltran, J. V. (2017). The emergence of the Philippine "anti-media": The Duterte factor. *Jurnal ILMU KOMUNIKASI, 14*, 61–74. https://doi.org/10.24002/jik.v14i1.833

Benson, K. A. (1984). Comment on Crocker's "An analysis of university definitions of sexual harassment". *Signs: Journal of Women in Culture and Society, 9*(3), 516–519. https://doi.org/10.1086/494083

Chen, G. M., Pain, P., Chen, V. Y., Mekelburg, M., Springer, N. & Troger, F. (2018). 'You really have to have a thick skin': A cross-cultural perspective on how online harassment influences female journalists. *Journalism*. https://doi.org/10.1177/1464884918768500

Cottle, S., Sambrook, R. & Mosdell, N. (2016). *Reporting Dangerously – Journalist Killings, Intimidation and Security*. London: Palgrave.

Coyle, K. (1996). 'How Hard Can It Be?' In: Cherny, L. & Reba Weise, E. R. (Eds.), *Wired Women: Gender and New Realities in Cyberspace* (p. 50). Seattle: Seal Press.

Duggan, M. & Smith, A. (2013, December 30). Social Media Update 2013. Retrieved October 6, 2019, from Pew Research Center: Internet, Science & Tech website: https://www.pewinternet.org/2013/12/30/social-media-update-2013/

Everbach, T. (2018). "I realized it was about them … not me": Women sports journalists and harassment. In J. R. Vickery & T. Everbach (Eds.), *Mediating Misogyny: Gender, Technology, and Harassment* (pp. 131–149). https://doi.org/10.1007/978-3-319-72917-6_7

Ferganchick-Neufang, J. K. (1998). Virtual harassment: Women and online education. *First Monday, 3*(2). https://doi.org/10.5210/fm.v3i2.575

Fox, J., Cruz, C. & Lee, J. Y. (2015). Perpetuating online sexism offline: Anonymity, interactivity, and the effects of sexist hashtags on social media. *Computers in Human Behavior*, *52*, 436–442. https://doi.org/10.1016/j.chb.2015.06.024

Gerbner, G. and Gross, L. (1976). Living with television: The violence profile. *Journal of Communication*, *26*, 172–199.

González de Bustamante, C. & Relly, J. E. (2016). Professionalism under threat of violence, *Journalism Studies*, *17*(6), 684–702, https://doi.org/10.1080/1461670X.2015.1006903

Heil, B. H. and Piskorski, M. (2009, June 1). New Twitter research: Men follow men and nobody tweets. *Harvard Business Review*. Retrieved from https://hbr.org/2009/06/new-twitter-research-men-follo

Høiby, M. (2016). Sexual violence against journalists in conflict zones. Gendered practices and cultures in the newsroom. In B. von der Lippe & R. Ottosen (Eds.), *Gendering War and Peace Reporting Some Insights – Some Missing Links*. Gothenburg: Nordicom.

Høiby, M. & Ottosen, R. (2018). Journalism under pressure in conflict zones: A study of journalists and editors in seven countries. *Media, War & Conflict*, *12*(1), 69–86. https://doi.org/10.1177/1750635217728092

Høiby, M. (2019). *Journalism under pressure: A cross-national study of antipress violence and journalist safety* (PhD dissertation). OsloMet – Oslo Metropolitan University, Oslo.

IFEX (2019). Is the internet a "safe place" for women journalists? (2017, June 8). Retrieved October 6, 2019, from IFEX website: https://ifex.org/is-the-internet-a-safe-place-for-women-journalists/

Keeble, R. (2004). Information warfare in in an age of hyper-militarism. In Allan, S. & Zelizer, B. (Eds.). (2004). *Reporting War: Journalism in Wartime*. Oxon: Routledge.

Kilman, L. (2017). *An attack on one is an attack on all: Successful initiatives to protect journalists and combat impunity* – UNESCO Digital Library (p. 98). Retrieved from https://unesdoc.unesco.org/ark:/48223/pf0000250430

Loader, B. D. & Mercea, D. (2011). Networking democracy? *Information, Communication & Society*, *14*(6), 757–769

Loyd, A. (1999). *My War Gone By, I Miss It So*. New York: Grove Press.

Mardorossian, C. M. (2014). *Framing the Rape Victim: Gender and Agency Reconsidered*. New Brunswick, NJ: Rutgers University Press.

Massanari, A. (2017). #Gamergate and The Fappening: How Reddit's algorithm, governance, and culture support toxic technocultures. *New Media & Society*, *19*(3), 329–346. https://doi.org/10.1177/1461444815608807

McLaughlin, G. (2002). *The War Correspondent*. London: Pluto Press.

McRobbie, A. (2008). *The Aftermath of Feminism: Gender, Culture and Social Change*. London: SAGE.

Megarry, J. (2014). Online incivility or sexual harassment? Conceptualising women's experiences in the digital age. *Women's Studies International Forum*, *47*, 46–55. https://doi.org/10.1016/j.wsif.2014.07.012

OSCE (2019). Safety of Female Journalists Online. Retrieved October 6, 2019, from www.osce.org/representative-on-freedom-of-media/safety-female-journalists-online

Paterson, C. (2014). *War Reporters Under Threat: The United States and Media Freedom*. London: Pluto Press

Rosales, R. G. (2006). Shooting the messenger: why radio broadcasting is a deadly profession in the Philippines. *Journal of Radio Studies*, *13*(1), 146–155. https://doi.org/10.1207/s15506843jrs1301_10

Suler, J. (2004). The online disinhibition effect. *Cyberpsychology & Behavior*, 7(3).

Tandoc Jr, E. C. (2017). Watching over the watchdogs. *Journalism Studies*, *18*(1), 102–117. https://doi.org/10.1080/1461670X.2016.1218298

Tuchman, G. (2013). Media, gender, niche. In C. L. Armstrong(ed.), *Media Disparity: A Gender Battleground*. Lexington Books.

Tumber, H. & Palmer, J. (2004). *Media at War* (1st edition). London; Thousand Oaks, CA: Sage Publications, Inc.

Tumber, H. & Webster, F. (2006). *Journalists Under Fire: Information War and Journalistic Practices*. London: SAGE.

UNESCO (2019a). Intensified attacks, new defences: developments in the fight to protect journalists and end impunity. Report. Retrieved March 23, 2020 from https://unesdoc.unesco.org/ark:/48223/pf0000371343

UNESCO (2019b). Standing Up against online harassment of women journalists – What works? Retrieved October 6, 2019, from UNESCO: https://en.unesco.org/events/standing-against-online-harassment-women-journalists-what-works

Waisbord, S. (2018). Why populism is troubling for democratic communication. *Communication, Culture & Critique*, *11*(1), 21–34. https://doi.org/10.1093/ccc/tcx005

Walsh-Childers, K., Chance, J. & Herzog, K. (1996). Sexual harassment of women journalists. *Journalism & Mass Communication Quarterly*, *73*(3), 559–581. https://doi.org/10.1177/107769909607300305

8

A WAY TO SILENCE JOURNALISTS?

Estonian female journalists' experiences with harassment and self-censorship

Signe Ivask

Introduction

Estonia is not considered to be a country where journalists face major danger; there is no news of Estonian journalists being detained, harassed, killed or having problems with online harassment (e.g. Council of Europe, 2019; Reporters Without Borders, 2019; UNESCO, 2019). Although international reports do not indicate that Estonian journalists have severe problems with insults, threats, harassment and self-censorship, this chapter argues that Estonian female journalists nevertheless experience threats and harassment, which affect the way they carry out their job.

The rationale for studying female journalists' experiences builds on international studies that indicate that female journalists are often attacked, insulted, criticized and targeted because of their gender. Misogyny towards female journalists is often expressed through the usage of insulting words (e.g. slut, bitch) (Löfgren Nilsson & Örnebring, 2016) and/or when sources refuse to give an interview to them because of their gender (e.g. sources saying that they only talk to a male sports journalist) (Hardin & Shain, 2005). International reports also indicate that female journalists receive more threats, insults and harassment than male journalists (Barton & Storm, 2018; OSCE, 2016). Female journalists tend to not take legal action against these issues in order to avoid making the situation more traumatic for themselves (Reporters Without Borders, 2015).

This chapter focuses on female journalists' experiences with harassment and whether such experiences result in self-censorship. Harassment is considered as "incidents where staff are abused, threatened or assaulted in circumstances related to their work, including commuting to and from work, involving an explicit or implicit challenge to their safety, well-being or health" (WHO, 2010, What is work-place violence? section, para. 2). This entails that harassment could come both from inside and outside of the workplace. Suffering from it could lead to emotional, psychological and physical problems (Ballard & Easteal, 2018). More precisely, this chapter mainly relies on a definition of *gender harassment*, which occurs if there is an unwanted behaviour or action related to one's gender, whose aim or effect is to degrade someone and establish a disturbing, hostile, degrading or insulting environment (Karu et al., 2014).

The structure of the chapter is as follows: first a theoretical and empirical background of offline and online behaviour towards journalists is presented. Then some recent Estonian regulatory cases concerning harassment toward journalists are sketched out, before the methods and analysis are presented. The chapter ends with a concluding discussion concerning female journalists' experiences with harassment and self-censorship.

Offline and online behaviour towards journalists

Self-censorship and harassment

One definition of self-censorship is that it is "an act of intentionally and voluntarily withholding information from others in the absence of formal obstacles" (Bar-Tal, 2017, p. 37). Another definition is that it is withholding one's true opinion from an audience because fearing that someone will disagree with it (Hayes et al., 2005). Cook and Heilmann (2013) distinguish between private and public self-censorship. Public self-censorship is an individual's reaction to a publicly existing external agent of censorship. Private self-censorship is a reaction within the individual, for example relying on one's value system whilst working, so the individual reacts to the interpersonal conflict without the external censor (Cook & Heilmann, 2013). Journalists could also self-censor themselves when they feel that there is information that could bring harm to the public, for example disseminating terrorist agendas (Mortensen, 2018). In this chapter I take a closer look into (private) self-censorship experiences where journalists voluntarily withhold information or avoid gathering information (e.g. reading comments, communicating with unpleasant sources etc.) in order to avoid harassment.

Comments that are criticizing the journalist could be considered the mildest form of harassment, yet they can include horrific threats towards a journalist. The common example of a harassing comment aims at undermining the intelligence and competence of the journalist. While such comments are not posed as direct threats, they can nevertheless have a negative influence on the journalist (Löfgren Nilsson & Ørnebring, 2016).

Harassment can vary a lot from calling journalists names with negative connotations, to even threatening them with sexual violence or death. Stalking or constantly calling journalists are also ways used to harass a journalist (Löfgren Nilsson &Ørnebring, 2016; Ivask, 2017a). These practices can be quite easily executed because journalists' contacts are available for readers; their names and photos are presented next to their articles or on the contact pages, making them recognizable to everyone. Additionally, journalists are active on social media as a part of their job. This makes them visible and approachable for the public (Chen et al., 2018; Löfgren Nilsson &Örnebring, 2016).

All in all, journalists are harassed by comments left in the comments' sections that contain threats towards journalists, calling journalists names that undermine their intelligence and competence and stalking or constantly calling journalists (Löfgren Nilsson & Örnebring, 2016; Ivask, 2017a).

Harassment is experienced by two-thirds of female media workers; sexual harassment is experienced by 46 percent of female media workers (International Women's Media Foundation, 2013). The International Press Institute (IPI), 2017) explained in a report that one out of four Finnish journalists have experienced harassing or other verbal abuse; most of the victims were women. Typical attacks were insults, rape threats and constant phone calls (IPI, 2017).

The reaction to harassment depends on the person on the receiving end. It is even said that some journalists could interpret negative attention as a positive thing – a sign that they are doing something right (Lischka, 2017). But these kinds of attacks usually have emotionally negative influence on journalists (Löfgren Nilsson & Örnebring, 2016). Thus, they might start looking for methods to overcome negative reactions, such as avoiding emotionally more triggering topics or not reading comment sections overall. Threatening journalists is a way to silence them (Löfgren Nilsson & Örnebring, 2016), as the fear can lead to self-censorship, which discourages critical reporting among journalists (Chalaby, 2000; Jungblut & Hoxha, 2017).

The reason why journalists do not react to harassment could lie in resilience, i.e. their ability to adapt to the negative situation (Williams, 2007). This also includes finding strategies of how to be resilient in threatening or challenging situations without spending too many resources (ibid. – in other words, finding a way to keep on working when attacked (Drury, 2011). This phenomenon occurs also collectively – people can overcome serious stress-inducing situations or traumatic incidents by relying on the "we" feeling that comes from the "relational bonds" between communities (Drury, 2011, p. 6).

It is clear that verbal attacks, whether offline or online, influence the way journalists do their jobs – ask questions, pick topics, identify sources and express themselves (Post & Kepplinger, 2019). These psychological reactions are connected to self-censorship (Waisbord, 2002). In order to avoid harassment, journalists could self-censor as a preventing mechanism – for example having experience that some topics bring along a lot of negative reactions from the audience, the journalist could start avoiding such topics in order to avoid harassment.

Self-censorship may undermine the press' responsibility to inform the public (Mortensen, 2018), because "it prevents free access to information, freedom of expression and the flow of information" (Bar-Tal, 2017, p. 37). In other words, harassment avoidance, or self-censorship, among journalists could not just have a negative effect on journalists themselves, but on the society overall.

Estonian cases and context

In order to provide context to the study, the following section explains a couple of regulatory cases in Estonia.

One of the cases is that of Leedo v. Delfi.[1] The case concerned 20 user comments (out of 185) in an online comment section under a news story about Estonian business man Vjatšeslav Leedo and his business. The content of the 20 comments was degrading and insulting towards Vjatšeslav Leedo. The outcome of the case was that Delfi as a media outlet is regarded as responsible for the content of the user comments left on their site (Swiss Institute of Comparative Law, 2015). After this decision, Delfi's editor-in-chief Urmo Soonvald raised worrying questions about freedom of speech and information, but also mentioned that they are putting more effort into moderating the comment section (Delfi, 2013).

Another important case is from 2018, when an Estonian actress Marika Korolev decided to sue the anonymous commentators of a public forum called Family School (Perekool), because of false information and slander that they spread about her. The Estonian Midwives Association, which moderates Family School, had to de-anonymize the commentators that were disseminating false information and slander and present their names to Korolev. Then a case was presented against the commentators and a settlement reached in favour of Korolev (Mihkels, 2018). A wider discussion arose in Estonia on the topic of anonymity, hateful comments and moderating the comments that contain hate, threats and attacks. A couple of other Estonian celebrities have also started a court case against Family School and anonymous commentators.

Most news outlets in Estonia have comment sections for the readers to react and discuss. Depending on the topic, the comment section can be either open or closed for commenting (e.g. in case if the news is about a very delicate issue, such as child molestation, where the identity of anonymous sources/sufferer could be exposed by the commentators). Although comment sections or forums have explanations of what is accepted and what not, hateful comments still make it to journalists and sources via forums and comment sections as most of the comments' sections are not moderated by the newsrooms in Estonia. Readers, commentators and sources can moderate the comments' sections by reporting hostile comments to the newsroom, who can then delete them. Journalists can also moderate the comments' section by reading the comments and deleting hostile ones.

Although the Leedo v. Delfi and Korolev cases show that the outlets/forum platforms are responsible for disseminating the comments and can be held accountable, moderating is not formally required in even the biggest newsrooms in Estonia.

Thus, journalists who write a news story or an article have to be ready to receive comments or messages on the topic or about themselves (Shanahan, 2017). Delfi's editor-in-chief Urmo Soonvald (Delfi, 2013) said that comment sections are platforms for freedom of speech and expression – two important rights that should not be restricted in any way. But this attitude raises important questions: if the newsroom accept any kind of opinion and expression, how can journalists react

118 Signe Ivask

against opinions or expressions that attack or undermine the journalists? Can the accepting approach result in self-censorship and thereby undermine free speech? It is also necessary to point out that hate speech is not criminalized in Estonia. Journalists in Estonian newsrooms have rarely reacted publicly to the comments they receive. This might be because freedom of expression carries such a great value among journalists and in newsrooms.

Data and method

Three studies were carried out: one in 2015, a second in 2016 and a third one in 2018 (Palgi, 2018). The sample consisted of (a) eight sports journalists – five male and three female (2015), (b) 12 female journalists from different fields (Palgi, 2018) and (c) 181 respondents (115 female, 66 male; 2016). All of the female journalists in the 2015 and 2018 studies were from a print or converged newsroom.

The 2016 study was carried out among 429 online, print and converged newsroom journalists in Estonia. I gathered answers from 181 respondents (response rate 42 percent). Among 181 respondents were 115 female and 66 male respondents. Most respondents were newspaper journalists (n=89), followed by journalists from converged newsrooms (n=79) and online journalists (n=12) (one respondent did not provide an answer). Most female respondents fell into the category of 18 to 37 years old, followed by 38 to 47 years old. The biggest age groups among male respondents were 18 to 27 and 38 to 47 year olds.

There were 61 respondents with five or less years of experience, 44 with six to ten years of experience, 19 with 11 to 15 years of experience, 15 with 16 to 20 years of experience and 42 with more than 20 years of experience.

The data were gathered by in-depth interviews (2015 and 2018), journalists' diaries (2015) and a questionnaire (2016). For the 2015 study journalists completed a seven-day diary explaining everything they did and felt during the days. In addition, in-depth interviews with all of the journalists were carried out. The diary did not have a concrete structure; all the journalists approached it in their own way. Journalists were asked to write about what they published (also the amount of time they had put in to producing the content), how they felt during the period stress-wise, if and what kind of incidents happened with sources (both negative and positive) and what felt stressful to them during the period.

Firstly, we collected the diaries and then we carried out the interviews. All of the interviews were carried out individually and contained questions that arose from the diaries. Afterwards we transcribed the interviews. The length of the interviews was approximately 45 minutes.

The in-depth semi-structured interviews that were carried out in 2018 (Palgi, 2018) consisted of questions about experiences with harassment and insults. The length of the interviews varied from 20 minutes to 50 minutes. All the interviews were carried out individually.

The data of diaries and interviews were analysed by qualitative content analysis. A code system was created and utilized in order to map out journalists' experiences of harassment and self-censorship. Codes such as "negative experience with a source", "negative experience with an audience member", "negative experience with a colleague", "negative feedback from comment sections", "negative feedback received via phone", "negative feedback received via email", "life-threatening situations", "fear", "indications of self-censorship" etc. were created and utilized.

After the coding, the data were analysed more thoroughly to see whether the experiences met the definitions and strategies of harassment. We considered as harassment experiences where journalists are abused, threatened or assaulted in work-related situations (WHO, 2010); and as gender harassment experiences where journalists are degraded or a disturbing, hostile, degrading or insulting environment is established because of their gender (Karu et al., 2014). Some of the strategies used to harass the journalists are threatening the journalist, calling the journalist names that undermine their intelligence and competence, stalking or constantly calling journalists (Löfgren Nilsson and Örnebring, 2016; Ivask, 2017a).

The questionnaire consisted of questions about experiences with negative or aggressive sources, burnout and stress among journalists. The data were collected from July to August 2016; afterwards it was cleaned, systematized and analysed in Excel, using statistics software.

Discussion of the methodology

To start out, the question of why is it difficult to map out Estonian journalists' problems has to be approached. Firstly, journalism is often described as a stressful profession that is embedded with negative emotions brought on by conflict coverage or aggressive sources (Backholm & Björkqvist, 2012; Careercast, 2018; Shanahan, 2017; Weidmann & Papsdorf, 2010). Journalists, therefore, are not willing to admit having problems or issues, because the job itself necessarily involves the basic principles of dealing with conflicts.

Secondly, the words harassment and (self-)censorship have very strong negative connotations in the Estonian language, so journalists might not want to label their own experience with such words. We used descriptive questions and asked about negative and/or stressful experiences with sources and audience in our studies in order to avoid overemphasizing the terminology.

Thirdly, as was indicated in our studies, journalists do not necessarily recognize the situations where they are suffering from harassment or are self-censoring. What is more, journalists usually deny the problem, because it is thought that no one can help and it is best to ignore the issue (Marshall, 2005). This is something that I faced in my studies as well: although journalists mentioned having problems, they still brushed it off as it was nothing and not worth mentioning.

As journalists might have avoided saying "harassment", the content analysis focused firstly on mapping the "negative experiences" instead of "harassment". As journalists described the situations without using the terms "harassment" and "self-censorship", it should be taken into account that the results are the interpretation of the researcher relying on the theoretical literature and definitions.

120 Signe Ivask

The avoidance of the words "harassment" and "self-censorship" could also mean that journalists do not experience the described situations as severely problematic either in terms of work or interpersonal relations, meaning, there might not be a problem after all for them. The avoidance could also be one of the strategies of collective resilience and could occur subconsciously (Williams, 2002). The reason why journalists avoid labelling their experiences is a topic that needs further investigation.

Results

The results of the questionnaire (N=181, female=115, male=66) carried out in 2016 showed that 17 percent (n=19) of the female respondents and 11 percent (n=7) of the male respondents said they *often* had experiences with abusive and/or aggressive people in their work. 28 percent (n=32) of female respondents and 24 percent (n=16) of male respondents said they had these kind of experiences at times.

Taking a more in-depth look into the statistics of people who said they *often* faced abusive and/or aggressive people in their work (N=26, female=19, male=7), there was a difference between how male and female respondents in this category felt towards burnout, phoning the sources and leaving the field. Male respondents did not indicate feeling burned out, not wanting to phone the sources nor did they think about leaving the field. Yet, eight out of 19 women felt burned out, seven out of 19 women did not want to phone the sources and nine out of 19 female respondents preferred email communication to other kinds of communication; 14 women out of 19 were exhausted by the communication with the sources; 12 out of 19 (63 percent) female respondents, who often had experiences with abusive or aggressive people in their work, considered leaving the field. Although I cannot directly claim that these issues are correlated to each other, these results should be subject to further research.

In conclusion, female journalists, who said they had experiences with aggressive and/or abusive people in their work, also reported having issues with contacting the source directly (via phone) and a high rate of intentions of leaving the field.

Experiences of female journalists

The female journalists' experiences with harassment varied. There were differences in why they were targeted, the strategy of the harassment and who targeted the journalist. Some of the comments were made on the preconception that a female journalist is not capable of doing her job as well as her male colleagues (especially in sports journalism), other comments arose from the stories arose from the stories that the journalist was covering (e.g. corruption cases).

As mentioned above, it was rather difficult to study harassment as journalists normalized their experience to something that went together with the profession (interviews of 2015 and 2018). The analysis showed that the main channels where journalists received comments that could be considered harassment were comment sections, personal emails, social media, face-to-face communication and phone calls.

The interviews carried out in 2018 among 12 female journalists led to a pattern: Comment sections were the first channels brought up in the interviews regarding where journalists were harassed. One female journalist mentioned that anonymous commentators take aim at her age and connect her success as a journalist to her being a prostitute at her workplace. The comments said, for example that the only way she – a young woman in her early twenties – got the reporter position, was by having sex with someone superior, who then had to hire her as a favour. She added that she had been repeatedly called stupid and a child-journalist in the comment section. Younger, less experienced journalists said that they were called a "child-journalist" often. This term emphasizes the age and experience of the journalist, trying to indicate that they are not professionals, rather novices. An older, more experienced female journalist said her articles also received comments about her looks.

> Commentators also say that I must be a wife of some rich Estonian man, how else would I be hired by the newsroom. [...] I think that male journalists do not receive these kinds of comments about sleeping with someone superior to get to their position.
>
> *(Interview, 2018)*

For female sports journalists, some of the insulting comments were connected to the preconception that sports journalism is a job for males, who understand sports better. Female sports journalists were also the ones who talked about insults being forwarded face-to-face. Some of the insults were about how female journalists should take on tasks and professions that are socially considered more female, such as knitting a sock or cooking.

> There have been several questions from the audience and sportsmen in a style of "How come football? Would you not be better off knitting a sock at home?" No, I would not. But I can knit a sock and speak about football at the same time. How many men are capable of that?
>
> *(Interview with a female sports journalist, 2015)*

Two male colleagues brought female sports journalists' problems up in their interviews (2015) as well. One said that there were jokes in the newsroom on the topic of female sports journalists or about female colleagues. The other admitted that female sports journalists have to prove themselves knowledgeable about sports and he was guilty of having preconceptions on that matter.

There was a repetitive pattern in the studies about female journalists – misogyny, insults and threats that emphasized the gender or gender features of the female journalist. Saying that someone is a beginner or not a professional, the commentators might try to indicate that the journalist should not be trusted because of the lack of experience and knowledge. It did not matter if a female journalist was covering sports, politics or social issues – the insults bore the same characteristics. This finding goes together with Örnebring's and Löfgren Nilsson's (2016) study: They also found that misogyny is s recurring theme when insulting female journalists.

Female journalists also mentioned delicate topics that caused strong reactions (e.g. audience commenting and sending messages that contain very aggressive and insulting content). These kinds of topics were, for example immigration, minority groups and refugees.

Female journalists also admitted in the 2018 interviews that harassing did not occur only via emails, phone calls or from the comment section of their stories, but was also forwarded via Facebook or on other social media platforms directly to the journalist. This meant that even if the journalists did not read the comments (as female journalists mentioned in the studies of 2015 and 2018), harassing, threatening, or insulting messages might have reached them other ways. One of these might have been by relatives, who read the comments, got frustrated and forwarded the comments with their negative emotions to the journalist.

Another problem was related to using a personal mobile phone number when contacting sources. By revealing a personal number, journalists are available to be contacted by the source at all times. One female journalist (2018) said that while she was on a bus ride home from work, a politician (source) called her on her personal mobile phone and yelled at her loud enough for the other passengers to hear him. Some sources started constantly calling the journalist; some started sending threat messages on the mobile phone during the night or random messages on the phone very often. One female journalist (2018) called it "psychological terror" aimed at making the journalist surrender and not write about the topic. The same was found in Löfgren Nilsson and Örnebring (2016) study, that the aim of harassing behaviour is to silence the journalist. Some journalists admitted (2015 and 2018) that harassments have led them to the verge of mental/physical breakdown. One journalist described how she could not sleep at night for a period of time. Many mentioned high stress and feeling uncomfortable.

Reactions of female journalists to attacks and self-censorship

Female sports journalists (2015) said that being watched constantly by their male colleagues and audience meant they were very fearful of making mistakes. Minor mishaps could lead to mental breakdowns (Diary of a female sports journalist). Not only because of failing in their work, but also because reactions from audiences towards mistakes could be extremely negative, including comments about how a "girl" did not manage with the job (Diaries of female sports journalists). Female sports journalists were very careful when picking the topics to write on and, if a topic was forwarded to them, they all felt extremely uncomfortable, because they were in an unknown territory (Diaries of female sports journalists).

But the female sports journalists mentioned that these kinds of situations, where they had to do someone else's job, were quite usual, because there was an attitude

Estonian female journalists' experiences **123**

in the newsroom that "she is a woman, she will do it anyways" (Interview with a female sports journalist, 2015) emphasizing the fact that women needed to prove themselves. Thus, all the topics "others do not want to cover" (Interview with a female sports journalist, 2015) ended up on their table.

This kind of moving from one topic that is familiar to another that is not meant that journalists had to surpass their competencies, which made them vulnerable to making mistakes or being inaccurate, hence leading to being attacked by the audience, sources and/or colleagues. Additionally, a female journalist in a 2018 interview mentioned that higher stress was also induced when an expert source expects that journalist knows everything about the field.

Male colleagues (2015 interviews and diaries) did not bring out such problems with sportsmen, colleagues or audience. Their problems with the job were mostly connected to the core of being a journalist, meaning that you take your job everywhere, you are away from home during nights, weekends and even work on holidays. Yet, there were indicators of self-censorship among both male and female sports journalist.

Most sports journalists in the sample of eight journalists (2015) admitted in their diaries and interviews that having a negative experience with a source could stop them from contacting the person again or covering a topic that the person was connected to. These negative experiences could be sources threatening to take legal actions, forwarding negative feedback to the editor-in-chief or saying that the journalists had done an extremely unprofessional job.

> When did I think about quitting? Well, there was a scandal with one of our top basketball teams. One of the players drove the car under the influence. I published the story. Then the manager of the team called me and threatened me by saying that I had lied and I will be sacked.
> *(Interview with a female sports journalist, 2015)*

Afterwards the female sports journalist mentioned that Estonian basketball was not a topic that she wrote on anymore; the topic was then covered by a male colleague by her own choice. A female journalist interviewed in 2018 described a similar situation. She explained that one of the sources threatened her with a court case. Afterwards he started to send messages on her mobile phone at night with the content indicating indirectly or directly that the journalist was a "slut". These kinds of situation where female journalists were threatened, combined with the fear of not being taken seriously and making mistakes, could lead to either self-censorship or female journalists leaving the field.

Journalists mentioned in diaries and interviews (2015) that if they had to phone a source who had been unpleasant or aggressive in the past, they hoped that the source would not answer the phone. But journalists also said that if the source had left an unanswered phone call, they felt the necessity to call back, because otherwise they might leave an unprofessional impression of themselves. Even in the case when the communication was achieved, the phone calls/email exchanges would

124 Signe Ivask

at times lack depth or omit critical questions. Self-censorship in this case was used as a strategy to remain resilient (Drury, 2011): to be able to work in the field and newsroom.

Trying to avoid a long in-depth communication with a person who has been unpleasant, insulting, etc., might lead to a poor quality of interviewing and reporting (Chalaby 2000; Jungblut & Hoxha, 2017). So some serious conflicts or issues are left without in-depth critical investigation. This is mentioned by Bar-Tel (2017) and Mortensen (2018), who say that withholding information from the wider society could damage it. What if the journalist is reporting information, but does not ask the "burning" questions because of former negative experiences with the source?

Relying on the definitions of public and private self-censorship by Cook and Heilmann (2013), the results of the studies 2015 and 2018 showed that journalists seemed to firstly react to the external agent of the censor, but negative experiences also evoked private censorship within the journalist, who started censoring themselves with the hopes of remaining resilient despite harassment.

But this leads to problems with fulfilling the "watchdog" role. The avoidance of writing on topics where a journalist has received harassment means that they start to censor themselves about what they write about and how. This is a threat to democratic society, because some important information may not be published, or information stays in the newsroom or with a journalist (Bar-Tel 2017). For example the international doping case of Estonian skiers in 2019 is a topic of discussion among journalism scholars and practitioners of why it was not discovered by (sports) journalists before the scandal exploded.

Journalists who have had faced harassment whilst working as journalists, might be leaving the field, because of the dissatisfaction caused by these kinds of incidents (Ivask, 2017b). This means having fewer and less professional journalists who mediate information and make editorial decisions about what kind of information should reach the audience and how.

Coping with negative experiences

Even though negative experiences were something that might have brought along stress and a feeling of being unsafe, female journalists, especially older and more experienced ones, foregrounded that the solution for online and offline harassment was to grow "a thick skin" (interviews of 2018). This could be considered as a resilience strategy (Drury, 2011) – in order for journalists to remain at work, they need to be emotionally passive towards attacks.

> Of course, there still occur situations where somebody does not like my story and then phones me, but I do not pay much attention to it. It is part of the job.
>
> *(Interview 2018)*

Female journalists said in interviews (2018) that another way of coping with negative experience was to use humour. This is a collective resilience strategy (Drury, 2011), which according to other journalism studies (e.g. Buchanan & Keats, 2011) is a common approach among journalists.

Another strategy was "to get over it". In other words, journalists foregrounded that receiving threats and insults was an everyday experience that went together with the profession. By choosing the profession, journalists said in the interviews (2015 and 2018), you had also agreed suffering from the negative sides of it, such as negative and aggressive sources, having to cover tragedies that evoke negative emotions and so forth.

A further strategy was avoidance. Female sports journalists said in their interviews (2015) that they did not pay attention to comments on their stories/news, because they did not consist of constructive criticism, but rather obscene insults about them as women covering sports, their age or looks. The behaviour of journalists contradicts the idea of commentaries/forums increasing interactivity between journalists and audiences and that it is a way for journalists to gather information for follow-up investigation (e.g. Chung, 2007; Bardoel & Deuze, 2001). Female journalists' choices of not reading or not paying attention to the comments might leave them without important additional information about the case/topic being covered and/or constructive feedback that the journalists could learn and develop from. Yet, journalists not reading the comments acted as a self-sustaining mechanism to avoid harassment. As mentioned before, these practices could also be connected to resilience strategies.

All in all, what connected the experiences was the uncertainty whether or not the harasser was serious about the threat. The issue here was that harassment led to female journalists feeling unsafe, because "You will never know if the harasser really means what he writes or says" (Interview, 2018). This entailed that a person who received threats or had been harassed could not feel safe in reality because of not knowing if the harasser was serious about carrying out the described act. On the other hand, as studies 2015 and 2018 indicated, female journalists normalized harassment and threats, and were spreading this behavioural pattern in the newsroom as a collective resilience strategy (Drury, 2011). This also meant that they did not take some of the messages seriously, by which they put themselves in a possible danger. For example an older more experienced female journalist talked about an experience, where the journalist was threatened face-to-face by one of the sources, when covering a corruption case.

> At one point he [the source] moved his jacket a bit and showed his gun that was on his belt. He asked me what I was going to do about the story.
>
> *(Interview 2018)*

The female journalist described that she started to laugh when the situation occurred. She did not react to the threat in any way and published the story without hesitation. Journalists also let the harassers continue with their behaviour, they did

126 Signe Ivask

not react to them. Very few of the threatened, harassed or insulted female journalists took legal actions (2015 and 2018 studies).

Conclusion

This chapter has explored female journalists' experiences with harassment and self-censorship on the basis of three different studies (2015, 2016 and 2018). In conclusion, female journalists suffer from harassment regardless of what field they cover, their age or experience.

Older, more experienced female journalists tended to normalize the acts of harassment more than their younger colleagues. This could be considered a resilience strategy: In order to remain working as a journalist, one has to adapt to the negative sides of it as well. The data suggest that journalists do not read comments on their stories not only because of lack of time, but to avoid harassment and remain resilient. Secondly, to avoid harassment from particular sources or audience, journalists show signs of self-censorship as they avoid writing on topics that bring along more negative attention (refugees, minority groups, etc.), topics that have brought on negative situations, or topics that involve a source that the journalist has had negative experiences with.

Journalists feel obliged to read the comments and interact with the public in order to create a trustworthy relationship with the public and strengthen job security by fulfilling a job task – interacting with the public. Another reason for reading comments is that audience members can offer hints for a follow-up story. If the journalist is in search of resilience strategies, then they might decide that their personal well-being outweighs interacting with the public. This means that journalist decides not to read comments because it brings them more harm than good.

Unless commenting is better moderated, journalists are still in danger of receiving harassment on their own territory – their media outlet. As journalists in all three studies said, this influences them and they start to censor themselves: Some of them start avoiding certain topics that bring in more negative attention, sources that behave in a negative way; some of the journalists feel threatened and fearful because of the comments they receive.

The questions remain: If the newsroom knows that there is a lack of appropriate discussion in the comment section, why should a journalist take part in the discussion? And if this leads to journalists' self-censorship, should newsrooms not do anything towards it? Although Estonian journalists' show signs of collective resilience, my studies also indicate that being passive towards threats could lead not only to self-censorship but to reckless behaviour as well (e.g. not being frightened when someone shows a gun on their belt). Journalists' unions could start discussions with the newsrooms in order to develop a strategy as to how the comments could and should be moderated on the outlet's pages. More and more outlets are trying out new automatic moderating systems in their comment sections, which could help to pick out and ban the comments that contain harassment. Journalists and media houses both could benefit from thorough moderating of the comments: On the

Estonian female journalists' experiences **127**

one hand, this could help to avoid future court cases with humiliated sources; on the other, journalists could interact with the public without fear of being harassed.

Self-censoring leads journalists to narrow the choice of topics they cover and sources they use. It also influences the way they practise reporting (e.g. superficial interviewing of unpleasant sources). All in all, self-censorship among journalists hinders fulfilling the "watchdog" role and this could have very serious consequences. Firstly, this could lead to the decline in trust towards journalists and journalism in society as public starts to notice the lack of in-depth critical investigation of topics and discussions among journalists and readers, also avoidance of some of the important topics (e.g. immigration, refugees etc.). Secondly, it could result in journalists leaving the field because self-censoring hinders them from reaching their full potential as journalists, leaving also because being afraid for their lives or psychological well-being.

Note

1 Initially Delfi AS v. Estonia in the European Court of Human Rights

References

Backholm, K. & Björkqvist, K. (2012). Journalists' emotional reactions after working with the Jokela school shooting incident. *Media, War and Conflict*, 5 (2), 175–190.

Ballard, A. J. & Easteal, P. (2018). The secret silent spaces of workplace violence: focus on bullying (and harassment). *Laws*, 7 (4), 35–52.

Bardoel, J. & Deuze, M. (2001). Network journalism: Converging competences of media professionals and professionalism. *Australian Journalism Review*, 23 (2), 91–103.

Bar-Tal, D. (2017). Self-censorship as a socio-political-psychological phenomenon: Conception and research. *Political Psychology*, 38, 37–65.

Barton, A. & Storm, H. (2018). *Violence and harassment against women in the news media: A global picture.* Retrieved from [accessed in June 2019]: www.iwmf.org/wp-content/uploads/2018/06/Violence-and-Harassment-against-Women-in-the-News-Media.pdf

Buchanan, M. & Keats, P. (2011). Coping with traumatic stress in journalism: A critical ethnographic study. *International Journal of Psychology*, 46 (2), 127–135.

CareerCast (2018). *The Worst Jobs of 2018*. Retrieved from [accessed in June 2019], www.careercast.com/jobs-rated/2018-worst-jobs?page=2

Chalaby, J. K. (2000). New media, new freedoms, new threats. *International Communication Gazette*, 62 (1), 19–29.

Chen, G., M., Pain, P., Chen, V., Y., Mekelburg, M., Springer, N. & Troger, F. (2018). *'You really have to have a thick skin': A cross-cultural perspective on how online harassment influences female journalists.* Austin, TX: The University of Texas, School of Journalism.

Chung, D. S. (2007). Profits and perils: Online news producers' perceptions of interactivity and uses of interactive features. *Convergence*, 13 (1), 43–61.

Cook, P. & Heilmann, C. (2013). Two types of self-censorship: public and private. *Political Studies*, 61 (1), 178–196.

Council of Europe (2019). *Estonia*. Retrieved from [accessed in June 2019]: www.coe.int/en/web/media-freedom/estonia

Delfi (2013). *Euroopa Inimõiguste Kohus tunnustas Delfi tasakaalustatud lugu, kuid lükkas portaali kaebuse tagasi.* Retrieved from [accessed in June 2019]: www.delfi.ee/news/paevauudised/eesti/euroopa-inimoiguste-kohus-tunnustas-delfi-tasakaalustatud-lugu-kuid-lukkas-portaali-kaebuse-tagasi?id=66883349

128 Signe Ivask

Drury, J. (2011). Collective resilience in mass emergencies and disasters: A social identity model. In Jetten, J., Haslam, C. & Haslam, S. A. (Eds.), *The social cure: Identity, health, and well-being*. Hove, UK: Psychology Press.

Hardin, M. & Shain, S. (2005). Female sports journalists: Are we there yet? "No". *Newspaper Research Journal*, 26 (4), 22–35.

Hayes, A. F., Glynn, C. J. & Shanahan, J. (2005). Willingness to self-censor: A construct and measurement tool for public opinion research. *International Journal of Public Opinion Research*, 17 (3), 298–323.

International Press Institute (2017). Journalists in Finland face 'unprecedented' levels of online abuse. IFEX, 22 September. Retrieved from [accessed in March 2019] www.ifex. org/finland/2017/09/22/journalists-online-abuse/

International Women's Media Foundation (2013) Global research project investigates violence against women journalists. Retrieved from [accessed in June 2019]: www. iwmf.org/blog/2013/12/02/global-research-project-investigates-violence-against-women-journalists/

Ivask, S. (2017a). TÜ meediauurija: Eesti ajakirjanikke ohustab läbipõlemine. *Novaator*, Retrieved from [accessed in June 2019]: https://novaator.err.ee/635625/tu-meediauurija-eesti- ajakirjanikke-ohustab-labipolemine

Ivask, S. (2017b). Stressed out print, digital and converged newsroom journalists consider leaving the field. *Media and Communication*, 8, 83–100.

Jungblut, M. & Hoxha, A. (2017). Conceptualizing journalistic self-censorship in post-conflict societies: A qualitative perspective on the journalistic perception of news production in Serbia, Kosovo and Macedonia. *Media, War & Conflict*, 10 (2), 222–238.

Karu, M., Soo, K., Biin, H., Lamesoo, K., Meiorg, M., Masso, M. & Turk, P. (2014). *Sooline ja seksuaalne ahistamine töökohal*. Tallinn: Poliitikauuringute Keskus Praxis

Lischka, J. A. (2017). Explicit terror prevention versus vague civil liberty: How the UK broadcasting news (de)legitimatise online mass surveillance since Edward Snowden's revelations. *Information, Communication & Society*, 20 (5), 665–682.

Löfgren Nilsson, M. & Örnebring, H. (2016). Journalism under threat: Intimidation and harassment of Swedish journalists. *Journalism Practice*, 10 (7), 880–890.

Marshall, A-M. (2005). *Confronting sexual harassment: the law and politics of everyday life*. London: Routledge.

Mihkels, G. (2018). Näitlejanna ristiretk. Anonüümne mõnitamine läks Perekooli "kägudele" kalliks maksma. *Eesti Päevaleht*, Retrieved from [accessed June 2019]: https://epl.delfi. ee/eesti/naitlejanna-ristiretk-anonuumne-monitamine-laks-perekooli-kagudele-kalliks-maksma?id=83856517

Mortensen, M. (2018). The self-censorship dilemma, *Journalism Studies*, 19 (13), 1957–1968, DOI:10.1080/1461670X.2018.1492880

OSCE (2016). New challenges to freedom of expression: Countering online abuse of female journalists. Retrieved from [accessed in June 2019]: www.osce.org/fom/220411?download=true

Palgi, G. (2018). *Estonian female journalists' experiences with harassment and aggression from their readers and sources*. Bachelor's Thesis. University of Tartu, Institute of Social Sciences. Retrieved from [accessed July 2019]: https://dspace.ut.ee/bitstream/handle/10062/60669/palgi_greete_ba_2018.pdf?sequence=1&isAllowed=y

Post, S. & Kepplinger, H. M. (2019). Coping with audience hostility. How journalists' experiences of audience hostility influence their editorial decisions. *Journalism Studies*, 1–21.

Reporters Without Borders (2019). *Estonia*. Retrieved from [accessed in June 2019]: https://rsf.org/en/estonia

Reporters Without Borders (2015). *Safety Guide for Journalists*. Retrieved from [accessed in June 2019]: https://rsf.org/en/guidelines-and-advice

Shanahan, M. (2017). *Journalism, Online Comments, and the Future of Public Discourse.* London: Routledge.

Swiss Institute of Comparative Law (2015). *Blocking, filtering and take-down of illegal internet content.* Retrieved from [accessed June 2019]: https://rm.coe.int/CoERMPublicComm onSearchServices/DisplayDCTMContent?documentId=090000168065497e

UNESCO (2019). *UNESCO observatory of killed journalists.* Retrieved from [accessed in June 2019]: https://en.unesco.org/themes/safety-journalists/observatory

Waisbord, S. (2002). Antipress violence and the crisis of the state. *Harvard International Journal of Press/Politics,* 7 (3), 90–109.

Weidmann, A. & Papsdorf, J. (2010). Witnessing trauma in the newsroom: Posttraumatic symptoms in television journalists exposed to violent news clips. *Journal of Nervous and Mental Disease,* 198 (4), 264–271.

WHO (2010). *What is workplace violence?* Retrieved from [accessed in October 2019]: www. who.int/violence_injury_prevention/violence/activities/workplace/background/en/

Williams, S. D. (2002). Self-esteem and the self-censorship of creative ideas. *Personnel Review,* 31 (4), 495–503.

Williams, R. (2007). The psychosocial consequences for children of mass violence, terrorism and disasters. *International Review of Psychiatry,* 19, 263–277.

9

RISK PERCEPTION AND NEGOTIATION OF SAFETY AMONG UGANDAN FEMALE JOURNALISTS COVERING POLITICAL DEMONSTRATIONS

Aisha Sembatya Nakiwala

Introduction

On March 1, 2016, one and a half weeks after Ugandan President Yoweri Museveni was re-elected for the fourth time in a row, Bahati Remmy, a popular Ugandan female journalist was brutally arrested by police. The arrest happened during a televised live report. Bahati and her colleagues had been covering a public protest at the home of the opposition leader and four-time presidential candidate (2001, 2006, 2011, 2016), Kizza Besigye. During her report, Bahati was surrounded by police, sprayed with pepper, arrested, and bundled into a waiting police van. She was then driven to an unknown location detained for hours and later released without charge. Bahati was one of the many Ugandan journalists who were caught up in a deliberate government crackdown on the media following a riotous election period and contested results. A year later, another female television reporter was kidnapped and beaten over coverage of an online protest by a famous social media activist against Uganda's first lady. Such intimidation has been seen as open victimization of women journalists which has become a usual occurrence, and which may push women to refrain from covering riots. Unlike other forms of violations against journalists, victimization of women is peculiar because in many cases a victim is at risk because of their gender. Yet, it is unknown how women journalists covering unruly political environments perceive their safety and how they negotiate the risks they encounter. The goal of this chapter therefore is to explore the safety risks that confront women journalists covering political protests in Uganda. It will assess the perceptions and experiences of journalists before unpacking the strategies for dealing with such risks. Understanding (potential) victims' perception of risk of future violations may be important for informing interventions to protect women journalists, and to prevent them from avoiding reporting certain topics or withdrawing from journalism altogether. Based on a qualitative study, the chapter sets out to answer two research questions: (1) How do women journalists perceive their safety when covering political demonstrations and do safety risks push them to self-censor? and (2) What mechanisms do women journalists use to negotiate risk and to avert self-censorship when covering political demonstrations?

This chapter was inspired by the need to contribute to scholarship on the importance of gender in understanding the safety and security issues that confront women working in the media across the world. In the following sections, the chapter progresses by giving a brief contextual and historical background on the state of the media as well as safety and security of journalists in Uganda. It further describes the status of women in media employment in Uganda, before the methodology of the study is briefly discussed. Thereafter, the analysis is presented, including the perception of risk, the effect of risk and the mechanisms for negotiating risk among Ugandan female journalists, and discussion of these vis-à-vis their linkage with self-censorship and resilience. In the conclusion, I argue the importance of an indulgent understanding and recognition of the nature of safety threats that women journalists face and the need for deliberate efforts to prepare journalists to handle such threats and to build collective resilience as a way to forestall self-censorship.

Risk, self-censorship and resilience

A universal definition of risk is elusive, but from a journalism perspective, Hughes and Márquez-Ramirez (2017) argue that it has to do with societal and anti-press practices that may have violent and traumatic effects on journalists. Like men, women journalists face risks and threats in the course of their work. Debates about the safety of female journalists, like the case is in this chapter, are commonly anchored in theoretical perspectives on gender and media. Such a framework takes into account the (mis)representation of women, and of issues that concern women, in the media. In general, feminist approaches to gender and the media focus on the liberation of women from any form of restrictions regarding access to the media and discrimination within journalism as a profession (Thornham, 2007). Researchers have argued that the world has moved to a post-feminist era in which feminist gains of the 1980s are now reinforced by the empowerment and agency of women, thereby making feminism irrelevant (Gill, 2016; McRobbie, 2004, 2007). However, several journalism researchers still argue for the continued value in understanding media from the perspective of feminism, arguing that powerful cultural and social stigma still make physical and moral threats against women a tolerated aspect within the media industry (Harris, Mosdell & Griffiths, 2016; North, 2016).

Departing from a general understanding of the Ugandan media as a male-dominated field and fusing it with the focus of this chapter, namely risk, feminism holds that risks and threats can cause further exclusion of women journalists and reinforce male dominance in the industry. Threats cannot only deprive women of media employment, but can also curtail their right to free expression. In addition, unsafe environments and risks may lead to self-censoring practices, thereby diminishing women's ability to report on issues that are relevant to the public. In particular, when risks and anti-press practices persist, they result in severe pressures on women which may give them reason to refrain from covering certain topics or covering those that are only related to feminine interest. Thus, based on this explanation, risk and risk perception may augment or inhibit one's ability to counteract threats in their work, thereby making resilience possible.

As a concept, *resilience* focuses on the ability to recover from difficulties (Houston, Schraedley, Worley, Reed & Saidi, 2019). In discussing resilience, Houston (2015) notes that it applies to both individuals and communities. In this regard, resilience can be seen not just as a product of personal risk perception but also as an important concept in understanding how women journalists collectively respond and thrive in the face of violations. Collective resilience – understood here as the adaptive capacities of a group that help them to endure and recover from adversity (Saul, 2013, p. 2) – can be exercised in different ways as a mechanism to counteract the impunity of those threatening journalists. For example in this chapter, collective resilience is important in understanding how mechanisms such as building teams, support and gendered training are useful not just for avoiding self-censorship, but for freedom of the press as well.

As a concept, *self-censorship* refers to non-externally compelled acts used by the media to avoid offending those holding power (Lee & Chan, 2009, p.112). At the level of an individual journalist, self-censorship can be exercised by choosing to remain silent on certain stories, without official directives, in order to avoid repercussions (Antilla, 2010). Thus, in the context of this chapter, women journalists could choose to ignore stories on political demonstrations, especially those that they perceive to pose particular safety risks. An important assumption can thus be that both individual and collective resilience could be adopted for preventing such self-censorship, so that the higher the degree of resilience, the less likely it is for self-censorship practices to occur, and vice versa.

Safety of women journalists: a focus on previous studies

In recent years, political protests have become a common occurrence in Uganda, especially during election campaigns, and so has incivility against journalists that report about political dissent. While researchers working on the subject of safety of journalists have extensively studied the aggression against journalists who work in dangerous political environments (Cottle et al., 2016), gender-specific aggression on its own remains largely unexamined. Studies of journalist safety and security are overly general in their outlook (Cottle et al., 2016; Hiltunen, 2017; Nilsson & Örnebring, 2016), which commonly results in an inadequate depiction of the gender dynamics that underpin the harassment and intimidation of journalists, particularly women. While studies of a general nature make an important contribution to our understanding of violence against journalists, they may also lead to insufficient attention being directed to issues pertaining to women journalists in particular.

The few studies that have focused on incivility against women journalists have been in contexts beyond Africa, including, for example Asia (Bulathsinghala, 2005; Orgeret, 2016; North, 2016). I argue in this chapter that this needs to change in order to address the disparity in the debate on safety of journalists in general and that of women in particular. This is important because the fundamental shortage of relevant information on women journalists' safety hampers not just efforts to provide important support mechanisms for women journalists, but also to keep them, as Bulathsinghala (2005) argues, in the male-dominated field of journalism. In addition, paying inadequate attention to women journalists' safety also hampers the public's right to access to information, as women have been reported to bring unique news stories to the world (Barton & Storm, 2014).

Thus, although harassment of journalists who report on protests is not unique to women, there are two important reasons to focus on the gendered safety issues prevalent in contexts of political disorder. First, women journalists working in various contexts across the world experience risks for the mere reason of their gender (Barton & Storm, 2014). North (2016) points out, for example, that sexual harassment and other gendered inequalities continue to be a systematic and persistent problem in many newsrooms. Women journalists encounter violations not just by their employers, but also from colleagues and sources (Lanza, 2017). Second, in order to guarantee the quality of media reports and support media pluralism and gender diversity in media production, the involvement of women is crucial. Research shows that, unlike men, women who report on insurgencies and disorder usually go beyond mere hard news reports, to include other angles such as the perspectives of those affected by conflict and human situations pertaining to the conflict (Bulathsinghala, 2005). Yet, as Bulathsinghala further contends, editors often discourage women journalists from reporting on dangerous situations because of their perceived vulnerability in unstable environments.

It is important to note that instead of reinforcing the long-held attitudes that women are fragile and better left to cover women issues as opposed to politics and hard news, the focus should be shifted towards understanding the threats and safety issues that confront them when covering politics, and how these can be removed. Reporting on protests is a dangerous activity for all journalists (Cottle et al., 2016). However, research shows that its chilling effect on women journalists is greater, due to the fact that efforts to mitigate violations lack a gender perspective (Article 19, 2016). In addition, women who work at the frontline of political protests are at a high risk of gendered aggression and overt harassment due to social expectations regarding what professional roles are suitable for women. For example, a survey by the International Women's Media Foundation in collaboration with International News Safety Institute (Barton & Storm, 2014) showed that nearly two-thirds of women who took part in the survey had experienced violations. In addition, according to the World Trends in Freedom of Expression and Media Development Global Report (UNESCO, 2018), the number of women journalists killed in the course of duty increased to ten in total in 2016, from five that were killed in 2012. The report points out further that African women journalists killed between 2017 and 2018 accounted for 24 percent of women journalist killed in the same period. While the number of women journalists killed is much lower than that of men, such a gender gap is perceived to be in part due to the under-representation of women reporting on insurgencies, wars, politics and crime (Harris et al., 2016).

The media and freedom of the press in Uganda

Prior to 1986, Uganda's media industry was almost non-existent, having been obliterated by war. However, the post-1986 period marked the onset of liberalization and privatization that saw rapid expansion of the media industry. Today, Uganda boasts of eight operational television stations and 292 licensed radio stations according to data from the Uganda Communications Commission (UCC, 2018). There are also five major newspapers and an array of online publications. It is this expansion that led to the establishment of Mama FM, the first women-only radio in Africa. The advent of a new government in Uganda in 1986 seemed to have ushered in a new promise for the respect of fundamental human rights, including the right to freedom of expression and the freedom of the press. In Uganda, press freedom is guaranteed by Article 29(1)a of the 1995 constitution, but this has continuously been eroded by the increasing tension between government and those who oppose it.

Between 1986 and 1996, the country did not have presidential elections, meaning there was no politically charged season during this period. However, the period following 1996 has been characterized by political unrest and disorder following increased pressure on the current government to relinquish power. These conflicts have often culminated into riots and demonstrations during electoral and non-electoral periods. For instance, during the 2001 general elections, there was election violence orchestrated mainly by state security agents. For the first time during this violence, the media and journalists became frequent and open victims of intimidation and harassment by security organs that had been co-opted by government to consolidate their grip on power. Civil and political disorder intensified after 2005 when the constitution was amended to allow multi-party democracy. Thus, the rapid expansion of the media industry between 1986 and the present time has barely been accompanied by a similar expansion in press freedom. In particular the constitutional guarantees for freedom of the press are restricted and undermined by the enactment of punitive laws. In East Africa, Uganda stands out for its violations of press freedom. For example, an assessment by the Federation of African Journalists (2010) showed that 12.4% of all press freedom violations in the East African region concerned Uganda. Further, the World Press Freedom Index by Reporters Without Borders (RSF, 2019) indicated that Uganda saw a drop in press freedom, and was ranked 117 out of 180 countries, down from 112 in 2017. In general, therefore, attacks on Ugandan journalists, intimidation, and impunity have become a daily occurrence. It is not uncommon for journalists to encounter brutal and arbitrary arrests, beatings and abduction perpetrated by mostly state security agents.

Ugandan women journalists in context

Nowhere in the media industry is gender inequality more pronounced than in media employment. The media in East Africa, Uganda inclusive, remain largely a male-dominated industry. Although the number of women joining news organizations has increased over the years, the number of women finding employment in the media in Uganda is by no means at parity with that of men. In terms of occupational status by gender, Ugandan men outnumber women in the media by 25%, according to the Global Report on the Status of Women in the News Media (IWMF, 2011). According to the Uganda Media Women's Association (UMWA, 2014), the majority of women working in the media in Uganda are accommodated in the lower occupational levels, with very few working in decision-making positions. For example, out of the five major media houses in Uganda, only one was headed by a woman by 2016 according to research by the indigenous non-government organization, Action for Development (ACFODE, 2016). The number increased to two with the appointment of one more woman at another news organization in 2018. The last five years have, however, seen an upsurge of female reporters on television, majority of whom are involved in news gathering and writing roles. For instance, research from the 2015 Global Media Monitoring Project (Macharia, 2015) focusing on the Uganda national report showed that 52% of journalists who delivered news were women. However, according to Uganda Media Women's Association (UMWA, 2014) data, even in such reporting roles, very few women journalists are likely to be engaged in writing hard news stories on complex issues such as politics, defence and the economy. Thus, the rising persecution of and violence against women journalists covering political disorder may mean that women may be discouraged and kept out of reporting certain crucial categories of news, particularly politics.

In the following section, drawing on qualitative interviews and focus group discussions, the risks facing women journalists when covering political demonstrations and the strategies to cope with such risks are analysed and discussed. The section starts with a brief description of how the information that is discussed was gathered.

Methodology

This qualitative research was accomplished in two phases. The first one was undertaken as part of a workshop organized by the Uganda Media Women's Association (UMWA), which I was invited to facilitate. The focus of the workshop was on sharing experiences about online and offline harassment, abuses and related safety risks as experienced by female journalists in Uganda. Three focus group discussions were conducted on the side of this event with women journalists who participated in the workshop. The focus groups comprised 17 women journalists altogether, who were asked to share details regarding their experiences of safety issues during political demonstrations.

In the second phase, in-depth interviews were carried out with six media managers, working with three newspapers, two commercial radio stations and one community radio station. They aimed to share their views on the safety of female journalists who cover political demonstrations and what is done to shield them from the risks they may encounter during their work. Those interviewed were media managers, specifically news editors, five of whom were male and one woman. The information collected from the two methods was thematically analysed. More specifically, a comparative technique was used to code the data. The transcripts were repeatedly read and pieces of information were arranged in categories in which ideas and responses were captured. A search for overlaps among categories was done after which the categories were sorted and labelled as themes. Three themes emerged out of the analysis, which included: risks facing women journalists, effects of risk on female journalists and mechanisms to mitigate risk.

Analysis

Risks facing women journalists

In order to understand the perception of risk, participants were asked to explain how they felt about their security and safety when covering political demonstrations. Three important issues concerning risk emerged out of the analysis, namely: that female journalists were targets of attack because of their gender, a perception that covering political demonstrations is a big risk and that young female journalists were at a greater risk. Participants also demonstrated great awareness of what violations women journalists are likely to encounter.

Concerning the gendered risks that they encounter, women journalists felt they were more likely to be targeted because of their gender and described themselves as vulnerable. For some, there was a strong sense of vulnerability especially because of what they had witnessed happening in the field. Others reported that their perceptions had been informed by what colleagues had told them. More specifically, there was an assumption that women who report about political demonstrations in Uganda were a target of perpetrators because women were less likely to retaliate. For some participants, women were more easy prey in the face of violators than male journalists because of the powerful stereotype, partly obtained through socialization, of the social weakness of women in a male-dominated world. This was what participants believed compounded the possibility of a female journalist being attacked during demonstrations. One participant who reported covering some of the most violent demonstrations following the 2016 elections commented thus during the focus group discussion:

> That is how I feel based on what I have witnessed in the field. It is that way most of the time because it is assumed women are an easy target. Police will beat you and they will assume you will not follow through with a complaint or charge.

Participants were able to identify cases where they felt women had been attacked because of who they were. For example, they talked of situations when the police chose to run after women journalists because, it is assumed, they cannot run fast, as well as the uncouth verbal attacks because it is assumed women are disoriented faster than their male counterparts. For some participants, the major reason for physical attacks was the style of dressing, which interviewees said in some cases could hinder easy pathway for the victims of harassment to escape. As one participant noted: "I mean, that is one thing you have to understand. [...] Sometimes it is a skirt, sometimes it is high, uncomfortable shoes that one is wearing. How can one respond fast in such circumstances?" Another participant, whilst seeing dress code as a risk factor for women journalists, had this to say:

> Right shoes, may sound silly. But I have seen women in high heels fall as they run away from danger. How one is dressed also matters [...], that way you get to run out fast, if you have to. Some girls wear miniskirts or tight dresses, which can make maneuvering from danger difficult.

It is clear from the foregoing quotes that in times of political demonstration, an uncomfortable dress style might act as a risk factor to increase exposure to violations. Nevertheless, some women pointed out that high heels are recommended for women journalists in the media organizations where they worked.

Several participants saw a great connection between gender and violations. Some participants foregrounded differences in expectations about men and women reporting about demonstrations, such as the unspoken rule requiring women journalists to only cover softer topics. Participants pointed out that it was more likely for women journalists to be attacked than men. On the contrary, there were participants who believed that male journalists covering political demonstration also encountered assault, but many were in a better position to take more clever choices, including for example operating further away from the hotbed of commotion. Many participants in the focus group discussions concurred with this view as this quote from one of the participants illustrates: "I think men tend to easily keep away from trouble spots, even in difficult circumstances. They seem to be more awake to what could go wrong and they maneuver easily". Thus, whilst the participants in this study understood that violations against journalists may sometimes target both men and women, a key issue of concern was that women, especially the young, tended to easily fall victims to attacks and violations during demonstrations because of the inability to perceive their vulnerability. However, while some participants thought women are not able to perceive their own vulnerability, some interviews indicated that women are very much aware of the risks and their vulnerability in reporting demonstrations.

Concerning risk awareness, several participants perceived covering of political demonstrations as a big risk. A number of comments during the discussion suggested a great awareness among participants of what risks women face when reporting political demonstrations. The violations that they highlighted as targeted at women journalists in particular included forced tearing of clothes, verbal abuse, sexual assault, groping and unwelcome sexual remarks. While some of these attacks may not be exclusively targeted at women, various participants in this study said they are more commonly inflicted on women journalists. Thus, whilst the studied women journalists generally pointed out that safety challenges were common to both women and men, a clear view emerging from the interviews was that women journalists were likely to be victims of particular kinds of violations that men seldom experienced. One participant, reporting to have regularly covered difficult situations, said the following about what nature of violations to expect when covering dangerous incidents:

> I have gotten used to what is done to women journalists. One time I was following run[ning] battles between the police and the rioters, and suddenly a man started to interrogate me, wondering about my decision to cover riots. Within a short time, our exchange had turned abusive and it was ridiculous the language he used against me.

Some participants talked of the risk of abuse when women journalists are arrested by police. Participants described the brutal, crude ways in which women journalists are handled, while some pointed out that women journalists are in many cases at risk of rape and sexual harassment when in police custody. For example, one participant said, "If you are unlucky, you can get sexually abused in a police cell. For us women, the assault is sometimes a deterrent, a kind of punishment for giving publicity to the riotous crowds".

Young women were perceived to be at a greater risk of being targeted, intimidated and violated. Some participants perceived young female journalists to be eager but inadequately prepared to handle riotous situations. This perspective is illustrated in this comment by one of the participants during of the focus group discussions: "Young women […] lack the ability to appreciate covering political demonstrations as a peculiar undertaking that warrants a certain level and a different kind of preparation". Young female journalists were also perceived by some participants as inexperienced: "I think they have a higher potential of underestimating risks when reporting demonstrations […] and many are unaware of the options available to them to cushion themselves from danger and attacks". Another stated: "I think they sometimes underrate what can go wrong during a riot. It is common for one to think they will handle somehow, but that is not how to prepare for a dangerous situation".

The above finding indicates that some interviewees perceived female journalists to be in themselves responsible for their safety and therefore blamed women themselves for being victims. Participants reasoned that if women learn to perceive the danger ahead of the assignments they are supposed to take on, then they can be able to take steps to avoid such danger. On the contrary, some participants perceived organizational factors, such as the lack of gender policy in newsrooms, and the hostile environment in which women journalists work, to have greater impact on their safety and ability to mitigate risks. As such, it viewed as important for media organizations to mind the safety of women journalists, and to earmark adequate resources to guarantee such safety.

Effects of risks on female journalists

The second theme concerned the effects of the risks discussed in the foregoing section. In this theme, participants spoke of the distressing and deterrent effect that violations have on women journalists' readiness to report on topics such as politics, crime and chaotic situations. A key perception on the effect of working in riotous situations was that dangerous and chaotic assignments are an impediment for many female journalists who would have otherwise been interested in reporting on riots and other complex issues. Participants who reported to have been assaulted during political demonstrations made strong statements about their disinclination to cover political demonstrations in the future, some insisting that they now only work through proxies to get information from the field.

Some talked about the negative ways in which colleagues who previously faced intimidation and harassment had been affected, indicating that some now prefer to work in less stressful environments, implying women journalists were resorting to self-censorship. One, for example, talked of a colleague who had abandoned journalism after being kidnapped. Whilst emphasizing this view, another participant noted, "Only those who have not been victims persist with reporting on riots – and I think that is a common view among many female journalists". More participants expressed a lack of enthusiasm to be at the centre of demonstrations as reporters, with one person commenting that: "If I must write about riots, it doesn't mean I must be present at the centre of things [riot], does it?"

Interestingly, some participants also indicated that they would be reluctant to encourage peers to nurture interest in political reporting because, in their assessment, it aggravates exposure to harassment. In general, participants' views suggested that female journalists remain apprehensive about the risks and challenges associated with covering political demonstrations in Uganda. Thus, concerning self-censorship, the above findings demonstrate how attacks on women journalists covering political demonstrations can have negative implications not just for individual victims, but for the wider journalism profession and media industry by reinforcing practices that prevent women from covering topics considered risky.

Mechanisms for negotiating risks

The third and last theme concerned mechanisms to mitigate risks that women face. Calls to guarantee the safety and security of journalists have been growing worldwide (Article 19, 2016; North, 2016). This study sought to explore women journalists' perceptions about the mechanisms that are and can be deployed in mitigating the risks that they face while reporting in contexts of political demonstrations.

140 Aisha Sembatya Nakiwala

Findings showed that participants believed three mechanisms were important for mitigating the risks that women face in covering political demonstrations. These comprised: speaking out, adequate risks assessment and working in teams. These are discussed below.

Speaking out

A key strategy that was pointed out by participants as essential for mitigating exposure to risk while covering political demonstrations was to speak out against the violations and their perpetrators. One participant noted that speaking out is important for creating a viable opportunity for soliciting and receiving support from fellow journalists and relevant authorities, including the international community. Participants observed that speaking out also facilitates the process of seeking help and assistance from a wide network of journalists, human rights activists and related agencies. The quotes below illustrates participants' views on the importance of speaking out:

> Once you speak out, some dangers are allayed. Once this happens, risks become fairly easier [sic] to overcome. At that moment they become a concern not just for an individual journalist, but also for some social groups, civil society and sometimes the international community.
>
> What easier way to get help than to make noise about one's bad moment! We always encourage them to talk, to speak out. But naturally some prefer to keep their suffering away from the limelight because they do not wish to attract attention. All in all, speaking out is important.

In discussing this strategy, the women talked about fellow women who had been released from police custody following the collective demands for their release from fellow journalists. They also talked of instances when women journalists were physically abused by politicians, then the media fought back with strongly worded commentary about such incidents and calls for the violators to be held accountable. The women reported that in some instances, politicians had been made to pay fines for their actions and one had to publicly apologize. Overall, participants held the view that speaking out was an effective mechanism that journalists can use to stand up for themselves.

Risk assessment

The findings revealed that the view of many of the participants was that female journalists need to undertake prior and adequate risk assessment to prepare them to handle risks appropriately. This was a common view and key to it was the idea that it is more dangerous for women journalists to be caught unawares when a political demonstration turns into a toxic environment. Participants reported that they normally felt that they were fairly out of harm's way and in control of hard situations, if they adequately anticipated and prepared to face certain risks. They noted that such preparedness required one to have a hunch to know how to respond in case of attacks, including ensuring that the response is fast enough to avoid danger. One of the media managers had this to say:

> Some media organizations create a climate in which women are indirectly discouraged from covering political demonstrations [...] But a better option should be to equip female journalists with skills to maneuver during hard situations.

Participants pointed out the Uganda Media Women's Association (UMWA) as an organization that conducts safety training for women journalists to prepare them for hard times. The organization has a media and gender training curriculum, but it was not clear how regularly training is done.

The general emerging perception from both the focus group discussions and the interviews with key informants was that a good level of preparedness, perhaps through training, was desirable to inculcate a sense of readiness to handle any eventuality. Respondents insisted that a strong sense of judgment on the part of a journalist is essential. One participant noted, for example that, "being in position to read and scan the environment to understand what might be ahead is key." Another had this to say in regard to the need for risk assessment:

> Political demonstrations are tricky, but our best weapon will always be our instinct. Because it is hard to know who will be hostile to us. Sometimes even a marked jacket or microphone will get you in trouble because someone in the crowd doesn't like it.

In general, the sense that a journalist's life comes first was perceived by participants as an important mark of awareness that one should have when covering riots.

Related to risk assessment, journalists were resorting to turning down assignments, which directly inculcates self-censorship as a safety mechanism. The women journalists and media managers interviewed in this study revealed that women journalists were choosing to refrain from covering certain events, especially those that they deemed dangerous. Some noted that this was due to lack of protection from their media organizations, but also lack of adequate support to be able to handle risks. For examples some participants stated that employers rarely engage with women journalists on issues of safety, which they noted was in itself a risk factor. They argued that there was need for media organizations to offer routine guidance on how women can guard against attacks when covering demonstrations, which was reported to be absent in various media organizations. Some held the view that their employers do not take attacks against women journalists seriously, thereby contributing to their vulnerability. Some of the interviewees reported that they had as a result excused themselves from covering political demonstrations and risky assignments as these quotes exemplify:

> In my case, being able to make a choice between covering demonstrations or not also makes a lot of difference for me. I feel in control when I get to choose whether to report on something or to leave. But again, this is not an option everywhere.
>
> Denying women the freedom to choose whether to report on demonstrations or not breeds dissatisfaction, resulting into costly mistakes sometimes. I am comfortable knowing that I can discuss the option of going to cover an assignment with my editor.

Working in teams

Participants indicated that many journalists were now choosing to work in teams and they noted this was a strategy that has effectively helped them whenever they were targets of abuse or unwanted advances from men. Participants noted that working in a team at a riot helps to create some level of psychological safety, as journalists know that they have colleagues to fall back on. Several participants acknowledged the importance of self-protection, but noted that individual self-protection was nothing without the assistance from a network of other journalists to consult in case of danger. Respondents held a strong belief that when they work in teams, there is always a sense that they are in it together, and team members are more likely to galvanize their energies to protect a team member who gets into danger as the quotes from the focus group discussions illustrate:

> Knowing that support is nearby helps to increase our readiness to cover demonstrations. Working in a group helps to reduce exposure to undue harm as colleagues are normally available to offer help. It is easier for them to make noise and get one of their own out of a situation.
>
> Working in a team helps in that it becomes easy to talk about it, and especially share information on how to cope. There is a calming effect, comforting effect to it. The trick is to watch out for where the hostile crowd is. Better stay in a group with fellow journalists. That way when the crowd throws stones at police, they don't aim at you and vice versa for the police.

Thus, concerning resilience, the above findings demonstrate that through working in teams, speaking out and by providing each other with support, women are able to build collective resilience which can serve to inspire their persistence in covering political riots – an activity that in many ways is male dominated. As a matter of individual resilience, the analysis shows that women journalists are able to gain the self-confidence that they need to remain active in covering riots, especially when their expectation of solidarity is fulfilled.

Discussion

A secure work environment is needed for all journalists, but it is of decisive importance to women – who are more often exposed to gendered violations – and to the fulfilment of a free press.

Throughout much of the research history on violations on media practitioners, the debate has often taken a general tone. It has been common to portray and articulate certain general forms of suffering of journalists, most often treating women as part of a homogenous group, thereby obscuring gendered issues concerning their safety. In this chapter, I have explored the safety risks confronting women reporting on political demonstrations in Uganda. Although the vast majority of journalists working in politically charged and risky environments are faced with overwhelming challenges (Cottle et al., 2016), paying inadequate attention to the barriers faced by women journalists exacerbates the violation of media freedom and a free press by further compounding the exclusion of women from the industry. Some respondents in this study reported that they knew and have encountered women journalists that have been victims of attacks during political demonstrations or have themselves experienced some sort of violation and incivility.

Whilst the perceptions held by participants were unquestionably shaped by their individual experiences, it is also important to take note of similarities in their perceptions and those discussed in other studies. For example the view that women journalists are violated because of their gender has been observed elsewhere (Lanza, 2017; North, 2016). In addition, previous research has revealed significant cases of violations against women journalists during the course of their work (Bulathsinghala, 2005). Despite the significant gains made in regard to freedom of the press in the majority of the developed countries, concerns about journalists' safety remain of key relevance in many countries in sub-Saharan Africa where women journalists remain largely unprotected.

The risks highlighted in this chapter have implications for interventions to enhance the safety and security of women journalists, their capacity to cope with the unfriendly work situations and to avert self-censorship. A notable finding is that risks were perceived to significantly impact the resilience of women who cover political demonstrations, further reaffirming previous findings that covering protests is a dangerous activity for journalists (Cottle et al., 2016). For example, risks were perceived to result in resentment for assignments that are perceived as risky. In some cases, both media managers and women journalists themselves prefer that women are assigned simple and less risky tasks. This further reaffirms earlier findings indicating that editors confine women journalists to reporting on soft issues for fear of their vulnerability to attacks (Bulathsinghala, 2005). The reported resentment of complex assignments suggests that this is a further possible implication of such violations on the work of female journalists, and its overall impact on journalism practice needs further analysis in specific social and cultural contexts. This is particularly important in Africa, where respect for human dignity and rights is curtailed by repressive political regimes.

The negative consequences of gendered violations, including self-censorship, illustrate the negative implications for freedom of the press, as Orgeret (2016) has also previously argued. From the evidence generated from the focus group discussions, it was perceived that when young female journalists experience violations during riots, they may find it difficult to deal with the situation, and therefore restrain themselves from covering certain topics. Media organizations need to take seriously the inadequate preparations on the part of their young women journalists. Thus, in the consideration of how to address violations on journalists reporting on political demonstrations, primarily in so-called developing nations, the contextualization of gender is important (North, 2016). At a practical level, media organizations and managers are key actors in supporting the safety of journalists and by so doing promote media freedom. Therefore, media managers can be enlisted to enhance the safety of women journalists instead of withdrawing them from working on complex issues. Media managers can be relied upon to put in place and to promote initiatives to protect women journalists and gender-related safety ideas in order to curb self-censorship.

Through speaking out, teamwork, support and training, women journalists are able to attain a good level of collective resilience (Houston 2015; Houston et al., 2019), instead of resorting to self-censorship. Based on Houston's articulation of resilience as capacity to cope with adversity, this chapter has illustrated mechanisms that help women journalists to counteract the effects of violations and to avert self-censorship. At the same time, the analysis shows that where the level of resilience was low, for example where there was insufficient emotional, informational and practical support, women resorted to self-censorship practices, particularly turning down assignments that were perceived as risky. This revelation builds on the notion of self-censorship (Antilla, 2010; Lee & Chan 2009) and illustrates how incivility against women journalists covering political demonstrations contributes to alienating women from the journalism profession in particular and from the media industry in general. Thus, considered together, the strategies highlighted above can help to build the required resilience among women to help them persist in the coverage of political demonstrations. The interventions need the attention of both individual journalists and media institutions. In particular, the findings in this study point to the need for better trained, better prepared, and better supported female journalists, who are protected from risks involved in covering political demonstrations and who are empowered enough to undertake their own risk assessment. However, my findings have shown that some young female journalists lack the competence to undertake such an assessment or to use creative techniques to manage violations that may confront them. In effect, the above strategies can be incorporated in more formal efforts aimed to enhance the safety of female journalists and to reduce self-censorship resulting from violations.

In terms of implications for theory, the issues discussed in this chapter are important for advancing research on the concepts of self-censorship and resilience. In particular, research could be advanced by developing understanding of the links between gender dynamics on the one hand and self-censorship and resilience on

Ugandan female journalists and risk **145**

the other. For example, the discussion in this chapter demonstrated a perception that male journalists who cover political demonstrations were likely to make more intelligent choices than their female colleagues to protect themselves in the face of risk, instead of self-censoring. Research could therefore be advanced by developing understanding of how gender influences self-censorship among journalists and what gender-specific self-censorship practices are induced, and which resilient practices are adopted among each gender.

Conclusion

The overall perception of the participants in this study appeared to be that women face unique risks when covering riots and demonstrations, and that there are long-term implications for women continuing to report hard and dangerous topics, if they are not to resort to self-censorship as a way to avert violations. There seemed to be a clear demand for better preparedness of women journalists planning to cover riots, but also a demand for media organizations to consider strategies for women journalists' protection in order to enhance their individual and collective resilience. Strategies to spur collective resilience, such as working in teams and speaking out, are particularly important because they engender a strong and wide network of support for victims of violations. Low levels of collective resilience can, however, heighten self-censorship as has been highlighted in the foregoing discussion. Thus, this points to the need for journalists to leverage collective resilience long before they set off to cover riots. This could be through sharing information on where to seek timely support to overcome adversity, as well as team building in order to help journalists to easily and effectively work together when covering riots.

Further, there seems to be a continued need for deeper analysis of the gender dimension of the safety of journalists from different contexts and perspectives. From a research context, studies need to adopt frameworks that take seriously the lived experiences of journalists, the impact, and resilience aspects related to the safety of female journalists. Both organizational-based interventions such as counselling and those that promote resilience to help prevent or overcome attacks on women journalists, as well as contextualized attention to violation in specific work contexts such as political reporting are needed. Without such interventions, society stands not to benefit from the important news stories that women bring to the world. More importantly, interventions of this type can go a long way towards averting self-censorship among women journalists.

As a way to enhance their resilience that effectively averts self-censorship, it is also important that women journalists make ample preparations prior to covering political demonstrations, build collaborative teams and strengthen their risk assessment competence. This they can learn through mentorship from senior colleagues. More critically, there is continued need for gendered training on risk assessment and management, something that can be undertaken by media organizations as part of their capacity development. By so doing, media organizations could contribute to building women's individual and collective resilience, which would in turn help women to overcome pressure and threats, and make self-censorship less likely.

References

ACFODE (2016). *Exclusion, misrepresentation and discrimination: Insights on the situation of women in the media*. Retrieved from www.kas.de/c/document_library/get_file?uuid=74f5c8e6-d786-f1f7-2453-4f951fa4814d&groupId=252038

Antilla, L. (2010). Self-censorship and science: A geography review of media coverage of climate tipping points. *Public Understanding of Science*, 19(2), 240–256.

OHCHR (2016). Article 19. *Submission to OHCHR for the report "Safety of journalists"*. Retrieved from www.ohchr.org/Documents/Issues/Journalists/GA72/Article19.docx.

Barton, B. & Storm, H. (2014). *Violence and harassment against women in the news media: A global picture*. International Women's Media Foundation & International News Safety Institute. Retrieved from www.iwmf.org/our-research/journalistsafety/.

Bulathsinghala, F. (2005). The role of women journalists in conflict reporting in Sri Lanka. *Media Asia*, 32(1), 31–33.

Cottle, S., Sambrook, R., & Mosdell, N. (2016). *Reporting dangerously: Journalist killings, intimidation and security*. London: Palgrave Macmillan.

Federation of African Journalists (2010). *Press freedom in Africa*. Retrieved from www.ifj.org/fileadmin/user_upload/Report_Press_Freedom_2010_Africa.pdf

Gill, R. (2016). Post-postfeminism? New feminist visibilities in postfeminist times. *Feminist Media Studies*, 16(4), 610–630.

Harris. J., Mosdell, N., & Griffiths, J. (2016). Gender, risk and journalism. *Journalism Practice*, 10(7), 902–916.

Hiltunen, I. (2017). Trouble in paradise? self-censorship, outside interference and harassment of journalists in Finland. *Media Asia*, 44(1), 66–70.

Houston, J. B. (2015). Bouncing forward: assessing advances in community resilience assessment, intervention, and theory to guide future work. *American Behavioral Scientist*, 59(2), 175–180.

Houston, J. B., Schraedley, K. M., Worley, E. M., Reed, K., & Saidi, J. (2019). Disaster journalism: fostering citizen and community disaster mitigation, preparedness, response, recovery, and resilience across the disaster cycle. *Disasters*, 43(3), 591–611.

Hughes, S. & Márquez-Ramirez, M. (2017) Examining the practices that Mexican journalists employ to reduce risk in a context of violence. *International Journal of Communication*, 11, 499–521.

International Women's Media Foundation (2011). *Global report on the status of women in the news media*. Retrieved from www.iwmf.org/wp-content/uploads/2018/06/IWMF-Global-Report.pdf.

Lanza, E. (2017). *Silenced zones: Highly dangerous areas for the exercise of freedom of expression*. Office for the Special Rapporteur for Freedom of Expression of the Inter-American Commission on Human Rights. Available at www.oas.org/en/iachr/expression/docs/publications/ZONAS_SILENCIADAS_ENG.

Lee, L. F. F & Chan, J. (2009). Organizational production of self-censorship in the Hong Kong media, *International Journal of Press & Politics*, 14(1), 112–133.

Macharia, S. (2015). *Who makes the news? Global media monitoring project*. World Association of Christian Communication. www.presscouncil.org.au/uploads/52321/ufiles/Who_makes_the_news_-_Global_Media_Monitoring_Project_2015.pdf

McRobbie, A. (2004). Post-feminism and popular culture. *Feminist Media Studies*, 4(3), 255–264.

McRobbie, A. (2007). Post-feminism and popular culture: Bridget Jones and the new gender regime. In D. Negra & Y. Tasker (Eds.), *Interrogating Postfeminism: Gender and the politics of popular culture* (pp. 27–39). Durham, NC: Duke University Press.

Nilsson, L. M. & Örnebring, H. (2016). Journalism under threat: Intimidation and harassment of Swedish journalists. *Journalism Practice*, 10(7), 880–890.

North, L. (2016). Damaging and daunting: Female journalists' experiences of sexual harassment in the newsroom. *Feminist Media Studies*, 16(3), 495–510.

Orgeret, K. (2016). Women in war: Challenges and possibilities for women journalists covering war and conflict. In U. Carlsson (Ed.), *Freedom of expression and media in transition: studies in the digital age* (pp. 165–176). Göteborg: Nordicom.

Reporters Without Borders. (2019). The world press freedom index. Retrieved from https://rsf.org/en/uganda

Saul, J. (2013). *Collective trauma, collective healing: Promoting community resilience in the aftermath of disaster*. Retrieved from https://content.taylorfrancis.com/books/download?dac=C2010-0-30937-2&isbn=9781136903915&format=googlePreviewPdf

Thornham, S. (2007). *Women, feminism and media*. Edinburgh: Edinburgh University Press.

Uganda Communications Commission (2018). *Post, broadcasting and telecommunications market and industry Q2 report*. Retrieved from www.ucc.co.ug/files/downloads/NEMPS%28N&E%29%20final%20report.pdf.

Uganda Media Women Association (2014). *Gender dimensions in Uganda's print media: A case for engendering practitioners*. Retrieved from www.umwamamafm.co.ug/wp-content/uploads/2016/03/Report-on-Gender-Dimensions-in-Ugandas-Print-Media-September-2014.pdf

United Nations Educational, Scientific and Cultural Organization (UNESCO) (2018). *World trends in freedom of expression and media development global report*. Retrieved from https://digitalcourage.de/sites/default/files/2017-11/unesco-bericht-meinungsfreiheit.pdf

10

FEAR, TRAUMA AND LOCAL JOURNALISTS

Implications for media development and peacebuilding

Michelle Betz and Paul Beighley

Introduction

Over the past decade issues surrounding the safety of journalists have gained increasing prominence in large part due to the numbers of journalists killed and to the advocacy of organizations such as the Organization for Security and Cooperation in Europe (OSCE),[1] UNESCO and the UN Plan of Action on the Safety of Journalists and the Issue of Impunity.[2]

Most of the journalists killed are locally based journalists and media workers. According to the Committee for the Protection of Journalists (CPJ) nearly 90 per cent of journalists killed since 1992 have been local journalists working in their own countries (CPJ, 2018).

Recently, psychosocial elements of safety such as the immediate effects of trauma and longer-term consequences of post-traumatic stress disorder (PTSD) have started to gain attention. International media and media support organizations are beginning to focus on the issue. Unfortunately, the predominance of research conducted on the subject has pertained to international war correspondents; much less discussed has been the situation of local journalists who live and work covering conflicts that impact them directly. These journalists must develop coping mechanisms particular to the context of working in the same environment where they live and have community. One area that needs to be explored is how self-censorship in these circumstances may influence these journalists' effectiveness and what mitigating strategies may promote resilience.

While there is general consensus that contemporaneous traumatic events have an impact, a review of the literature reveals inadequate discussion of the impact of historical trauma in areas of protracted conflict or genocide such as Afghanistan or Rwanda, and what effect such trauma may have on local journalists in these contexts. Historical trauma refers to "complex and collective trauma experienced over time and across generations by a group of people who share an identity, affiliation, or circumstance" (Mohatt et. al., 2014, p. 128).

Understanding the effects that fear and psychological trauma have on journalists is critical in understanding how covering violence and conflict may affect not only those tasked with reporting news events and serving as watchdogs but also how it may affect peacebuilding in conflict-affected and transitional areas.

This chapter examines the chain of causality between traumatized journalists, self-censorship and peacebuilding and how self-censorship has a negative effect on journalistic content and the potential for conflict resolution and peacebuilding in conflict-prone environments.

Method and theory

This chapter uses a cross-sectoral documentary analysis in that it draws on documents from such disparate fields as medicine and psychology, peace and security, communications and freedom of expression, and provides a holistic perspective on a complex problem. Documents included UN documents, grey literature from international and local NGOs, academic literature and news media.

The findings draw on grounded theory to help elucidate the chain of causality between traumatized journalists, self-censorship and peacebuilding. Glaser and Strauss (1967) introduced grounded theory to legitimize qualitative research. The theory is grounded in actual data with analysis and development of theories happening *after* the data has been collected. In this case, the research process involved examining data and documents from a wide array of sectors and it was only pulling them all together that led to the conclusion that trauma and fear could lead not only to self-censorship but to negative impacts on peacebuilding.

The chapter begins with an examination of the increasing reliance on local journalists by international news outlets, then outlines how fear and trauma can affect the work of journalists. The chapter next moves on to issues of self-censorship: why journalists self-censor and the implications of such self-censorship on peacebuilding. The chapter concludes with suggested solutions to bolster journalistic communities in the context of trauma, fear and self-censorship.

Reliance on local journalists

Increasingly, the reporting of conflicts such as those in Syria and Afghanistan is being carried out by local journalists. Foreign news bureaus have been closed and fewer international correspondents report on these conflicts as they are deemed simply too dangerous to send in internationals.

When the security situation deteriorates, so making foreign journalists' access to conflict hot spots more difficult and unsafe, media outlets use news material, particularly visuals, from local journalists and photographers who are already at the scene (Høiby and Mitra, 2018).

150 Michelle Betz and Paul Beighley

In Afghanistan, the last foreign bureau chief for the Associated Press in Kabul left in late 2016 after receiving a death threat by the Islamic State. The BBC closed its English-language bureau in 2015 and no US broadcast network or British paper has a full-time foreign presence in the country (O'Donnell, 2018). Today, international news bureaus in Afghanistan are staffed almost exclusively by local journalists.

Local journalists have the language skills, contextual knowledge and contacts to get the job done. But their expertise comes at a price. Globally, around 95 per cent of journalists killed in armed conflict are locally based journalists (UN, 2015). In Syria, for example, 90 per cent of journalists killed have been local (Dlewati, 2016).

Writing about the experience of conflict-torn Mexico, Canadian psychiatrist Dr Anthony Feinstein says that, unlike international correspondents who are able to leave a war zone after several weeks and "return to a safe home environment", Mexican journalists were unable to leave (Arellano, 2016). This creates a challenge for Mexican journalists who may also face threats to themselves and their families. War correspondents "can climb on a plane to a home country where it's safe and get therapy" while the Mexican journalists and their families are often targeted by drug cartels (Arellano, 2016).

Clearly, there is a need to put the spotlight on local journalists not just as fixers for internationals, but also for the work they do, the content they produce and the role they play in their country's development, conflict resolution and peacebuilding.

Journalists, fear and trauma

Over the past two decades, there has been increasing research by trauma experts and journalism educators to better understand how covering violence and conflict might affect journalists. Researchers, including Feinstein, have shown how journalists, particularly war correspondents, are affected by the work they do (Feinstein et al., 2002). But there has been little examination of the effects on local journalists or fixers for international media who live and work covering violence, conflicts or disasters that impact them directly.[3] Unlike their international colleagues, they usually have no escape from the threats and intimidation or the traumatic environment and may be both witness and victim. Local resources for mental health support are likely to be scarce or non-existent. Cultural barriers and a lack of awareness about expected responses to psychological trauma and its aftermath complicate matters, as does the existence of historical trauma in some instances resulting in journalists not only dealing with work-related fear and trauma but trauma that is pervasive in many conflict-affected countries. Journalists working in dangerous conditions may be affected by fear or trauma or even both. But what is fear? What is trauma and how are they different or related?

Fear may be operationally described as an emotional experience in direct response to a readily identifiable threat to health or well-being. Experts have called the emotions and physiological changes related to this as the "fight or flight" response (originally coined by Walter Cannon in 1915) and describe this as a

Fear, trauma and local journalists **151**

potentially adaptive response leading the individual to either flee the external threat or take actions to defend themselves.[4]

In defining trauma for the purposes of meeting the diagnosis of post-traumatic stress disorder, the Diagnostic and Statistical Manual of Mental Disorders, Fifth Edition (DSM-V) describes it as experiencing events which result in death, threatened death, serious injuries, or sexual violence, including things like natural disasters, murders, assaults, fires, and natural deaths. The person must have been exposed to death, threatened death, actual or threatened serious injury, or actual or threatened sexual violence in one or more of the following ways:

1. Direct exposure, i.e. a traumatic event is personally experienced or witnessed.
2. Witnessing, in person, the event(s) as it occurred to others.
3. Indirectly, by learning that a close relative or close friend was exposed to trauma. If the event involved actual or threatened death, it must have been violent or accidental.
4. Repeated or extreme indirect exposure to aversive details of the event(s), usually in the course of professional duties (for example, first responders, those collecting body parts or professionals repeatedly exposed to details of child abuse).

Notably, DSM-V highlights that exposure to trauma may be related to one's work and specifically mentions first responders. Although war correspondents and local journalists covering conflict or disaster, violence, accidents, physical or sexual assault are not technically first responders (defined as those among the first to respond to an accident or disaster to provide assistance) they are often exposed to similar events and thus would easily fit into this category. DSM-V is clear, however, that such trauma "does not include **indirect non-professional** [emphasis added] exposure through electronic media, television, movies or pictures" (American Psychiatric Association 2013, p. 271). DSM-V, in the discussion and description of symptoms related to PTSD, lists behaviours which have a pattern of persistent avoidance of reminders of the traumatic event as a key feature. Such avoidance could lead to self-censorship to reduce thinking about and/or re-experiencing the traumatic event.

Local journalists may be affected by traumatic exposure at one or more of the four levels described above. Dworznik (2008) explains: "Near constant exposure to people in trauma coupled with long or irregular work routine, deadline pressure, and lack of social support make journalists a prime candidate for secondary traumatic stress, burnout and compassion fatigue" (p. 71). It is also likely that many journalists in conflict-prone countries such as Syria, Afghanistan and Gaza are candidates for primary traumatic stress.

> In addition, the relationship between history, memory and contemporary contexts, highlights the dual nature of historical trauma—on the one hand, historical trauma refers to events and experiences that many people consider

traumatic; on the other hand, these events are carried forward through public narratives that not only recount the events but individual and collective responses to them.

(Mohatt et al., 2014, p. 5)

In many cases these public narratives are created or reported by journalists. As such, journalists could be faced with a double dose of historical trauma – simply by being a part of the affected community, but also faced with the daily task of covering this affected community. So, what happens when a journalist is affected by fear, PTSD, historical trauma or a combination of these?

(Local) journalists, censorship and self-censorship

Censorship, or the action of silencing, in the media occurs in two ways. The first happens when "an authoritative body imposes censorship in order to obscure information it believes to be harmful either to itself or to others" (Anthonissen 2008, p. 401). The second is self-censorship when an individual intentionally and voluntarily withholds from others "information believed to be harmful to themselves or to others" (Anthonissen, 2008, p. 401). Some argue that self-censorship is more harmful than censorship by the state for it shuts down conversation completely (Scruton, 2016).

Self-censorship of information, according to Bar-Tal (2015), is an obstacle to the proper functioning of a democratic society because it prevents freedom of expression, free flow of information and access to information. The key implication of self-censorship, writes Bar-Tal, is that information that may shed new light on various issues is blocked.

Bar-Tal, whose research focused on Israel, believes that self-censorship is especially prevalent in violent contexts. In conflict-prone African societies, as Skjerdal (2010) points out, self-censorship is often morally justified and instinctively applied while covering ethnic conflict or national security issues. In many transitional societies, self-censorship is employed as a coping mechanism and often as a survival strategy (both literally and figuratively) (Skjerdal, 2010; Tapsell, 2012).

Trauma and self-censorship

Overtly, journalists may consciously avoid situations which put them at risk. However, it is also likely that journalists who have been traumatized will be impaired occupationally which may lead to unconscious self-censorship. Clinically, PTSD symptoms fall into four domains: re-experiencing (e.g., intrusive recollections, nightmares, flashbacks, etc.), avoidance (e.g., of feelings, thoughts, place, activities, and other reminders of event), emotional numbing (e.g., loss of pleasure, feeling detached from others), and hyperarousal (e.g., sleep disturbance, irritability, poor concentration, hypervigilance). While intuitively it might seem that avoidance symptoms would most likely lead to occupational impairment, research suggests that rather those symptoms related to re-experiencing and emotional numbing lead to the greatest degree of impairment in work function (Taylor et al., 2006). How this finding might result in an informed approach to treatment which has as a goal the improvement of occupational functioning of affected journalists is unknown and warrants research.

In addition to research showing occupational impairment from re-experiencing and emotional numbing, anywhere from 15 to 30 per cent of individuals with PTSD experience significant dissociative symptoms of depersonalization (feeling as though one is separated from one's own body) and derealization (feeling as though things around you are strange or unfamiliar). Boyd et al. (2018) note in their research that this population can suffer from significant occupational impairment. While this chapter acknowledges Boyd et al.'s findings as preliminary, it may well be that targeting this subgroup may help facilitate improvements in traumatized journalists who are experiencing dissociative symptoms and may be occupationally impaired.

Why journalists self-censor

Fear and trauma of local journalists working in violent contexts may result in self-censorship but for different reasons. While there has been extensive research that suggests journalists do self-censor (Høiby and Ottosen, 2016; Media Matters for Democracy, 2018), less is understood about why journalists self-censor. There is strong evidence that fear can result in self-censorship as pointed out by Hannoush (2017):

> Fear from the punishment of governments and terror from death threats that the journalist receives from extremist organizations in the Middle East, such as ISIS and its ilk. This is indirect censorship that forces the reporter to stop his writing out of fear for his life.

One recent study that surveyed journalists in Nepal, the Philippines, Uganda, Tunisia, Nigeria and Nicaragua suggested that over the past several years the working environment for journalists has changed significantly, particularly with regards to security. Høiby and Ottosen (2016) say these safety issues result in a reluctance on the part of journalists to produce information from conflict or other high-risk zones. Self-censorship, Høiby and Ottosen write, is particularly common among journalists who are especially vulnerable in their local setting.

Honduras' high-pressure media environment exacerbates the problem of self-censorship among the country's journalists. Wendy Funes, an investigative reporter in Honduras, puts the blame on fear. "I lived it when I was working for the monopoly media corporations; I self-censored, as did a lot of my colleagues, in order to be able to keep working in these companies", she says, explaining that the reasons differ from region to region (Index on Censorship, 2018). "Journalists in the Atlantic coast self-censor for the fear of organized crime, and in other places they self-censor when there are protests, because of the risk or danger this might put them in" (Index on Censorship, 2018).

Clearly, there are a number of reasons, including fear, vulnerability, newsroom pressures and editorial lines and national interest, that can influence and explain why local journalists may censor or self-censor. Fear, be it of violence, physical harm to themselves or their families, or fear of legal action, appears to overwhelmingly be the most significant factor and is highly dependent on the local context.

Human Rights Watch (2015, p.33) has noted that in Afghanistan "violence, impunity, and lack of legal and institutional safeguards for the media have fuelled fear, self-censorship, and attrition among Afghanistan's media professionals". Intuitively it seems likely that fear and self-censorship are connected. This awareness is important if organizations seek to address self-censorship as they must initially address the causes behind it.

A recent report from the Afghan Journalists' Safety Committee (AJSC, 2018) says that the Taliban and ISIS cultivate fear with the objective of ensuring that the media follow their narrative and interests. The report continues:

> By creating fear among journalists and the media, terrorist groups try to prevent the media from exposing their crimes...in provinces like Helmand, Ghazni, Kandahar and Khost, journalists tend to cover the crimes of the Taliban group with much caution and at times even refrain from covering them. This has placed tremendous challenges ahead of the very principles of free journalism.
>
> *(AJSC, 2018, p. 6)*

Several journalists in northern Afghanistan have stopped investigative reporting for fear for their own or their family's safety (Pajhwok Afghan News, 2017). In Pakistan, journalists face numerous pressures in the pursuit of their professional duties including censorship and "threats of physical harm, vilification campaigns on social media, abductions, psychological stress, and physical violence including murder" (Media Matters for Democracy 2018, p. 10).

Effects of trauma

Self-censorship usually involves a deliberate, conscious decision on the part of the self-censor. However, it is also likely that some journalists who have suffered from trauma are not even aware that they self-censor and due to trauma will be impaired occupationally which may lead to unconscious self-censorship.

Anthonissen (2008) writes that trauma can often result in a kind of silence in which a person who has experienced pain withdraws as she simply is unable to relate what is intolerable, even in memory. For the media, such silence

> would be effected by means of omission (as when details are left out, when critical aspects of a story are simply not told) or more visibly through

leaving blank spaces, or deleting offensive words and phrases – but also by relexicalizing, by retelling in terms that are perhaps ambiguous, perhaps obscure.

(Anthonissen, 2008, p. 404)

Trauma influences the working performance of journalists in a number of ways. Irritability, distrust of others, lapses in memory or concentration are common and all can lead to poor decision-making and errors in news judgement (Rees, 2013, p. 421).

In Mexico self-censorship has been enforced by threats, abductions and attacks against journalists by drug cartels in conflict. There is an information blackout "after a journalist is killed, fuelled by the fears of the victims' surviving colleagues" (Medel, 2010, p. 18). According to one Mexican journalist, "the self-censorship that many media outlets have adopted to protect its [sic] journalists has meant turning a blind eye to corruption and possible links between authorities and drug trafficking" (Medel, 2010, p. 29). A 2013 study found that journalists in Northern Mexico have fallen into a state of fear, creating a silenced media that is less willing to report crime and take on investigative pieces (Relly and González de Bustamante, 2014).

In Afghanistan it is clear that fear is a strong motivator for self-censorship as mentioned above, with journalists increasingly concerned about their safety and increasingly stressed. The "psychological warfare" against Afghan journalists "has extensively disrupted the practice of free reporting in Afghanistan and reduced the effectiveness of journalism" (AJSC, 2018, p. 7).

Historical trauma

The fear and PTSD experienced by some Afghan journalists is likely coupled with historical trauma. The country has experienced decades of armed conflict, widespread poverty and social injustice. Health care has been severely crippled as have the community networks of social support; large-scale surveys have shown that substantial mental health problems exist in the adult population including depression, anxiety and PTSD – all associated with long-term exposure to traumatic events (Panter-Brick et al., 2009).

One meta-analysis of conflict-affected populations published in the *Journal of the American Medical Association* suggested that half of a population exposed to extremely high rates of torture and political terror will meet the criteria for one or more mental disorders. Afghanistan has met those criteria for decades (Steel et al., 2009).

Historical trauma may also mean that families transmit trauma from one generation to another while individual responses to trauma may impact the broader society with patterns of social behaviour.

> Societies can become deeply divided on social, political and economic issues. People may come to see conflict as "us" versus "them" or "good" vs. "evil" without a real understanding of the issues driving the conflict.

> Communication between groups is difficult, making negotiated political processes difficult, increasing the chance that individuals and groups will use violence to achieve their goals.
>
> *(Schirch, 2016, p. 259)*

It is likely that such difficulties in communication extend to journalism.

Historical trauma such as that experienced in Afghanistan, a country that has experienced 40 years of ongoing conflict with at least two generations knowing nothing but conflict, means that people may lose trust in public order while trauma influences the society's ability to address problems and conflicts.

Implications of self-censorship for peacebuilding

One of the major values in any democratic society is freedom of expression which guarantees the free flow of information. In order to function properly, the public sphere must have free-flowing access to information, enabling the views of ordinary citizens to be heard. To make this happen, policymakers need to "focus on the media's role in constituting the public sphere of society – how that can be fostered and nurtured in such a way as to allow non-violent resolution of conflict" (Pudephatt, 2006, p. 10).

The Institute for Economics and Peace (IEP) developed a holistic framework consisting of eight "pillars of peace" which together were associated with peaceful environments. These eight pillars are inter-dependent and mutually reinforcing to the extent that improvements in one factor would tend to strengthen others and vice versa (IEP, 2013, p. 1–2).

One of these pillars is the free flow of information,[5] which includes how easily citizens can access information, whether the media is free and independent and the extent to which citizens are informed and engaged in the political process. As such, free flow of information "is an attempt to account for the degree of access to information as well as the independence of that information from vested political and economic interests" (IEP, 2011, p. 24). IEP argues that a flow of information that is restricted would have a negative impact on financial transparency which, in turn, would affect business, the functioning of government and lead to corruption (IEP, 2013, p. 1–2).

In volatile or challenging environments self-censorship limits the free flow of information and could have negative implications for peacebuilding. Ultimately, self-censorship has a negative impact on press freedom due to degraded quality, and possibly quantity, of information from conflicts (Høiby and Ottosen, 2016, p. 8).

An understanding of media, conflict and the interaction between the two can assist in leading to further understanding of the media's roles in conflict prevention and peacebuilding. At its most basic, conflict is:

> an extreme form of communication. Where the media can play a vital role in allowing a peace process to develop is by enabling the underlying conflicts

in a society to be expressed and argued through a non-violent manner. This requires the creation of a suitable media space in which this can happen.

(Pudephatt, 2006, p. 11)

The media space can improve governance, make public administrations more transparent and accountable and enable citizens to understand policies and use information to ensure the exercise of their other human rights, making them active stakeholders. All of these are critical for conflict prevention and peacebuilding.

If the goal of peacebuilding is to move from polarization to positive relationships, the media can be an effective tool to build these relationships by changing behaviours and attitudes. The media's impact on behaviour is complex and more likely to work on attitudes and opinions that shape behaviours rather than directly affecting people's actions (Bratic and Schirch, 2007).

But if there is self-censorship, whether due to fear or trauma, the media will be unable to play any of these roles and freedom of expression and the free flow of information are in jeopardy. "Self-censorship serves as a barrier, blocking information that could potentially facilitate various constructive and functional processes of improving society" (Bar-Tal, 2015, p. 16). This would include peacebuilding which is a constructive, functional process of societies in conflict.

Self-censorship prevents free access to information, freedom of expression, and free flow of information. According to Bar-Tal (2015), self-censorship protects the hegemonic narrative and prevents alternative information from being revealed. This self-censorship becomes destructive as it maintains the conflict supporting narrative and continuation of the conflict.

Self-censorship blocks relevant information, thereby decreasing access to relevant and important information, which is particularly important during both conflict and peacebuilding. Bar-Tal (2015) suggests that self-censorship hurts public debate by jeopardizing transparency, blocking critical views and thereby reinforcing norms, beliefs and practices which may have been changed had information not been withheld. This, contends Bar-Tal, "may also lead to moral deterioration, because it prevents information about societal misdeeds" (p. 63).

It is therefore critical that the media are free of self-censorship, thereby enabling accountability and transparency and ensuring that all members of society have the information required to make informed decisions. Only with these characteristics present in a society, particularly one that has seen years of conflict, can the development of tolerance be facilitated, the likelihood of free and open discussions increased, and fair, violence-free elections can be held – all critical to peacebuilding.

Going forward

Clearly, psychosocial issues are a safety issue but have much broader implications. In developing concrete recommendations for considerations going forward there is the presumption of causality from fear or trauma leading to self-censorship and when self-censorship prevails then it is difficult, if not impossible, to ensure professional

158 Michelle Betz and Paul Beighley

journalism standards and ethics are met – standards that are critical for responsible reporting that can contribute to peacebuilding. As such, journalists must have psychosocial support available to them and an understanding of the implications of self-censorship.

In this context psychosocial issues must be viewed from a broader perspective than as primarily a safety concern. Interventions would logically focus on addressing underlying threats causing the journalist to experience fear, helping journalists recognize and address that fear, and if actual traumatizing events have taken place addressing the emotional aftermath and lingering consequences which may even include psychiatric diagnoses. Recognition of cultural factors such as historical trauma is required. Efforts to immunize against the psychological consequences of trauma and fear in advance are the aims of resiliency programs.

There must be a realistic view that such efforts are largely situational and have tenuous evidence supported by our current knowledge base. Those who would provide support would be wise to acknowledge that past efforts, which were considered as standard of care at the time, turned out after further research to have the potential to cause harm. Efforts to help which are based on untested assumptions by well-meaning individuals and organizations should be avoided while thoughtful interventions and methodologies based on demonstrated effectiveness should be implemented. When possible, such efforts should include meaningful data collection to help advance our knowledge.

Additional actions include:

Addressing fear

In addressing fear, local journalists should have and use digital safety skills. In some cases, digital safety literacy may be enough to prevent potential attacks. Media support organizations can provide support in both of these areas. Moreover, local journalists should continue work to address impunity and encourage governments and donors to do the same.

In addition, local journalists can share information they are likely to self-censor with other reporters to ensure that the news gets reported. This may not always be possible at larger media houses, but if reporters are able to collaborate and support each other to prevent self-censorship broader collaborations between news media organizations and journalist collectives could be made possible to resist the pressures of self-censorship.

If possible, local journalists should work to encourage organizational collaborations which can minimize risks for each partner while ensuring important stories are told. Similarly, efforts should be made to ensure unity among various journalist unions and associations so that they operate from a point of commonality and support rather than friction. Finally, local journalists need to work with journalist associations and unions to advocate for media owners to change the working environment, respect the work of journalists, ensure safety and a living wage. If the structure does not change then self-censorship will continue.

Addressing trauma

Culturally sensitive support for journalists suffering PTSD or trauma-related psychological conditions is needed. While formalized mental health treatment might be beneficial it may also be that general support by peers and their community can be helpful. Moreover, there is a need for greater understanding of the extent that journalists may face potentially traumatic experiences. The challenge then is to build resilience and to understand that post-traumatic recovery is linked to prior preparation, and how post-traumatic support can strengthen a journalist for future incidents.

Mental health and psychosocial activities should be mainstreamed in the work of INGOs and others and should also include educational efforts regarding the same (and donors should be encouraged to support this).

It is important to highlight that "immediately after a traumatic event, simple practical, pragmatic support provided in a sympathetic manner by non-mental health professionals seems most likely to help" while some interventions targeted at providing for individuals to have a cathartic expression of emotions might actually have deleterious consequences rather than be restorative (Bisson, 2007, p. 399). As such it is important that efforts to support traumatized individuals be offered by providers of care who have specialized training and expertise in working with trauma victims.

Some researchers have suggested that the most effective way of detecting and treating most people may be to educate those who are most likely to be in contact with them about the recognition of problematic responses. This would include friends, families, colleagues, managers, general practitioners and occupational health practitioners (Bisson, 2007).

Finally, media support organizations and donors should understand the impact that trauma can have not only on journalists but also on peacebuilding. As such, they should consider support to local mental health initiatives, journalism safety initiatives and research.

Addressing historical trauma

Journalists should understand the impact of historical trauma and acknowledge and work on understanding such trauma and how it may affect their work as a journalist.

There is a need for restorative justice and community building, and this may be effective in some cases as part of conflict resolution. Media support organizations can work with journalists to adopt best practices regarding coverage of such efforts and of historical trauma.

Those working with journalists in these cases, including therapists and media support organizations, should recognize that spiritual, religious and/or cultural healing services may be appropriate tools in some cases either in addition to or separately from traditional psychosocial support.

160 Michelle Betz and Paul Beighley

Further research

More research needs to be undertaken to provide a clearer picture of the linkage between fear, trauma, self-censorship and peacebuilding, its prevalence and effective mitigation. The current instrument most used to assess self-censorship is the Willingness to Self-Censor Scale (Hayes et al., 2005). While it is a validated instrument used to evaluate the presence of self-censorship in participants, the theoretical underpinning on which it is based does not consider that journalists are a specific population which may not be represented in the original research cohort. Future instruments developed should target journalists as a specific cohort and consider the three domains discussed in this chapter: self-censorship due to fear of reprisal, self-censorship related to the aftermath of psychological trauma which may not be conscious, and the influence of historical trauma.

There is a need for further understanding of historical trauma, historical trauma response and the role of journalists in both. It is likely that in some cases resilience strategies have developed; however, this too is an area ripe for research.

Case studies could provide valuable information. For example, an examination of the narratives of historical trauma in places like Afghanistan, Rwanda or Gaza/Palestine and the implications of understanding historical trauma as narrative. This is particularly important considering the role of journalist as storyteller; ethnographic studies may be useful here.

Research suggests that those symptoms that are related to re-experiencing and emotional numbing lead to the greatest degree of impairment in work function (Taylor et al., 2006). How this finding might result in an informed approach to treatment which has as a goal the improvement of occupational functioning of affected journalists is unknown. As such, more research in this area is warranted.

Notes

1 See for example information on recent OSCE conference on safety of journalists: www.osce.org/fom/151466.
2 See the UN Plan of Action here: www.unesco.org/new/fileadmin/MULTIMEDIA/HQ/CI/CI/pdf/WPFD/UN%20Plan%20of%20Action_Safety%20of%20Journalists.pdf.
3 There are some exceptions. See for example Feinstein's work on Mexican journalists covering drug wars in that country and his research on Kenyan journalists.
4 See for example: www.health.harvard.edu/staying-healthy/understanding-the-stress-response.
5 The other seven are: a well-functioning government; a sound business environment; equitable distribution of resources; acceptance of the rights of others; good relations with neighbours; a high level of human capital; and low levels of corruption.

References

Afghan Journalists Safety Committee (2018). Six-month report: 1 January – 30 June. Report: Kabul. Available at: http://ajsc.af/summary-of-six-month-report-2018/.

Fear, trauma and local journalists **161**

American Psychiatric Association (2013). Diagnostic and statistical manual of mental disorders (5th ed.). Arlington, VA: American Psychiatric Publishing.

Anthonissen, C. (2008) The sounds of silence in the media: Censorship and self-censorship. In Wodak, R. and Koller, V. (Eds.), *Handbook of Communication in the Public Sphere*. Berlin: De Gruyter Mouton, 401–428.

Arellano, P. (2016). More than physical violence: Experts warn that Mexican journalists also face trauma, mental health problems. Austin, TX: Knight Center for Journalism in the Americas. Available at: https://knightcenter.utexas.edu/blog/00-17832-more-physical-violence-experts-warn-mexican-journalists-also-face-trauma-mental-health.

Bar-Tal, D. (2015). Self-censorship as a socio-political-psychological phenomenon: Nature, antecedents, consequences. Available at: www.researchgate.net/publication/280732289_Self-censorship_as_a_Socio-political-psychological_Phenomenon_Nature_Antecedents_Consequences.

Bisson, J.I. (2007). Post-traumatic stress disorder. *Occupational Medicine* 57(6), 399–403. https://doi.org/10.1093/occmed/kqm069.

Boyd, J.E., Protopopescu, A., O'Connor, C., Neufeld, R.W.J., Jetly, R., Hood, H.K., Lanius, R.A. and McKinnon, M.C. (2018). Dissociative symptoms mediate the relation between PTSD symptoms and functional impairment in a sample of military members, veterans, and first responders with PTSD. *European Journal of Psychotraumatology* 9(1).

Bratic, V. and Schirch, L. (2007) *Why and When to Use the Media for Conflict Prevention and Peacebuilding*. The Hague: European Centre for Conflict Prevention.

Committee to Protect Journalists (2018). Journalists killed. Available at: https://cpj.org/killed/ (accessed 28 September 2018).

Dlewati, H. (2016). Few journalist deaths in Syria – because there aren't many left. Available at: www.newsdeeply.com/syria/community/2016/08/31/fewer-journalist-deaths-in-syria-because-there-arent-many-left (accessed 1 April 2019).

Dworznik, G.J. (2008). *The psychology of local news: compassion fatigue and posttraumatic stress in broadcast reporters, photographers, and live truck engineers*. PhD Thesis, Kent State University, USA.

Feinstein, A., Owen, J. and Blair, N. (2002). A Hazardous profession: War, journalists and psychopathology. *American Journal of Psychiatry* 159, 1570–1575.

Freedom House (2018). *Freedom in the world 2018: Democracy in crisis*. Available at: https://freedomhouse.org/sites/default/files/2020-02/FH_FIW_Report_2018_Final.pdf.

Glaser, B. and Strauss, A. (1967). *The Discovery of Grounded Theory: Strategies for Qualitative Research*. Mill Valley, CA: Sociology Press.

Hannoush, R. (2017). Self-censorship: Silencing the voice to stay alive. Asharq al-Awsat, 21 August. Available at: https://eng-archive.aawsat.com/ranim-hanoush/features/self-censorship-silencing-voice-stay-alive.

Hayes, A.F., Glynn, C.J. and Shanahan, J. (2005). Willingness to self-censor: A construct and measurement tool for public opinion research. *International Journal of Public Opinion Research* 17(3), 298–323, https://doi.org/10.1093/ijpor/edh073.

Høiby, M. and Mitra, S. (2018). Why we must pay attention to the death of journalists in Kabul. *The Globe and Mail*, 3 May 2018. Available at: www.theglobeandmail.com/opinion/article-why-we-must-pay-attention-to-the-death-of-nine-journalists-in-kabul/.

Høiby, M.H. and Ottosen, R.O. (2016). Reduced security for journalists and less reporting from the frontline. In Carlsson, U. (Ed.), *Freedom of Expression and Media in Transition. Studies and Reflections in the Digital Age*. Gothenburg: Nordicom, 183–191.

Human Rights Watch (2015). *Stop reporting or we'll kill your family: Threats to media freedom in Afghanistan*. USA. Available at: www.hrw.org/report/2015/01/21/stop-reporting-or-well-kill-your-family/threats-media-freedom-afghanistan.

Index on Censorship (2018). Wendy Funes defies pressures to silence Honduran journalists. Available at: www.indexoncensorship.org/2018/09/wendy-funes-defiant-honduran-journalists-silent/. (accessed 1 April 2019).

Institute for Economics and Peace (2013). *Pillars of Peace: Understanding the key attitudes and institutions that underpin peaceful societies.* Available at: http://visionofhumanity.org/app/uploads/2017/04/Pillars-of-Peace-Report-IEP2.pdf (accessed 1 April 2019).

Institute for Economics and Peace (2011). Structures of Peace: Identifying what leads to peaceful societies.

Medel, M. (2010). Journalism in Times of Threats, Censorship and Violence: Report from the Seminar "Cross-border Coverage of U.S.–Mexico Drug Trafficking", 26–27 March.

Media Matters for Democracy (2018). *Surrendering to Silence: An account of self-censorship among Pakistani journalists.* Pakistan.

Mohatt, N.V., Thompson, A.B., Thai, N.D. and Tebes, J.K. (2014). Historical trauma as public narrative: a conceptual review of how history impacts present-day health. *Social Science & Medicine* 106, 128–136.

O'Donnell, L. (2018). Afghanistan journalism continues to suffer after its deadliest attack. Available at: www.cjr.org/analysis/afghanistan-journalism.php?_cldee=bWljaGVsbG ViZXR6QHlhaG9vLmNvbQ%3d%3d&recipientid=contact-296457ab4f30e71180d 9005056a456ce-72003da91e5c4ebc9a9c7c7b569efe4f&esid=f05e6261-a3b2-e811-80f8-005056a456ce (accessed 29 August 2018).

Pajhwok Afghan News (2017). Fear cited behind self-censorship in the north. Available at: www.pajhwok.com/en/2017/02/08/fear-cited-behind-self-censorship-north (accessed 1 April 2019).

Panter-Brick, C., Eggerman, M., Gonzalez, V. and Safdar, S. (2009). Violence, suffering, and mental health in Afghanistan: a school-based survey. *Lancet*, 374(9692), 807–816.

Pudephatt, A. (2006) *Voices of war: conflict and the role of the media.* Denmark: International Media Support.

Rees, G. (2013). The Trauma Factor: Reporting on Violence and Tragedy. In Fowler-Watt, K. and Allan, S. (Eds.), *Journalism: New Challenges.* Bournemouth: Centre for Journalism & Communication Research Bournemouth University.

Relly, J. and González de Bustamante, C. (2014). Silencing Mexico: A study of influences on journalists in the northern states. *The International Journal of Press/Politics* 19(1), 108–131.

Scruton, R. (2016). Self-censorship and the loss of reasoned argument. *Eurozine.* Available at: www.eurozine.com/self-censorship-and-the-loss-of-reasoned-argument/ (accessed 1 April 2019).

Schirch, L. (Ed.). (2016). Handbook on human security: A civil–military–police curriculum. The Hague, The Netherlands: Alliance for Peacebuilding, GPPAC, Kroc Institute.

Skjerdal, T.S. (2010). Justifying self-censorship: a perspective from Ethiopia. *Westminster Papers in Communication and Culture* 7(2), 98–121. Available at: www.westminsterpapers.org/articles/abstract/10.16997/wpcc.149/ (accessed 1 April 2019).

Steel, Z., Chey, T., Silove, D., Marnane, C., Bryant, R.A. and van Ommeren, M. (2009). Association of torture and other potentially traumatic events with mental health outcomes among populations exposed to mass conflict and displacement: A systematic review and meta-analysis. *JAMA* 302(5), 537–549.

Tapsell, R. (2012). Old tricks in a new era: Self-censorship in Indonesian journalism, *Asian Studies Review* 36(2), 227–245.

Taylor, S., Wald J. and Asmundson, G.J.G. (2006). Factors associated with occupational impairment in people seeking treatment for posttraumatic stress disorder. *Canadian Journal of Community Mental Health* 25(2), 289–301.

UN (2015). Adopting resolution, Security Council condemns violence against journalist, urges end to impunity. Available at: www.un.org/apps/news/story.asp?NewsID=50980#. VWbAOPmqpBc (accessed 28 September 2018).

UN Plan of Action on the Safety of Journalists and the Issue of Impunity (2013). Available at: www.unesco.org/new/fileadmin/MULTIMEDIA/HQ/CI/CI/pdf/WPFD/UN%20Plan%20of%20Action_Safety%20of%20Journalists.pdf (accessed 1 April 2019).

11
SAFETY AND SELF-CENSORSHIP[1]

Examining their linkage to social media use among Uganda journalists

Florence Namasinga Selnes

Introduction

Journalism can be regarded as a dangerous profession in Uganda due to the growing number of cases of violence against journalists and the media. Journalists grapple with physical attacks, arrest and arbitrary detention as well as harassment, a situation worsened by existing punitive legal provisions that impinge on journalism practice and freedom of the media. News organizations operate under pressure due to fear of prosecution and of being shut down. Any reportage that is perceived as negative can result in intimidation, warnings and legal action while journalists who criticize authorities, risk being attacked or even losing their jobs. Accordingly, journalists are forced into self-censorship to avoid being targeted. A UNESCO report (2018) shows that there are high levels of self-censorship in Uganda as journalists and media organizations avoid reporting on certain issues due to fear of retaliation.

This chapter is an offshoot of a separate study about how journalists in Uganda use social media in routine news coverage, which suggests that social media present opportunities and challenges related to safety and self-censorship. As a further interrogation of these issues, this study explores the relationship between safety, self-censorship and Uganda journalists' appropriation of social media. The chapter is, therefore, concerned with how journalists and media organizations negotiate insecurity and censorship in an environment characterized by hostility and suppression. Anchored in research on safety, media freedom and self-censorship, the chapter explores how journalists and news organizations creatively use social media to circumvent repression and practise journalism. The question guiding this research is: how does Uganda journalists' employment of social media relate to (their) safety and self-censorship?

The data that informs this research were collected from two focus group discussions and 23 semi-structured interviews with print and broadcast media journalists located in Kampala, Uganda's capital. The chapter is organized as follows: the first section gives an overview of Uganda's media landscape followed by a discussion about safety, media freedom and self-censorship. This is followed by an elaboration of the data collection procedures, a presentation of the main findings and a discussion of the implications of the findings on safety and self-censorship for journalism practice in Uganda.

The Ugandan media landscape, safety and media freedom

Uganda's media landscape has expanded since the early 1990s when the government under President Museveni liberalized the media. Today, the country's media landscape can be described as dynamic, with over a dozen publications, hundreds of radio stations and scores of TV stations. The broadcast media, particularly radio, have expanded more rapidly than print and as such, Uganda can rightly be described as a radio nation with statistics showing close to universal access to the medium at 99% (Mwesige, 2009; UCC, 2017). Newer media formats including mobile phones, the Internet and social media are also available. The number of Internet users was estimated at 18.5 million as of June 2018, according to the media regulator (UCC, 2018). Social media applications such as Facebook, Twitter, YouTube, Instagram and LinkedIn are among the top ten websites in the country and these have debatably influenced the face of public communication.[2] While Internet access is low compared to the country's population of about 41 million, there is no doubt that social media have become important channels through which users express their views on a range of issues. Social media play a significant role as alternative channels for individuals and groups with limited access to mainstream media.

The expansion of the media has mainly been quantitative in terms of the number of media outlets rather than the quality of journalism and the level of media freedom (Mwesige, 2009). Although murders of journalists are rare in Uganda, the state uses direct and indirect means to suppress media freedom. Media freedom violations are widespread, and safety of journalists is increasingly becoming a critical issue.

Research about journalists' safety has become topical in recent years due to the prevalence of violations against journalists and the media. Journalists all over the world face violence, threats, harassment, intimidation and death (UNESCO, 2018). In Africa, journalists must surmount multiple media laws, which politicians justify on grounds of strengthening national security and fighting terrorism (Hengari, 2017). Freedom of expression and freedom of the media are constitutionally guaranteed in most countries on the continent but the same rights are limited by regulations on sedition, criminal defamation, publication of false news and public order related laws. The public order and security laws restrict activities of political opponents and of journalists (Freedom House, 2016b). In Uganda, for instance, security agencies invoke the Public Order Management Act to block opposition politicians from holding public rallies and meetings. These laws limit journalists' newsgathering practices as security officials use teargas and force to disperse demonstrations or meetings. Several journalists have been targeted, injured and had their equipment confiscated and/or destroyed during such fracas.

Violations against journalists have become common in Uganda with indications that the state of freedom of the media is worsening (HRNJ-U, 2018; Freedom House, 2017). Journalists grapple with laws of sedition, public order, computer misuse and cyber harassment and interception of communication in addition to physical and verbal assault by security agencies and individuals (HRNJ-U, 2018). The violations are often perpetrated by state security agencies – the police, the army, and individual politicians and civilians working on their behalf. For example after the February 2016 elections, police arrested seven journalists for covering former presidential candidate Kizza Besigye. In May of the same year, government banned the coverage of opposition protests (Wesonga & Bwire, 2016). Two journalists, James Akena (Reuters) and Alfred Achol (*The Observer*) were attacked and beaten by security agents in August 2018 while covering anti-government demonstrations. The journalists had their cameras destroyed in the process. In March 2016, a government minister attacked and beat up female journalist, Judith Naluggwa, of Bukedde TV, as she covered a court case in which he was accused of corruption (*Daily Monitor*, 2016). In April 2019, a court registrar assaulted two journalists (from Smart 24 Television and Salt TV) (*Daily Monitor*, 2019). The perpetrator was caught on camera slapping and destroying the cameras of the journalists as they covered a story in which he was accused of stealing land.

Independent media organizations must sometimes conform to avoid sanctions and closure. *Daily Monitor*, the leading privately owned publication has faced the wrath of government for publishing stories that criticize its policies and officials. Together with *The Observer*, *Daily Monitor* is repeatedly accused of promoting the agenda of opposition politicians and for publishing stories that highlight the weaknesses of the government. Consequently, the news organization has faced siege by security agencies and shutdown, in addition to an advertising ban. The closure of *Daily Monitor* headquarters in Kampala and the main offices of *Red Pepper* over a story about presidential succession in May 2013 left the entire media industry shaken. The story was sparked off by a letter written by the former government chief spy in which he claimed that there were plans to kill senior government officials who did not support Muhoozi[3] to succeed his father Yoweri Museveni as Uganda's president. Security forces raided and disabled the printing press and computer servers of *Daily Monitor* and *Red Pepper* as well as transmission equipment of sister radio stations, Dembe FM and KFM. The premises of the two media organizations were declared crime scenes and subsequently shut down.

Safety and self-censorship

Self-censorship is a common phenomenon in journalism practice, which entails inclusion and exclusion (of information) during the writing and editing processes. In this sense, self-censorship is related to professional standards where media practitioners voluntarily leave out certain information on grounds of taste and morality. Self-censorship can be caused by commercial pressures (from advertisers and media owners), cultural expectations and lack of professionalism on the part of the media (Skjerdal, 2010). However, journalists sometimes avoid covering and reporting on certain issues due to fear of interference from authorities. This kind of self-censorship is what this chapter is concerned with. Empirical research shows that journalists and the media around the world self-censor to avoid dangers that occur or may occur as a result of their work (HRW, 2019). Whereas self-censorship is justified in journalism out of professional conviction, restrictions in addition to intimidation, harassment, threats, imprisonment, advertisement bans and closure push journalists and media houses to avoid covering and publishing some journalistic material. Journalists adopt this kind of self-censorship as a survival tactic and coping mechanism (HRW, 2019; Skjerdal, 2010; Tapsell, 2012), which means that self-censorship is practised to thwart any undesirable responses and ensure safety. This type of self-censorship is common in countries where freedom of expression and freedom of the media are restricted. Other studies also regard self-censorship in relation to undue external interference (e.g. Hayes, Glynn, & Shanahan, 2005; Lee, 1998). Lee (1998, p. 57) further regards self-censorship as "a set of editorial actions" taken by journalists and media organizations to avoid punishment.

Self-censorship has been proven to be a result of interference from external forces such as government, and other actors outside media's control. Chin-Chuan Lee, for example explains self-censorship as:

> A set of editorial actions ranging from omission, dilution, distortion, and change of emphasis to choice of rhetorical devices by journalists, their organizations, and even the entire media community in anticipation of currying reward and avoiding punishment from the power structure.
>
> *(1998 in Skjerdal, 2010, p. 99)*

This definition regards self-censorship as a result of pressure exerted on journalists and the media. Indeed, self-censorship is pervasive in countries where the media are highly controlled and characterized with a repressive legal framework (e.g. Aaron, 2007 in Skjerdal, 2010, p. 100; Thompson, 2007a). The phenomenon is rife in semi-democratic contexts with oppressive regimes in which government authorities are hostile towards journalists. In such contexts, the media are targeted for reporting stories that throw government and individual politicians into disrepute. Governments use tactics including: direct and indirect attacks on individual journalists and media organizations; legal action against the media to target their business interests in addition to withholding their advertising revenue.

Self-censorship is connected to the political context within which journalism is practised (e.g. Simons & Strovsky, 2006; Nadadur, 2007; Amin, 2002 in Skjerdal, 2010, p. 100). This chapter emphasizes this line of thinking, arguing that repressive political regimes are responsible for widespread self-censorship through draconian laws and sets of actions targeting the media and journalists. Reports by organizations such as Human Rights Watch and Freedom House show a persistent

168 Florence Namasinga Selnes

trend of censorship at different levels in Uganda (Freedom House, 2016a; HRW, 2017).There is evidence of widespread self-censorship which results from restrictive media laws and attacks on journalists. Moreover, the increasing government crackdown on the media results in self-censorship due to fear of prosecution, persecution and loss of livelihood.

Insecurity and censorship problems have also extended to the Internet with indications of digital surveillance, which threaten the practice of journalism (IFEX, 2018). There are reports that the government of Uganda sometimes employs intrusion malware to incapacitate websites of media that are perceived as carrying negative coverage. For example CIPESA (2015) reported that *Daily Monitor's* website was disrupted during the post-election demonstrations in 2011. Internet and mobile communication surveillance under such laws as anti-terrorism and interception of communication empower security forces to monitor computers and other communication devices of opposition politicians, perceived enemies, activists and journalists. Additionally, the Computer Misuse Act 2011 criminalizes what it calls offensive communication and gives security agencies a freehand to arrest Internet users whose communication is perceived as offensive particularly to the president and members of his family.Victims of this law include ordinary citizens and journalists.

Cronau's (1995, p. 11) description of self-censorship as the most corrosive and insidious form of censorship underscores the undesirable impact of the phenomenon on journalism. Self-censorship not only restricts freedom of speech and inhibits free expression but threatens independent journalism and media freedom in general.This chapter focuses on self-censorship as a practice in which journalists and media organizations consciously refrain from covering certain issues for fear of retribution. Safety is taken to mean the ability of journalists and the media to do their work without physical or moral suppression – in other words, a situation where journalists can gather, write and publish news without facing violence, assault, loss of property, imprisonment, kidnap, or without fear for their lives.

This chapter is not oblivious to safety challenges associated with social media but focuses on opportunities related to the production, distribution and branding of journalism especially in contexts where practising the profession is a risky endeavour. Newer technologies have generally been found to facilitate journalistic work in settings where freedoms of the media are controlled, with anecdotal evidence suggesting that (even) traditional media sometimes turn to the Internet during state crackdown (e.g. Hem, 2014; Namasinga, 2018). Social media have been found to play an important role in journalism practice in Uganda's newsrooms (ACME,[4] 2013; Namasinga, 2018). While Information and Communication Technologies and social media continue to attract scholarly attention in relationship to their influence on journalism, little is known about how journalists in semi-democratic contexts creatively use the applications for safety and how the deployment of the Internet platforms relates to phenomenon of self-censorship.

Methodology

This chapter set out to explore the relationship between safety, self-censorship and journalists' deployment of social media. It addresses the question: how does Uganda journalists' deployment of social media relate to safety and self-censorship? The data for addressing the question were obtained through in-depth interviews and focus group discussions that were conducted in Kampala, Uganda's capital. The initial data collection covered the period between June 2015 and March 2016 when focus group discussions and interviews with journalists from *New Vision*, *Daily Monitor* and *The Observer* were carried out. The data collection procedure started with two focus group discussions in June 2015. The focus groups included journalists from *New Vision* and *The Observer* and each of them comprised six respondents. Afterwards, nine interviews were conducted with journalists at *Daily Monitor* and six additional interviews with journalists at *The Observer*. Four interviews were conducted in October 2018 and four more email interviews in July 2019 to update the data. The journalists in this sample were selected from newspapers (four), radio (two) and television (two). In total, two focus group discussions and 23 semi-structured interviews were conducted.

As mentioned in the introduction section, this chapter springs from an earlier study (Namasinga, 2018) that examines journalists' deployment of social media in routine coverage. Respondents in that study (2015/2016) were purposively selected based on their willingness and potential to provide relevant information that illuminated the investigation. The additional eight interviewees (for the interviews conducted in 2018 and 2019) were selected based on their knowledge and experience with social media and how that relates to safety and self-censorship. Two of the journalists in this sample were selected from the earlier sample of respondents who were interviewed in 2015/2016. The remaining six were picked through snowball sampling. Snowball sampling was employed in the sense that the first respondents recommended potential further interviewees. As Patton (2002) asserts, the snowball (sample) grows bigger as new information-rich cases accumulate and as key names or incidents are mentioned repeatedly.

The empirical material was analysed qualitatively using cross-case analysis as described by Patton (2002). Cross-case analysis enabled me to put together and analyse responses to common questions from different interviewees. The cross-case analysis technique was also employed to develop central themes such that respondents' views were categorized into themes drawn from the research question.

Findings: Social media and safety for news organizations

Safety in this study was taken to mean freedom for journalists and media to operate without attacks, threats, intimidation, fear and closure from any forces. News organizations in Uganda are not immune to attacks and closure for publishing news that offends authorities. The study shows that news organizations employ social media to remain in operation when their premises are shutdown. In May 2013,

170 Florence Namasinga Selnes

security agencies raided and cordoned off two Ugandan media houses: Monitor Publications and Red Pepper Publications. Their premises remained occupied and their printing presses halted. *Daily Monitor* and *Red Pepper* were out of circulation for 10 days. They had published a letter authored by Uganda's former chief spy David Sejusa. In the letter, Sejusa made several allegations including that there was a plan to have President Museveni's son, Muhoozi, succeed his father as president and a plot to assassinate senior politicians opposed to the plan. The analysis of interviews suggests that social media served as alternative channels for reporting and publishing and that journalists deployed social media to manoeuvre the shutdown. The interviewees pointed out that they used Facebook to communicate with each other since their work spaces had been shut down. The role of social media and how journalists used them during the shutdown is reflected in sentiments by *Daily Monitor's* digital content editor in the excerpt below:

> When we were shut down, the journalists could not access the premises. Facebook helped in a way that it was used to coordinate journalists [...] people were able to talk to each other [...] because people were not coming to work. Journalists were using Facebook to stay in touch with editors or call to consult about ongoing stories. We posted all kinds of reportage on social media (which) helped a lot because the only means of reporting then was via the Internet, through Facebook, Twitter and our website.
>
> *(Personal communication, July 12, 2019)*

This excerpt highlights the different functions social media served in the face of state suppression. The functions included facilitating coordination and communication among journalists and enabling reporting and publishing. The interview extract also suggests that social media served as a virtual newsroom where reporters and editors converged to file and report stories as they would have done in a physical space. It is also evident in the above quotation that social media and the Internet in general were employed to distribute stories in the absence of machines to print newspapers for circulation.

For individual journalists, social media was relevant during the closure of physical premises of news organizations. The findings showed that journalists affected by the incident also deployed social media to report about the siege in order to draw attention to the state of the media organization to attract assistance from human rights organizations and foreign missions. Via social media, the media organization remained connected to its readers. A journalist[5] who witnessed the attack and the subsequent shutdown of *Daily Monitor's* premises described how social media was useful:

> I posted pictures of the siege, police officers taking position in different corners of the building and the subsequent protests of journalists along the road. The more pictures and posts we put up on Facebook, the more the

world got to know. So, social media was a great way to keep the world abreast with what was going on at Monitor.

(Personal communication, July 11, 2019)

The closure of *Daily Monitor* was intended to censor and curtail its operations. Declaring the premises of the news organization a crime scene aimed at scaring journalists into self-censorship. With their working space occupied by security forces, journalists turned to social media to not only report about the invasion but to continue working. *Daily Monitor's* shutdown highlights the difference social media made for journalists and their news organization in the face of state censorship. Social media and the Internet facilitated the journalistic roles of publishing and disseminating which had been blocked by the shutdown of the organization's premises. It is, therefore, arguable that social media facilitated journalism practice which the news organization could not execute through the traditional means because the printing machines and premises had been shut down and occupied by security agencies. *Daily Monitor* remained relevant to its readers even if the newspaper itself was not circulated on news stands. In sum, journalists and the news organization used social media to manoeuvre during the period of shutdown, thereby overcoming censorship.

That news organizations' and journalists' resort to social media in face of shutdown underscores the relevance of social media in enabling journalism in times of uncertainity. Journalism does not necessarily need to be produced from particular physical buildings or newsrooms. Social media can ease the coordination of groups of individuals that may be geographically dispersed so that they can produce and publish information for public consumption as *Daily Monitor* did during the 11 days when its premises were a crime scene. Additionally, the news organization managed to stay in operation, produce and publish news online through its digital platforms. Otherwise *Daily Monitor's* business operations would have been adversely affected, hence threatening the newspaper's survival.

Social media as safe spaces

The interviewees pointed out that they deploy social media for safety reasons and to keep themselves from physical harm. Some of the interviewees regarded social media as a safer alternative compared to face-to-face encounters with some news sources and physical presence at news scenes. Moreover, some of the journalists were aware of the degree of safety afforded by social media and the advantages of some of the platforms over the others. For example the findings indicate that journalists use WhatsApp to share sensitive information and communicate with sources because communication via the application is encrypted and, therefore, regarded as a safer platform than other social media applications. The analysis also shows that news organizations are concerned about safety in relation to journalists' deployment of social media in routine coverage as reflected in the following extract by *Daily Monitor's* digital content editor:

> Social media can be used to keep someone safe. For example, I know that WhatsApp is fairly safe so I encourage journalists to use WhatsApp more for messages and calls because it is encrypted so the chances of having your communication intercepted by a third party is low.
>
> *(Personal communication, July 12, 2019)*

The above interview extract highlights three points related to safety and journalists' appropriation of different social media applications: (i) journalists' knowledge of safety features of the different social media applications, (ii) journalists' knowledge of the challenges linked to the use of social media, (iii) their alertness to the possibilities of intrusion into their activities via social media. Reference to the encryption ability as enabled by WhatsApp is evidence of the importance journalists attach to the platform in relation to safety. Communication via digital platforms is susceptible to monitoring and/or intercepted by state agents in Uganda because of the interception of communication law. That journalists weigh up the advantages afforded by a particular social media application in relation to safety shows how journalists creatively and selectively appropriate social media to minimize harm to themselves, their news organizations and sources.

It emerged from the findings that journalists' deployment of social media in relation to safety is conditioned by the preferences of their sources. There were indications in the findings that sources, just like journalists, are wary of the possibilities for interception of their interactions and communications via digital platforms. Some sources sometimes prefer to communicate through WhatsApp to avoid having their conversations monitored because of the encryption afforded by the platform. The WhatsApp application offers end-to-end encryption such that all forms of communication remain between or among parties involved.[6] The use of WhatsApp in regard to safety is reflected in the quotation below by a senior editor at *Daily Monitor:*

> Sources now also use WhatsApp to provide information, documents and so on. I think they feel it is safer and cannot be easily tracked. Also, if they are on the record, they use it as proof, in case a journalist has misquoted them [...]. In fact, some sources might not pick [up] your call, but they will reply [to] your WhatsApp messages.
>
> *(Excerpt taken from Reddit[7])*

Journalists are driven to deploy social media applications such as WhatsApp because of the encryption – a safety feature afforded by the platform. They share documents, videos, pictures, voice and text messages with each other and their sources with minimal risk to their safety. The affordance of WhatsApp in the context of this chapter is that it enables secure communication between journalists and sources thereby contributing to reducing self-censorship on both sides.

Social media and physical safety

Journalists also indicated that they employ social media for safety in coverage of public demonstrations, outlawed events and hostile sources. The findings suggest that some journalists turn to social media to follow such events instead of physically attending them for fear of being targeted by security forces. A *New Vision* reporter narrated the circumstances in which he has been forced to resort to social media to stay safe:

> I was assigned to cover a public demonstration in the city but I had to run away from the field after a short time because the police started to beat people. When I realized that it was not safe, I had to leave the scene. To me, life and safety come first. I started monitoring the story on social media because during riots people tweet and write about incidents that have happened to them and their neighbours during such events [...]. Another incident was the raid on Edith Byanyima's home. It was unsafe. I wasn't sure about what was happening. So, I went to her Twitter account, picked her comments and later called her on [the] phone. I turned to social media.
>
> *(Personal communication, October 18, 2018)*

This quotation raises several points relating to journalists' safety in Uganda. Firstly, public demonstrations in Uganda (especially organized by the political opposition) turn violent because they are outlawed. Secondly, journalists are among the victims when violence erupts during such demonstrations with evidence that the police target journalists. Several journalists have been attacked, injured and had their tools destroyed while some are arrested by security forces for covering such events. Thirdly, the temptation to resort to social media is high because one does not necessarily need to be on the street to endure teargas or risk being beaten to get information and pictures pertaining to the event. The findings are in line with previous studies pointing to how social media provide easy access to sources (Marwick & Boyd, 2011; Namasinga, 2018), and enable journalists to identify, connect with and contact sources and learn about potential stories as they occur (Broersma & Graham, 2012; Vis, 2013). Based on the findings presented in this chapter, it can be argued that social media become even more relevant in newsgathering when journalists' safety is at risk.

The interviewees further regarded some individual sources as threatening, and indicated that they would be afraid of meeting sources again for safety reasons. While most attacks and threats to journalists emanate from state security agencies, the analysis shows that journalists face intimidation and assault from individual politicians who beat and warn journalists about stories they pursue. The threats aim to scare journalists to self-censor. The findings suggest that journalists avoid face-to-face encounters with aggressive sources but would resort to social media as an alternative newsgathering tool for safety purposes.

174 Florence Namasinga Selnes

The findings also suggest that journalists deploy social media as tools for alerting colleagues, their supervisors and the world about their safety status. Several respondents recounted incidents in which they have used social media to avoid situations that put them in harm's way or to give updates regarding their whereabouts as evident in the quotation below by one of the respondents:

> During the 2017 Age Limit consultations my cameraman and I travelled to Nakaseke district, Central Uganda to attend one of the consultation meetings, because there was doubt on whether legislators were consulting the public on their views. We arrived early and waited for the legislator to arrive. We had made several calls to the legislature and she confirmed she would hold the meeting. But an hour before her arrival, her handlers started quizzing us and asked us why we were there with no invitation. We tried to explain in vain. Before we knew it, they had called in a police team who then bundled up my cameraman onto the van, but I fought back. I quickly texted a group I am on, via Signal and they spread the word fast on other social media. By the time I left the venue and got to the town centre, my cameraman had been released and we left the location.
>
> *(Personal communication, July 11, 2019)*

The excerpt above shows that journalists face safety challenges in routine news coverage including being arrested for doing their work. It also shows the deliberate use of social media for highlighting their dilemma when the journalists got into trouble. Making phone calls to the newsroom for help would not have been feasible or accorded the journalists the immediate assistance they needed, considering the distance between Kampala – where the journalists travelled from – and Nakaseke district. In deploying social media, the journalist was able to alert a wider audience about the status of her colleague and indeed got assistance within a few hours. This reflects social media as omnipresent with the ability to help users to overcome geographical and time limitations and enable many-to-many simultaneous communication.

The findings further suggest that journalists sometimes use social media to inform the public about the dangers they face in order to get support to fend off threats. For instance, one journalist narrated how she used social media to alert the world about her arrest:

> In 2009, I think, I had also gone to visit a media colleague, radio presenter to be exact because I was working voluntarily on the side as a representative for journalists with a human rights defenders' committee. I took out my camera and took a photo of our colleague through a window of the room he was being kept in and the officer in charge of the Police Station, Wandegeya Police, quickly ordered for my arrest. I was arrested and put into a cell with a man. In there, I quickly posted on Facebook about the incident and many

media houses ran the story. After an hour, the police officer was asked to let me out.

(Personal communication, July 11, 2019)

The above narrative reflects the seriousness attached to social media by journalists and violators of journalists' freedoms. By posting pictures of herself in a police cell on Facebook, the journalist believed that she would be freed. The post on Facebook alerted her employers and probably piled pressure on her tormentors leading to her release. This points to the potential of social media to spread information and attract action because the reporter was freed in a short time. The immediate release of the journalist as indicated in the quotation above also shows that Ugandan authorities regard social media as valid communication channels. This reflects the importance of social media when journalists' lives are threatened, when they are arrested or kidnapped, because the applications make it easier for journalists to inform the world of their situation and to advocate for their freedom.

Related to the above view is the notion that journalists and news organizations use social media to mobilize towards safety-related causes in which colleagues are under threat or when journalism is under attack. For example some interviewees noted that social media were widely used to condemn the government closure of *Daily Monitor* in 2013 and to highlight the fate of the media house as stated at the beginning of this section. Human rights defenders converged online and offline and pressured the government through social media to re-open the news organizations. Whether government yielded to this pressure by opening the media organization is beyond this chapter's consideration but we can argue that social media's ability to bring together large numbers of people who can instantly propagate information, makes it possible and easier to advocate for journalists' rights as a crowd instead of scattered individual efforts.

The research also revealed that social media give journalists the leeway to share stories that are regarded as unsafe to publish through the mainstream channels. Some of the journalists explained during interviews that they are sometimes forced to drop stories for security reasons or because the assigning editor has interests. Moreover, journalists sometimes do not publish some stories in the mainstream media for fear of backlash from parties involved. This in itself points to tendencies of self-censorship, but the analysis suggests that journalists regard social media as an alternative channel through which they can share such censored information. The allure of social media in this case relates to the anonymity afforded by some of the applications. The idea that social media afford users anonymity, and free them from the limitations of space and time is of relevant here. It is arguable that the existence of avatars and anonymous accounts enables journalists and other users to share information and express their views more freely than they would have done in an open public setting. This helps to alleviate self-censorship among journalists which makes the use of social media in disseminating information important to journalism in contexts where freedom of expression and of the press are controlled.

176 Florence Namasinga Selnes

While anonymity poses ethical-related challenges to journalism, the finding echoes the view that people are generally less inhibited when using social media and that sources might be more open to divulge information or might just be more informal when communicating via social media (Jordaan, 2013, p. 32).

Discussion and conclusion

This chapter is concerned with how journalists and media organizations in Uganda navigate through insecurity and at the same time surmount self-censorship. The findings indicate that reporters devise solutions to remain in operation. The study specifically found that journalists and news organizations sometimes resort to using social media for newsgathering, reporting and dissemination for safety reasons and to overcome self-censorship.

Safety challenges arise during newsgathering as journalists are required to go to news scenes and also meet sources. As indicated earlier, journalists in Uganda operate in a climate of fear and suppression, pushing them to self-censor. Covering political rallies and demonstrations has become dangerous as journalists are targeted and assaulted by security forces. Journalists risk being assaulted and arrested and have their cameras confiscated or destroyed at the hands of security forces who target them to prevent them from accessing news events. Moreover, journalists face harassment and intimidation by individual politicians and organized gangs. As such, social media are deployed as substitutes for face-to-face interactions with violent sources and physical presence at news events to avoid dangers that arise during coverage of such events and meetings with unfriendly sources. Journalists turn to social media to bypass blockage to news scenes, thereby circumventing self-censorship. While social media do not replace the enduring journalistic practice of shoe-leather reporting and physical interactions with sources, they provide journalists with an option when conventional methods are unfeasible. Additionally, social media enable publishing and dissemination of journalistic material when media houses are under state-perpetrated suppression. This study regards the closure of *Daily Monitor* and cases of attacks and intimidation of journalists as attempts by the perpetrators to scare journalists into self-censorship. As other studies about the safety of journalists indicate, suppression of news media and journalists usually lead to self-censorship (HRW, 2019; IFEX, 2018; Morrison, 2016). The closure of *Daily Monitor* in 2013 highlights the role of social media in enabling journalists and news organizations to remain in practice during periods of clampdown. Here social media served as virtual working spaces when *Daily Monitor's* newsroom was shut down; they were used for communication purposes and for coordinating news production activities and finally for publishing the final journalistic product. The publishing opportunity, aided by social media and the Internet in general, kept the news organization in operation until it was reopened.

Furthermore, the findings show that social media are essential in mobilizing masses to issues relating to journalists' safety. Journalists encounter many safety problems including intimidation, kidnapping and arrest, hence the need to continuously discuss these issues in the public domain. It emerged in the findings that journalists tap into the power of crowds brought together on social media to condemn the violations and to advocate for freedoms of colleagues who may be in trouble. It is not possible to ascertain whether authorities yield to criticism from users but there were indications that journalists overcome security-related challenges such as being freed from prison as a result of sharing their safety situation on social media.

The insecurity that arises during public political demonstrations makes the use of social media justifiable on grounds of safety to reduce the attacks on journalists, which have become rampant in recent times. Social media's relevance in relation to journalists' safety can be argued in two ways. Firstly, social media serve as a tool which journalists deploy for immediate safety from physical harm during newsgathering. A journalist can opt to follow an event via social media instead of being physically present for fear of being assaulted or arrested as is usually the case.

Secondly, the suppression of journalists and violations of media freedom reflect the society of Uganda overall, which is characterized by the censoring of critical voices. Censorship is not confined to the media but also extends to opposition politicians, activists and ordinary citizens. These have limited avenues for expression due to a plethora of laws that hamper freedom of expression in addition to the high-handedness of security agencies. One such piece of legislation is the Public Order Management Act which regulates and limits public gatherings. This law specifically targets people with agendas and views that are contrary to those of the government. The same regulation hampers journalists' ability to access particular sources and to obtain news from outlawed newsworthy events. Social media have, therefore, become useful deliberative spaces for newsmakers whose activities are restricted and for news media and journalists whose ability to access the said sources is inhibited. For instance, there have been cases in which sources are left with social media as the only means to communicate with the public and with journalists. This is particularly true when sources fear being arrested or because their movements are tightly controlled. One such example occurred after the February 18, 2016 general election when presidential candidate Kizza Besigye was put under house arrest for more than a month. In the immediate aftermath of his confinement, journalists were denied physical access to him.

In addition, politicians and activists who criticize the government resort to passing information to the public through social media instead of appearing in public for fear of arrest. A case in point is when presidential aspirant Amama Mbabazi announced his candidature in the February 2016 election in a video circulated on social media instead of the traditional press conference after a series of run-ins with the police. Mbabazi had become a police target since he showed interest in running for the presidency and his subsequent fallout with the ruling government. While the use of social media shows the importance politicians attach to the platforms, the intimidation from security operatives of his former allies as well as harassment of his supporters prompted the politician to announce his presidential bid through

178 Florence Namasinga Selnes

social media. This means that social media are not only useful to journalists but also to sources who have a message to pass on to the public but cannot because their freedoms of assembly and expression are curtailed. Social media, therefore, play an important role in promoting reporting as they enable journalists to obtain information they would not otherwise have accessed due to censorship and unfriendly legislation. This study's findings support Hem's (2014) view that new media are relevant tools that journalists and media organizations in authoritarian societies deploy to bypass state repression.

The author is not oblivious to safety problems associated with information and communication technologies. Digital surveillance has become widespread in Uganda as the government invokes laws such as interception of communication and computer misuse to arrest and prosecute journalists. Journalists have also fallen victim to such surveillance. Moreover, the government of Uganda has joined several others on the African continent to suppress access to the Internet and social media through stringent legislation, shutdown and, more recently, the social media use tax. The findings in this chapter are not generalizable because of the perennial digital divide linked to inequalities in Internet access among journalists and the entire country. As Banda (2010) and other African media researchers such as Moyo D (2009) and Gicheru (2014) contend, there is a gap between the utopian ideals expected of the Internet and reality. Apart from the widely documented challenges related to unequal access to ICTs, the government of Uganda has devised means to control access to and the use of social media and the Internet. In addition to Internet regulations and shutting down of the Internet on two occasions in early 2016 and in May 2017, the government introduced a social media use tax in July 2018. Justified on the grounds of raising revenue and to counter what the president called "gossip", the levy is an attempt to extend suppression of discourse to the newer digital platforms. While the direct impact of the levy on journalism is yet to be measured, there are reports that it has already led to a reduction in access to the Internet. Social media are, therefore, a double-edged sword for Uganda's journalism, posing both opportunities and challenges related to safety and self-censorship.

Notes

1 Note: Special thanks to Annet Kizza Rønningsbakk for assisting me to collect some of the data that informed this chapter.
2 www.alexa.com/topsites/countries/UG. Accessed June 02, 2014.
3 Muhoozi Kainerugaba is President Yoweri Museveni's only known son.
4 The African Centre for Media Excellence – a Kampala-based independent, non-profit media and communication support organization. See http://acme-ug.org/about-us/who-we-are/. Accessed December 10, 2016.
5 Freelance journalist for Voice of America – Africa Desk at the time of this interview. She was a reporter at *Daily Monitor* at the time of the shutdown.
6 https://faq.whatsapp.com/general/28030015/. Accessed October 14, 2019
7 www.reddit.com/r/IAmA/comments/9lc5fo/i_am_carol_beyanga_managing_editor_of_digital/. Accessed July 13, 2019.

References

African Centre for Media Excellence [ACME] (2013). Annual Report.

Amin, H. (2002). Freedom as a value in Arab media: perceptions and attitudes among journalists, *Political Communication 19*(2): 125–35.

Banda, F. (2010). Citizen journalism & democracy in Africa: An exploratory study. Rhodes University. School of Journalism and Media Studies, Highway Africa.

Broersma, M., & Graham, T. (2012). Social media as beat. *Journalism Practice, 6*(3), 40–419.

CIPESA (2015). State of Internet Freedom in Uganda 2015, August 2015. At www.cipesa. org/?wpfb_dl=209. Accessed May 21, 2019.

Cronau, P. (1995). Self-censorship: the most insidious gag. *Pacific Journalism Review, 2*(1), 11–15.

Daily Monitor (2016). Minister Byandala beats up journalists. 24 March. At www.monitor. co.ug/News/National/Minister-Byandala-beats-up-journalist/688334-3131160-b3llt3/ index.html. Accessed July 13, 2019.

Daily Monitor (2019). Court registrar under fire over assault on journalists. 29 April. At https:// mobile.monitor.co.ug/News/Court-registrar-under-fire-over-assault-journalists/ 2466686-5091960-hokfpwz/index.html. Accessed July 13, 2019.

Freedom House (2016a). Uganda: Freedom of the press 2016. At https://freedomhouse.org/ report/freedom-press/2016/uganda. Accessed October 10, 2019

Freedom House (2016b) Freedom in the World report: Anxious dictators, wavering democracies: Global freedom under pressure. At https://freedomhouse.org/report/freedom-world/freedom-world-2016. Accessed January 25, 2019.

Freedom House (2017). Freedom of the Press 2017 – Uganda Profile. Freedom House. https://freedomhouse.org/report/freedom-press/2017/uganda. Accessed March 13, 2019.

Gicheru, C. W. (2014). The challenges facing independent newspapers in Africa. Reuters Institute for the study of journalism, University of Oxford.

Hayes, A. F., Glynn, C. J., & Shanahan, J. (2005). Willingness to self-censor: A construct and measurement tool for public opinion research. *International Journal of Public Opinion Research*, 299–323.

Hem, M. (2014). Evading the censors: Critical journalism in authoritarian states. Reuters Institute for the study of journalism, University of Oxford.

Hengari A. T. (2017). Democracy in Africa: Reversing backsliding after ten years of the African Charter on Democracy. *L'Afrique en Questions, 41*. Paris: Ifri.

HRNJ-U (2018). Impunity: A cry for media freedom. Press Freedom Index Report. Kampala: Human Rights Network for Journalists-Uganda.

HRW (2017). World report 2017 – Ethiopia: Events of 2016. At www.hrw.org/world-report/2017/country-chapters/ethiopia. Accessed April 12, 2018.

HRW (2019). Afghanistan's Media Self-Censors to Survive: Press Freedom at Risk in Deadliest Country for Journalists. At www.hrw.org/news/2019/04/11/afghanistans-media-self-censors-survive. Accessed October 10, 2019.

IFEX (2018). Pakistani: Journalists and activists increasingly self-censor due to rampant surveillance. At https://ifex.org/pakistan-journalists-and-activists-increasingly-self-censor-due-to-rampant-surveillance/. Accessed October 10, 2019.

IREX (2008). Media Sustainability Index (MSI)–Uganda 2008. At www.irex.org/system/ files/2-Africa_08_uganda.pdf. Accessed October 10, 2019.

Jordaan, M. (2013). Poke me, I'm a journalist: The impact of Facebook and Twitter on newsroom routines and cultures at two South African weeklies. *African Journalism Studies, 34*(1), 21–35.

Lee, C.-C. (1998). Press self censorship and political transition in Hong Kong. *International Journal of Press/Politics, 3*(2), 55–73. DOI https://doi.org/10.1177/1081180X98003002005.

Marwick, A. & Boyd, D. (2011). I tweet honestly, I tweet passionately: Twitter users, context collapse, and the imagined audience. *New Media & Society, 13*(1), 114–133.

Morrison, R. (2016). Watching our words: Perceptions of self-censorship and media freedom in Fiji. At https://reutersinstitute.politics.ox.ac.uk/sites/default/files/research/files/Watc hing%2520our%2520Words%2520-%2520Perceptions%2520of%2520Self-Censorship% 2520and%2520Media%2520Freedom%2520in%2520Fiji.pdf. Accessed October 7, 2019.

Moyo, D. (2009). Citizen journalism and the parallel market of information in Zimbabwe's 2008 election. *Journalism Studies, 10*(4), 551–567.

Mwesige, P. G. (2009). The democratic functions and dysfunctions of political talk radio: The case of Uganda. *Journal of African Media Studies, 1*(2), 221–245.

Nadadur, R. D. (2007). Self-censorship in the Pakistani print media, *South Asian Survey 14*(1): 45–63.

Namasinga, F. (2018). *Sourcing in converged media spheres: A study of how print journalists in Uganda use social media in routine news coverage* (unpublished doctoral dissertation). University of Oslo, Norway.

Patton, M. Q. (2002). *Qualitative Evaluation and Research Methods.* Thousand Oaks, CA: Sage.

Simons, G. & Strovsky, D. (2006). Censorship in contemporary Russian journalism in the age of the War against Terrorism, *European Journal of Communication 21*(2): 189–211.

Skjerdal, T. S. (2010). Justifying self-censorship: a perspective from Ethiopia. *Westminster papers in Communication and Culture, 7*(2), 98–121.

Tapsell, R. (2012). Old tricks in a new era: Self-censorship in Indonesian journalism. *Asian Studies Review, 36*(2), 227–245.

ULII (2011). The Computer Misuse Act 2011. At https://ulii.org/ug/legislation/act/2015/ 2-6. Accessed March 24, 2020.

Thompson, A. (2007a). Journalism training and media freedom in Rwanda. *Media Development, 54*(4), 24–8.

UCC (2017). Post, Broadcasting and Telecommunications Market & Industry Q3 Report, 2017. At www.ucc.co.ug/wp-content/uploads/2018/02/Market-Industry-Quarterly-Report-for-the-Quarter-ending-September-2017-Final.pdf. Accessed April 13, 2018.

UCC (2018). Post, Broadcasting and Telecommunications Market & Industry Q2 Report, 2018. At www.ucc.co.ug/wp-content/uploads/2017/09/Communication-Sector-Performance-for-the-Quarter-ending-June-2018.pdf. Accessed August 10, 2018.

UNESCO (2018). World Trends in Freedom of Expression and Media Development. Paris: UNESCO and University of Oxford.

Vis, F. (2013). Twitter as a reporting tool for breaking news. *Digital Journalism, 1*(1), 27–47.

Wesonga, N. & Bwire, N. (2016). Government bans live broadcast of FDC defiance campaigns. *Daily Monitor,* 05 May. At www.monitor.co.ug/News/National/Government-bans-live-broadcast-of-FDC-s-defiance-campaign/688334-3189888-65hgqwz/index.html. Accessed November 08, 2016.

12

DEFENDING THE WATCHDOG

How local NGOs build journalists' resilience by combating threats to their safety and security

Gerald Walulya

Introduction

On 11 February 2019 a journalist, Moses Walugembe, wrote on a Facebook page of Ugandan journalists commending the local non-governmental organization (NGO) Human Rights Network for Journalists-Uganda (HRNJ-U) for the work it does to defend journalists. He also implored his colleagues to appreciate this organization:

> Peeps, isn't it ripe [that] we make a loud noise appreciating Human Rights Network for Journalists–Uganda for becoming almost the only true independent non-profit organization that promotes press freedom in Uganda. They defend the rights of journalists to do their job of reporting without fear of reprisal. To me they are the only insurance for journalists.
>
> *(Facebook post)*

In the comments that followed, several journalists expressed their appreciation to HRNJ-U for the work it does for the journalism community in Uganda. In fact, a few journalists in the same comments testified how they too had been assisted by this organization when their rights as journalists were violated.

This chapter investigates the role of two NGOs in Uganda, HRNJ-U and Uganda Media Women's Association (UMWA), in protecting journalists against threats they face while doing their work. The chapter further considers how this form of support encourages journalists to minimize cases of self-censorship as well as making journalists more resilient when faced with adversity.

The media and NGOs, particularly the ones in the field of human rights, enjoy a symbiotic relationship. The media publish information upon which NGOs conduct advocacy. At the same time NGOs advocate for the freedom of the media

182 Gerald Walulya

to operate independently without interference from either the state or non-state actors. Thrall, Stecula and Sweet (2014) have noted that historically, NGOs have relied on mainstream news media to expose human rights violations and encourage governments to pressure the perpetrators.

There are hundreds of local and international NGOs worldwide involved in the assessment of the media operating environment with a view to promoting freedom of the media. Some of these organizations, for example Freedom House, Committee to Protect Journalists, Reporters Without Borders are international, while the majority of others operate locally and sometimes in affiliation with international organizations. The mandate of these organizations includes promoting free and independent media through activism, monitoring media freedom violations, evaluating media systems through indices and written reports, and defending and protecting journalists working in conflict zones and under repressive governments. Becker, Vlad and Nusser (2004) acknowledge that these organizations have invested a lot of effort in evaluating media systems, pointing out violations and other policy concerns in areas of media freedom and independence.

This chapter contributes to the debate about journalists' safety and security by highlighting how support to journalists from NGOs contributes to minimizing cases of self-censorship and how this form of support encourages journalists to become resilient.

Worldwide, journalists face numerous threats in the process of executing their duties. On the basis of these threats, UNESCO (2018) has noted that journalism is one of the most dangerous professions in the world. According to the 2019 World Press Index released by Reporters Without Borders (RSF), there is a growing trend of hatred for journalists that has culminated in increased violence against journalists, which in turn has led to a chilling effect (RSF, 2019). Freedom House has reported that part of the assault on journalism is coming from elected leaders, who should instead have been the ardent defenders of media freedom. (Freedom House, 2019). Berger (2018) notes that there are several instances of mobilization of mobs by elected leaders at rallies and online, creating an environment in which journalists are treated as liars and trouble-causers who deserve the ill treatment they receive.

In Africa, media freedom remains fragile, with threats, harassment, kidnaps and detention of journalists being a commonplace across several countries. Although there has been a marked improvement in some countries such as Ethiopia, following the coming of a new government in 2018, in other countries such as Tanzania, Chad, Libya and Ghana the situation has further deteriorated. In the first half of 2019 alone, three journalists were killed in Africa. These include a Ghanaian investigative journalist, Ahmed Hussein-Suale who was shot dead early in 2019 on his way home; Obed Nangbatna, a Chad TV reporter; and Mohamed Ben Khalifa, a Libyan freelance journalist who was killed in crossfire in January 2019.[1] According to the African Freedom of Expression Exchange (AFEX, 2018), 11 journalists were killed in different countries in Africa in 2018. These included three journalists from each of Guinea and Somalia, two journalists from Togo and one journalist from each of Gambia, Senegal and Liberia.

In Uganda, media freedom violations continue to be highly prevalent, with acts of harassment of journalists, intimidation, assault, detention, kidnaps and destruction of journalists' equipment being a commonplace (Freedom House, 2019). Police and the army – the major perpetrators of media freedom violation (HRNJ-U, 2018) – often target journalists during riots and demonstrations, assaulting them, damaging or confiscating their equipment and ordering them to delete all recorded information about whatever they may have been covering. For example in August 2018, while covering the parliamentary by-election in the north-western town of Arua and subsequent protests against the arrests of two members of parliament and other opposition supporters, several journalists were beaten or arrested by authorities and had their equipment damaged or confiscated.[2]

Some of the most common incidents of media freedom violations in Uganda are arrests and assault of journalists and blocking of access to news scenes. In 2018 for instance, 40 incidents of blocking access to information, 37 cases of assault and 31 cases of detention of journalists were recorded (HRNJ-U, 2018). Increasingly, the police and the army in Uganda are reliant on the strategy of restraining journalists from accessing important news scenes (such as riots and demonstrations) that the police and the army suspect may cast the government in a negative light. Similarly, the government media regulatory agency, the Uganda Communications Commission, frequently writes to media houses restraining them from covering some incidents and threatening them with closure if they insist on covering banned incidents (HRNJ-U, 2018). For instance, in May 2019, UCC ordered 13 media houses to suspend 39 workers, including news managers, producers and heads of programmes, accusing them of breaching minimum broadcasting standards.[3] Media owners of the affected media houses went into dialogue with UCC over the matter while journalists under their umbrella organization, Uganda Journalists Association, decided to drag UCC to court. In general, the range of threats journalists face seems to be expanding every passing day, including repressive laws, such as the Computer Misuse Act (2011)[4] whose target seems to be limiting public discourse of state affairs online.

This chapter is organized into four sections; including theoretical framework, methodology, findings, analysis and conclusion. In the next section, I present a theoretical reflection on media freedom and self-censorship, and the concept of resilience.

Theoretical perspectives

Media freedom and self-censorship

Media freedom is one of the contentious concepts in mass communication literature. Some scholars, such as McQuail (2000) observe that media freedom encompasses both the level of freedom enjoyed by the media to publish and the degree of freedom with which citizens have access to this media content. He argues that the media should have enough independence to protect the free expression of ideas and information as well as a diversity of media content that does not originate from limited concentrated owners. This notion has been supported by other scholars such as Rozumilowicz (2002) who also argues that the question of who controls the media is an important determinant of whether the media is free and independent. Other scholars, for instance, McChesney (1999) and Doyle (2002) are mostly concerned with the impact of economic pressures and media concentration on a free press and effects of censorship on media freedom. Freedom of the media, generally understood as the right to publish or broadcast without interference from government or other private actors, has been widely regarded as the hallmark of democracy (Barendt, 2005). Freedom of the media is also regarded as essential for the protection of all other human rights because the media often publicizes breach of other freedoms through, for instance, abuse of power, leading to corrective measures. Without a vibrant free media, it is almost impossible to have an informed and active citizenry (Frere, 2011). Due to diverse challenges, media houses and journalists have sometimes had to censor themselves in order to remain secure or to protect some interests.

In some countries, especially in Africa and other developing countries, there exists a deep-rooted tradition within the media of withholding information from the public for fear of certain negative consequences if such information is released. There is a strong relationship between the political environment and *self-censorship* (Skjerdal, 2010). In countries where the political environment is restrictive, self-censorship is highly prevalent (Nadadur, 2007; Simons & Strovsky, 2006). According to Skjerdal (2010), discourses of fear play a significant role in the reproduction of self-censorship in media organizations. Although self-censorship is associated with societies that are tightly controlled by the state, such as Eritrea (Aaron, 2006) and Zimbabwe (Mukundu, 2006), it is also seen in countries such as Kenya (Ongong'a, 2010) and Ghana (Kafewo, 2006), which are regarded as generally more democratic, in an African context. Similarly, although self-censorship is mostly linked to state media in Africa, private media have also been observed restraining their reporting for fear of legal and sometimes economic reprisals (Skjerdal, 2010).

Laws such as defamation, anti-terrorism and protection of national security that attract severe punishments are a major source of self-censorship. For example according to Nassanga (2007), self-censorship increased within the Ugandan media following the passing of the Anti-Terrorism law. Anxiety about criminal charges remains a major stumbling block to the work of journalists in tightly regulated media environments, which cultivates self-censorship. For example in a study conducted by Peter Mwesige among Ugandan journalists, more than half of the journalists cited official laws such as sedition and libel as a "major limit on journalistic freedom" and a source of self-censorship (2004, p. 80).

Apart from laws that involve political interests, self-censorship is also a function of commercial pressures and cultural norms and expectations. As scholars such as McChesney (1999) and Craig (2004) have warned, advertisers and commercial interests in general represent a major threat to independent journalism world-wide. In Kenya and Uganda, for instance, negative stories are not published because of the need to protect the media's revenue sources (IREX, 2008, p. 276; Khamalwa, 2006). According to Schiffrin (2009), in Nigeria the oil industry is a major source of journalistic self-censorship – probably more so than media laws.

In regard to cultural expectations, journalists are constrained by socio-cultural limitations. Self-censorship is a common operating system for journalists when covering gender (Tom, 2008) and religion (Banda, 2003). Self-censorship is also applied in coverage of conflicts of ethnic nature. For instance, in Rwanda, it is a taboo to mention issues of ethnicity in the media or any other public forum, (Waldorf, 2007). Self-censorship is sometimes used as a mechanism of resilience to counter adversity towards journalists. As Skjerdal (2010) has observed, self-censorship is a difficult vice to eradicate in any given media system as long as there are external parties which have an interest in what is covered in the media.

Resilience and journalists

Resilience has been defined as the capacity to recover from extremes of trauma and stress (Atkinson, Martin & Rankin, 2009). Masten (1994, p. 3) has defined resilience individually as a "successful adaptation despite risk and adversity." According to the American Psychological Association (APA, 2019), resilience is the process of adapting well in the face of adversity, trauma, tragedy, threats or significant sources of stress such as serious health problems or workplace and financial stressors.

The concept of resilience is relevant to journalism professionals because, despite threats, journalists are often involved in covering stories that put them in harm's way. Although this concept has been applied in a wide range of disciplines, it has not been extensively used in journalism. In one of the studies related to journalism, McMahon and McLellan (2008) have emphasized that journalists and their employers need to be cognizant of the impact of trauma and natural disasters on victims and journalists themselves. They note that the road to building resilience is greatly enhanced where individuals have a significant amount of knowledge of the potential impacts of trauma or threats to an individual.

Key factors in building resilience

There are a number of factors that contribute to a person or an organization's resilience. Mark, Al-Ani and Semaan (2009) looked at disaster recovery in wartime Iraq and identified several factors for resilience, including reconfiguring social networks, self-organization, redundancy, proactive practices, and repairing trust in information. Powley (2009) notes that an organization's ability to be resilient is dependent on its social capital and networks. Doerfel, Chewning and Lai (2013) contend that social capital accrued through long-standing partnerships and efficient pre-disaster networking through building communities of practice significantly impact post-disaster resilience. This affirms the need to establish supportive systems that can be activated in times of crisis. As APA (2019) has noted, relationships that create love and trust, provide role models and offer encouragement and reassurance, which bolster a person or an organization's resilience.

Another factor that helps people and organizations to build resilience is planning ahead of disasters and crises. According to APA (2019), it is important that people and organizations build capacity to make realistic plans and make strategies towards implementing them. In the context of journalism, media organizations and journalists that do not make contingent plans to counter unexpected attacks and disasters are likely to be less resilient compared to the ones that plan ahead of time. In his focus on National Resilience, Bean (2018) has noted that, in recent years, countries such as Australia, Israel and Malawi have formed national resilience frameworks to prepare their countries to be resilient during traumatic situations. He notes that these strategies offer citizens a mental cushion in the wake of disaster and during adversity.

Apart from proactive planning, resilience can also be attained by developing a positive attitude. According to APA (2019), a positive view of yourself and confidence in your strengths and abilities are important properties in achieving resilience. Shing, Jayawickreme and Waugh (2016) observe that one's experience of harnessing positive emotions, even during an especially trying or stressful time, is a major factor that contributes to resilience. Shing Jayawickreme and Waugh (2016) argue that positivity contributes to resilience by helping one to build up social, psychological, and physical resources over time, which could help you develop coping skills during future times of stress. According to Fredrickson's broaden-and-build theory (Fredrickson, 2001), positive emotions can help broaden your momentary thoughts, actions, and attention to your surroundings.

All in all, responding to situations of adversity differs from person to person. Therefore, building resilience is a personal experience. According to APA (2019), people react differently to the same traumatic and stressful situations. This means that a framework of building resilience that works for one person might not work for another. The adaption variations may reflect cultural differences. With growing cultural diversity, the public is now exposed to different approaches to resilience (APA, 2019).

Methodology

The data presented in this chapter is based on interviews with four representatives of two NGOs involved in protection of journalists in Uganda; HRNJ-U and Uganda Media Women's Association (UMWA). This has been supplemented by interviews from ten purposively selected journalists in Uganda. The selected journalists had received support from NGOs after being involved in incidents of media freedom violations in the last four years. These journalists include three print journalists, one online journalist, two radio journalists and four television journalists. I have also included photojournalists and TV camera journalists (four) because they tend to be at the center of controversy in most of the incidents that have happened. In terms of gender, I have included three female journalists and seven male journalists, which reflects the ratio of male to female reporters in Uganda.

The interviews were conducted in May 2019. Most interviews were conducted at journalists' places of work for the convenience of the interviewees. One of the interviews was carried out at a location where the journalist had been assigned. Using an interview guide, journalists were asked about incidents threatening their safety and security in which they have been involved and how the assistance from NGOs gave them encouragement. NGOs were mainly asked about what kind of assistance they offer to journalists who face safety and security challenges related to their work.

Analysis

Roles of NGOs in protecting journalists

The two NGOs under review perform several roles that contribute to reducing self-censorship and protecting journalists. These include advocacy and networking for improving journalists' working environment, training journalists in safety and security, and providing free legal support for journalists who are pursuing violators of media freedom. Other roles include financially supporting journalists who have been affected by violations of media freedom, and carrying out research into and documenting violations of media freedom.

Advocacy and networking

The NGOs interviewed conduct advocacy and networking work to influence policy and laws pertaining to the media. They lobby different actors for a liberated press environment. For instance, they engage security agencies, media owners and other stakeholders in dialogue with the aim of ensuring that journalists have freedom to publish without prior restraint. This is done together with other human rights organizations. There are many human rights organizations in Uganda that are not exclusively working on press freedom but when they are networked with media freedom NGOs, those generalist organizations also use their spaces and platforms to talk about press freedom. This serves to amplify the issue of media freedom. In some cases, this networking extends to international organizations. For instance, one journalist narrated how a local NGO; HRNJ-U linked him to an international NGO, the Committee to Protect Journalists, that gave him money to leave Uganda because his life was in danger after a story he wrote about targeted deaths of Rwandan refugees in Uganda.

> HRNJ-U came to know about my plight and they had an interview with me and after that interview they put my case on the forum of human rights organizations and immediately I received a call from Nairobi, from the Committee to Protect Journalists asking about my situation. The next call

came from New York asking me what the problem was. They told me that it is safer to get out of Uganda. At first, they gave me \$1,000 but I told them I cannot leave my children with nothing. I stayed around for about two months, meanwhile they were raising another \$1,000 that I left with the children and then I left. I went to Nairobi and I stayed there for three years.

(Personal communication, 17 May 2019)

While in Nairobi, this journalist lived a reclusive life to evade whoever was targeting him. He did not practise journalism but instead did manual jobs to support himself. The journalist did not indicate why he was unable to find a journalism job in Kenya, but it is possible that he wanted to live a more private life. The above case demonstrates how NGOs provide practical assistance to journalists in times of need. Minimal as it may appear, this kind of assistance is important to journalists in helping them remain resilient. As APA (2019) has observed, people are more likely to be resilient if they have established relationships that create love and trust, and offer encouragement and reassurance. Apart from networking, the NGOs' advocacy for media-friendly laws is critical in reducing self-censorship. As Mwesige (2004) has noted, the fear of strict media laws is a major source of self-censorship among Ugandan journalists. While acknowledging the work of these NGOs, one journalist noted that:

The work of these organizations is so much useful because it gives me courage to continue with my work because I know there is someone who is giving me back up. Someone who is doing litigation for me in case certain problems come, so it encourages me to go on with my work.

(Personal communication, 30 May 2019)

His opinion did not differ from that of another journalist who said:

When you know that you are a bit secure, when you know that you have someone to help you, to relieve you in any problem as long as you are right, you get courage. You do even beyond your expectation. What makes us fear is that if these organizations decide to step back we don't have any other organized group that can help journalists.

(Personal communication, 30 May 2019)

Training

NGOs provide training to journalists in areas of safety and security. They also train journalists in aspects of media ethics to mitigate the security concerns that journalists face due to their own unethical behavior. Many journalists in Uganda still learn journalism on-the-job with no formal education background in this field. It becomes important for such journalists to have some training in the area of ethics. Secondly, many journalism schools have not yet incorporated safety and security into their curriculum, which means that even journalists from journalism schools do not know how to protect themselves. UMWA Executive Director explains how their work helps journalists.

> Under the skilling of female journalists, we do training on safety for professionals in the media so that they are not caught within the crossfire but also to stay safe and secure while they are doing their job. Meaning that we take them through how secure they would be while at work.
>
> *(Personal communication, 24 May 2019)*

The HRNJ-U Executive Director also explains what aspects of training his organization handles:

> We build professional capacity of journalists through training on the legal framework in order to make sure that they move within the legal framework but also to prepare them as paralegals. They can be their own lawyers in case lawyers are not readily available. So, people will know how to go to plead at police, if taken to court they will know how to ask for bail, they know the arguments, they even know how they must be treated and they put up an informed argument and we have really seen a fundamental shift in the way police treats journalists in the countryside who are informed compared those who are less informed.
>
> *(Personal communication, 25 May 2019)*

The Executive Director of UMWA also believes that the work of organizations like the one she heads have kept many journalists in the profession longer than they would have stayed, as she explains below.

> It gives them some confidence because now they know how they can cope and if you have that coping strategy then they become more confident. They stay longer in the field because somebody told them what to do and how to do it, so eventually they become resilient and stay on longer in the profession than when they had no such kind of exposure.
>
> *(Personal communication 24 April 2019)*

Training journalists in ethics, legal and safety issues is important in reducing self-censorship because it equips them with knowledge of what they can and cannot do based on the law and a professional code of conduct. Sometimes journalists may self-censor themselves over unfounded fears. Journalists who are well trained in their rights and responsibilities are less likely to self-censor compared to their colleagues who lack this kind of awareness.

Providing free legal aid and financial support

NGOs not only train journalists about the law, they also offer free legal services to journalists who cannot afford them. In Uganda, many media houses, especially

190 Gerald Walulya

radio stations, do not have lawyers. But even the ones who have them sometimes do not get the emergency assistance when they need it because of the bureaucratic nature of organizations. HRNJ-U has a standby legal team available on call to represent any journalist who has been harassed, unlawfully arrested, detained, intimidated or fictitiously charged. This is particularly important in the fight against impunity. In the past, many perpetrators of violence against journalists have got off scot-free due to their political and financial standing in the country. One of the many cases HRNJ-U succeeded in prosecuting was that of a police commander, Joram Mwesigye, who assaulted a TV journalist causing him bodily harm.[5] The affected journalist, who now moves on crutches and can no longer practise journalism due to the bodily harm he sustained, explains how the NGO helped him.

> If it wasn't for HRNJ-U, I would not have received justice in courts of law. They were the people who were running my court files. Remember I was in hospital or at home but each time court came up, they had to find means of me being in court, they gave me a lawyer who was always in court. The entire team of HRNJ-U was always in court. With HRNJ-U, I always felt like, 'yes I have someone to run back to.' Time came when I was under threats. Those threats were horrible, I was being followed, receiving anonymous calls all the time, being beaten. Actually, I was once beaten at the home gate. I could not even go to the police to record a statement because everyone knew me by face. So I could only report to HRNJ-U. HRNJ-U would send me a car to take me wherever I wanted to go. I would always feel safe under HRNJ-U.
> *(Personal communication, 24 May 2019)*

Although the above journalist is no longer able to practise journalism, his case remains a major source of inspiration to journalists in Uganda, a reminder that there is someone who cares for you in such difficult times. Support of this nature minimizes journalists' fear of reprisals after reporting. Skjerdal (2010) has identified fear as one of the major causes of self-censorship. As long as journalists know that there is someone willing to freely represent them in court when a case against them comes up, they become less likely to self-censor themselves. This assurance may also give them boldness to report on issues they would otherwise have feared to venture into.

Although the primary focus of these NGOs is not to provide money to journalists, sometimes they have done it out of necessity in difficult financial situations. For example in the case mentioned above, HRNJ-U contributed more than $1,000 in medical expenses for this journalist to receive treatment.

> HRNJ-U were the first to deposit money on my account for my medical bills. My bill had accumulated up to 2.6 million Uganda shillings [$700]. They were the first people to make a deposit of about 1 million ($300) towards clearing of this bill. They gave me that financial assistance and I really needed it. When I was discharged, HRNJ –U didn't give up on me. I started

visiting the hospital as an outpatient. As I was improving I fell sick again and I was admitted at Norvik hospital. HRNJ-U came in with money as well. My bill at the hospital was fast accumulating because every day I was using 400,000 [$110] for one injection. So HRNJ-U still came in to save my situation. They were the first people to deposit about 2 million [$550] because now my bill was so huge.

(Personal communication, 24 May 2019)

Assistance of the above nature is likely to contribute to building a positive attitude among journalists in times of adversity, which according to Shing, Jayawickreme and Waugh (2016) may make journalists more resilient. This positivity is reflected in one journalist's response who noted:

The assistance I received from these organizations encouraged me because they cared about what I was going through. They come at the scene and see what has happened, whether you are the one in the wrong, they will do something accordingly and things will normalize. They have encouraged me by demonstrating that they are together with me.

(Personal communication 24 April 2019)

Research and documentation

NGOs also conduct research on the media freedom landscape in Uganda. Within this mandate, they conduct research into and analysis of proposed media laws and raise red flags if such laws infringe on people's right to free expression. As Nadadur (2007) has noted, self-censorship tends to thrive in restrictive media environments. Efforts of this kind are therefore likely to counter media restrictions, thereby reducing incidents of self-censorship. Another important aspect of this function is the documentation of violations of media freedom. Since 2009, HRNJ-U has released a local media freedom index that highlights violations of media freedom and the major perpetrators of these violations. These reports have put media freedom violators on the spot, thereby alerting them that someone is watching their actions. Although journalists continue to receive attacks from the same perpetrators, it may be said that without these efforts, such attacks would be at an even higher magnitude. Yet, the more journalists are attacked, the more they are likely to self-censor themselves due to fear of attack. The press freedom index reports have also become a major basis for other researchers to conduct more research into the safety and security of journalists.

In general, NGOs that defend press freedom perform important roles that contribute to the reduction of self-censorship among journalists. The contribution of these NGOs has attracted wrath from political and economic interests that stand to benefit from self-censorship. Recently, many perpetrators of media freedom violations have started directing their attacks to these organizations, as the Executive Director of UMWA notes:

Sometimes you also attract abuses from the perpetrator because I have gone through that. I remember one time there were some people who were calling me 'why don't you drop this case of Nalugwa,[6] what interest do you have? You want money, blah, blah, blah.' I didn't know this would happen but I am sure that even other activists who are doing this kind of work get such threats.

(Personal communication, 24 May 2019)

HRNJ-U Executive Director further narrates threats that his organization has received:

Our office has been broken into three times in three years – 2013, 2015, 2016 – and all these didn't come off as ordinary robberies because at every occasion they targeted information. We had a lot of valuable property which was never touched. The last one of 2016 we even had footage captured by our CCTV cameras which we presented to police. They did not generate any interest in hunting down these criminals. So you have an impression that maybe these are state-managed attacks on offices of human rights organizations. Unknown people also trail our staff. Sometimes we have had to relocate them from one place to another. People they stay with in their homes are bribed to poison them. Our bags are stolen from our cars under very mysterious circumstances, people sending us lots of malware in our emails to crash our emails and information, regular hacking into our mails.

(Personal communication, 25 May 2019)

It remains important that organizations like HRNJ-U and UMWA continue to defy such threats from elements that want to silence journalists. Otherwise, if NGOs start withdrawing from pursuing certain cases, self-censorship among journalists may unfortunately become inevitable. When journalists get discouraged due to lack of support when they are threatened, thoughts of self-censorship surface.

Reflections and conclusion

This chapter has examined the role of NGOs in reducing self-censorship among journalists. Through interviews with representatives of NGOs and journalists I have indicated that NGOs play five major roles that contribute to the reduction of self-censorship as well as promoting safety and security of journalists. These include: advocacy and networking, training, providing free legal aid to journalists, providing financial assistance to journalists in crisis situations, and documentation and research. In turn, this work of NGOs has built resilience among journalists to stay on the job as well as limiting incidents of self-censorship. The protection and support journalists receive from NGOs reduces fear among journalists, thereby minimizing incidents of self-censorship.

The NGOs studied in this chapter form what Powley (2009) has called social capital and networks for journalists, which contribute towards their resilience.

As APA (2019) has observed, these networks and relationships with NGOs offer encouragement and reassurance, which contribute towards the reduction of journalistic self-censorship and resilience. Working on behalf of journalists, these NGOs proactively plan in anticipation of threats to journalists. As Bean (2018) has noted, this planning, which includes training journalists how to deal with threats, helps to mentally and physically prepare journalists ahead of threats to their safety and security. Additionally, as a result of the encouragement journalists derive from the NGOs' support, journalists gain self-belief and confidence to publish information they would otherwise have censored. According to APA (2019), a positive view of yourself and confidence in your strengths and abilities are important properties in achieving resilience.

As Becker et al. (2004) have observed, NGOs make a considerable contribution to promoting a free media. However, there remains the challenge of how some of this work can be sustained in the absence of such organizations. Secondly, there remain questions of the ethics of having a media that is supported by NGOs most of which are foreign-funded, especially after some critics have suggested that this may limit the type of stories journalists can tell.[7] Given that the organizations studied in this chapter are local NGOs in which journalists participate and feel represented, some of the shortcomings related to foreign NGOs may not hold. However, progressively, there may be a need to develop mechanisms through which media houses and organized journalist unions can take on some of the responsibility these NGOs are currently shouldering. This may help to forestall the challenge of sustaining the work done by these organizations. Moreover, funding opportunities for NGOs continue to dwindle, implying that they may at some point have to scale down the amount of work that they do.

In the context of self-censorship, NGOs make an important contribution by advocating for a free media environment. Through providing journalists with financial assistance in crisis situations as well as free legal aid, NGOs contribute towards reducing discourses of fear among journalists that, according to Skjerdal (2010) are a major driver of self-censorship in several countries in Africa. Through advocacy, NGOs encourage the amendment of laws such as defamation and libel that Mwesige (2004) has identified as a major cause of self-censorship. Overall, although NGOs alone cannot end self-censorship nor ensure journalists are completely safe, the cooperation between journalists and NGOs may build resilience and potentially decrease practices of self-censorship, especially if these efforts are supported by media owners.

Notes

1 International News Safety Institute, Journalists under attack https://newssafety.org/casualties/journalists-under-attack/?tx_bbgnews_articleindex%5B%40widget_0%5D%5BcurrentNumberOfitems%5D=50&cHash=a0308570df8d1312f6d9b3f9ef1d4dab (2/7/2019)
2 www.hrw.org/world-report/2019/country-chapters/uganda (3/7/2019).

194 Gerald Walulya

3 https://observer.ug/news/headlines/60575-ucc-orders-suspension-of-39-journalists-at-13-media-houses (1/7/2019)
4 The Uganda Legal Information Institute, Computer Misuse Act, 2011, 2010 Accessed at https://ulii.org/ug/legislation/act/2015/2–6 (15/11/2019).
5 Betty Ndagire, Former Old Kampala DPC Joram Mwesigye guilty of assaulting journalist www.monitor.co.ug/News/National/Former-Old-Kampala-DPC-assaulting-journalist/688334-3844742-gu0g9jz/index.html (6/7/2019).
6 Judith Nalugwa is a journalist who was assaulted by a Ugandan minister after a court session in which the minister was accused of corruption
7 http://theconversation.com/donor-funded-journalism-is-on-the-rise-in-africa-why-it-needs-closer-scrutiny-119894?utm_source=facebook&utm_medium=facebookbutton&fbclid=IwAR1BHZT5LvGqox0tUrlEm-1r7OJ4wThLfjuimsLpMekvmCchwliETn6qPiM (8/7/2018).

References

Aaron B. (2006). *The state of the media in Eritrea*, report presented at the Sub-Regional Journalists' Conference, Entebbe, Uganda, 27–29 November.

AFEX (2018) *Annual Freedom of Expression Situation in Africa Report*. www.africafex.org/afex/wp-content/uploads/2019/04/Annual-FOE-Situation-in-Africa-Report-2018.pdf.

American Psychological Association (2019). *The road to resilience*. Retrieved from www.apa.org/helpcenter/road-resilience (15/10/2019).

Atkinson, P.A., Martin, C.R. and Rankin, J. (2009). Resilience revisited. *Journal of Psychiatric and Mental Health Nursing*, 16(2), 137–145.

Banda, F. (2003). *Community radio broadcasting in Zambia: a policy perspective* (Unpublished Doctoral dissertation). Pretoria: University of South Africa.

Barendt, E. (2005). *Freedom of Speech*. Oxford: Oxford University Press.

Bean, H. (2018). National resilience. *Journal of Applied Communication Research*, 46(1), 23–25, doi:10.1080/00909882.2018.1426709

Becker, L.B., Vlad, T., and Nusser, N. (2004). *Media freedom: Conceptualizing and operationalizing the outcome of media democratization*. A paper presented at the International Association for Media and Communication Research, at the conference in Porto Alegre, Brazil, July 25–30, 2004.

Berger, G. (2018). UNESCO's safety of journalists agenda: what impact? *Australia Journalism Review*, 40(2), 29–39.

Craig, R.L. (2004) Business, advertising, and the social control of news. *Journal of Communication Inquiry*, 28(3), 233–52.

Doerfel, L.M, Chewning, L.V., and Lai, C-H. (2013) The evolution of networks and the resilience of interorganisational relationships after disaster. *Communication Monographs*, 80(4), 533–559, doi:10.1080/03637751.2013.828157

Doyle, G. (2002). *Media Ownership: The Economics and Politics of Convergence and Concentration in the United Kingdom and European Media*. London: Sage.

Fredrickson, B.L. (2001). The role of positive emotions in positive psychology: The broaden-and-build theory of positive emotions. *American Psychologist*, 56(3), 218–226.

Freedom House (2019). *Democracy in retreat. Freedom in the world report*. https://freedomhouse.org/report/freedom-world/freedom-world-2019 .

Frere, M.-S. (2011). *Elections and the media in post-conflict Africa: Votes and voices for peace?* London: Zed Books.

HRNJ-U (2018) *Impunity: A Cry for Media Freedom*. www.hrnjuganda.org/?wpfb_dl=79.

IREX (2008). *Media sustainability index 2006/2007: The development of sustainable independent media in Africa*. Report by the International Research and Exchanges Board. Washington, DC: IREX.

Kafewo, S. (2006). Ghana: Research *findings and conclusions*. *Report for African Media Development Initiative*. London: BBC World Service Trust.

Khamalwa, J.W. (2006). Uganda: Research *findings and conclusions, Report for African Media Development Initiative*. London: BBC World Service Trust.

Mark, G., Al-Ani, B., and Semaan, B. (2009). Resilience through technology adoption: Merging the old and the new in Iraq. In *Proceedings of the 27th international conference on human factors in computing systems* (pp. 689–698). New York: ACM. doi:10.1145/1518701.1518808

Masten, A.S. (1994). Resilience in individual development: Successful adaptation despite risk and adversity. In Wang, M. C. & Gorden, E.W. (Eds.), *Educational resilience in inner-city America* (pp. 3–25). Hillsdale, NJ: Erlbaum.

McChesney, R. (1999) Rich Media, Poor Democracy: Communication politics in dubious times. The New Press, New York.

McMahon, C., and McLellan, T. (2008). Journalists reporting for duty: Resilience, trauma and growth. In Gow, K & Paton, D. (Eds) *The phoenix of natural disasters: Community resilience*, pp.101–22 New York: Nova Science Publishers

McQuail, D. (2000). *McQuail's mass communication theory*. 4th ed. London: Sage.

Mukundu, R. (2006) Zimbabwe: Research *findings and conclusions, Report for African Media Development Initiative*. London: BBC World Service Trust.

Mwesige, P. (2004). Disseminators, advocates and watchdogs: A profile of Ugandan journalists. *Journalism*, 5(1), 69–96.

Nadadur, R.D. (2007). Self-censorship in the Pakistani print media. *South Asian Survey*, 14(1), 45–63.

Nassanga, G.L. (2007). Peace journalism applied: an assessment of media coverage of the conflict in Northern Uganda. *Conflict and Communication Online*, 6(2), available at www.cco. regener-online.de/2007_2/pdf/nassanga.pdf (Retrieved 18 January 2019).

Ongong'a, S.O. (2010). The challenges for Kenya's journalism education, in Josephi, B. (ed.) *Journalism Education in Countries with Limited Media Freedom*, New York: Peter Lang, pp. 137–54.

Powley, E.H. (2009). Reclaiming resilience and safety: Resilience activation in the critical period of crisis. *Human Relations*, 62(9), 1289–1326. doi:10.1177/0018726709334881

Reporters Without Borders [RSF] (2019). *World press freedom index – A cycle of fear* https://rsf.org/en/2019-world-press-freedom-index-cycle-fear (2/7/2019).

Rozumilowicz, B. (2002). Democratic change: A theoretical approach. In Price, M.E., Rozumilowicz, B. & Verhulst, S.G. (Eds.), *Media reform* (pp. 9–26). London: Routledge.

Schiffrin, A. (2009). Power and pressure: African media and the extractive sector. *Journal of International Affairs*, 62(2), 96–107.

Shing, E.Z., Jayawickreme, E., and Waugh, C.E. (2016). Contextual positive coping as a factor contributing to resilience after disasters. *Journal of Clinical Psychology*, 72(12).

Simons, G., and Strovsky, D. (2006). Censorship in contemporary Russian journalism in the age of the War against Terrorism. *European Journal of Communication*, 21(2), 189–211.

Skjerdal, T. (2010). Justifying self-censorship: A perspective from Ethiopia. *Westminster Papers in Communication and Culture*, 7(2), 98–121.

Thrall. A.T., Stecula. D., and Sweet. D. (2014). May we have your attention please? Human-Rights NGOs and the problem of global communication. *International Journal of Press/Politics 2014*, 19(2), 135–159. doi:10.1177/1940161213519132.

Tom, T.O. (2008). *Enhancing gender equality in the media in Eastern Africa.* Djibouti: Eastern Africa Journalists' Association.

UNESCO (2018). *World Trends in Freedom of Expression and Media Development.* Paris: UNESCO and University of Oxford.

Waldorf, L. (2007). Censorship and propaganda in post-genocide Rwanda in A. Thompson (ed.) The Media and the Rwanda Genocide, pp. 404–16. London: Pluto Press.

13

CONCLUSION

Researching self-censorship caused by inadequate safety of journalists. Causes, solutions and future research

Ingrid Fadnes, Roy Krøvel and Anna Grøndahl Larsen

As stated in the Introduction, the purpose of this book is to contribute to a better understanding of the relationship between the safety of journalists and self-censorship. In addressing this relationship, the book illuminates causes and consequences of self-censorship in different contexts and under different circumstances. In so doing, the various chapters also point to what can be done to minimize self-censorship, and how self-censorship can be conceptualized and studied empirically. As noted in the introduction, self-censorship is a broad concept, that in and of itself is not inherently good nor bad. However, this book focuses on self-censorship in relation to the safety of journalists, conceptualizing self-censorship as instances where journalists avoid certain topics, angles or perspectives that may be in the public interest, due to perceived physical or psychological risks that publishing could entail.

We started working on this book almost two years ago. Preparing for the Annual Safety of Journalists Conference at Oslo Metropolitan University, we invited original research papers dealing with self-censorship from a variety of angles. We asked: Can we talk about self-censorship? We were well aware of the double meaning of the question. On the one hand, we wondered if self-censoring journalists are able to talk about self-censorship. Talking about what cannot be said could be seen as a contradiction in terms. On the other hand, we wondered how researchers can talk about and empirically explore self-censorship if journalists cannot or will not talk about it – or are unaware of what self-censorship actually is, and how it may affect their work practices.

As mentioned in the introduction, previous scholarship on self-censorship is ripe with comments on the difficulties of researching and understanding self-censorship. Nevertheless, it also seems clear from the growing body of literature on the phenomenon that it plays an important role for those who wish to understand journalism and free speech. Moreover, UNESCO (2015) has included "self-censorship effects on journalistic work, contents and products (chilling)" on the list of topics

198 Fadnes, Krøvel and Larsen

on the academic research agenda proposed to strengthen research on the safety of journalists. By inviting scholars from around the world and providing scholarships for the best proposals, our aim was to get an impression of how scholars in different contexts and geographies see issues related to safety and self-censorship today. It could perhaps be framed as a small experiment in itself, not to produce a representative selection of cases and contexts, but one that could capture some of the diversity in issues and challenges related to safety and self-censorship. For this book, we received more than 20 papers from around 15 countries, of which 11 are presented in the book. These chapters firmly establish that self-censorship does indeed exist and is possible to study empirically. Moreover, the chapters do, in our opinion, capture a broad variety of issues related to self-censorship that need to be addressed – by the journalistic community, by academics, politicians, and organizations-in order improve the working conditions of journalists and secure healthier information environments.

Simultaneously, during the work with the aforementioned Safety of Journalists Conference and this book, we became aware that linking safety for journalists and self-censorship is not a straightforward task. The authors in this book have previously studied safety for journalists, but not necessarily self-censorship *per se*. Yet, self-censorship in some form tends to be an implicit part of works concerning the safety of journalists. Thus, this book is a collective effort in linking safety and self-censorship. In our opinion, the book is a step forward in gaining empirical insights into self-censorship – an issue that we would argue is as important to understand as censorship when we talk about the safety of journalists, freedom of the press and free speech.

While the chapters illuminate how self-censorship indeed is a fruitful concept in studying the safety of journalists, and show that it is indeed possible to gain empirical insights into self-censorship practices, there are certainly conceptual and methodological issues that should be further discussed. For example the term *self-censorship* has so far mainly been used to refer to individual processes. However, several of the studies presented in this book identify and discuss broader structural factors relating to self-censorship. In sum, although self-censorship may be regarded as the result of (routinized) journalistic decision-making processes, self-censorship is often the result of structural factors, thus pointing towards collective solutions. This further elucidate how self-censorship should be studied in context, paying attention to the variety of contextual factors affecting journalistic work.

Contextualizing self-censorship today

Traditionally, *self-censorship* has quite often been understood and studied in relationship to *censorship* (Çipuri, 2015; Jungblut and Hoxha, 2017). To some extent, the two concepts have been mutually defined. However, what we observe are important historical shifts in the environment of media and journalism around the world since some of the seminal studies on safety of journalists and self-censorship were first published. Especially since the end of the Cold War, political and social environments have changed – in many localities, from repressive and undemocratic regimes

Causes, solutions and future research **199**

to (at least formal) democracies. However, the shift away from authoritarian regimes has not always led to open societies, but to various forms of authoritarian democracies where elections tend to serve the interest of governing elites more than the majority population, or to states dominated by violent illegal groups such as the drug "cartels" of Latin America. A few decades ago, numerous strong states with one-party systems, for instance in Eastern Europe and Mexico, or the military dictatorships in African and Latin-American countries and European countries such as Spain, had in place apparatuses to enforce media censorship. The literature demonstrates that regimes censoring the media could expect many journalists "to stay within the limits", to avoid repression and persecution. Historically, self-censorship has undoubtedly been closely related to state repression. However, many of the chapters in this book demonstrate that self-censorship because of safety concerns is now prominent in many (formal) democracies that have constitutions and laws in place to protect free speech. In places such as Guatemala and El Salvador, authoritarian regimes have been replaced by what José Luis Benitez, in Chapter 2, calls "insecure democracies". Violence and threats against journalists are commonplace, and many journalists have to be very cautious to stay safe. Such a situation is similar to, but at the same time different from, the situation under military dictatorship or other forms of authoritarian regimes. It is possible to conclude that the context and thus causes of self-censorship have changed and become more complex, diffuse and fragmented. Yet, the effects of self-censorship are similar to the effects of censorship. Self-censorship — like censorship — silences journalists and works to limit the flow of information, thereby also limiting open public debate.

As discussed in this book, these processes of change in the environment of journalism pose challenges for traditional understandings of self-censorship. As the number of regimes with apparatuses in place to censor the media dwindles, the usefulness of defining self-censorship in relationship to censorship also diminishes. Self-censorship itself does not necessarily diminish, but it becomes less related to the formal functioning of the state. This does not mean that self-censorship becomes less important to study or that journalists today can more easily and safely navigate the environment of possible dangers related to journalism. As the formal forms of censorship have dwindled, the challenges posed by non-state actors or illegal actors such as drug "cartels" partly in control of state apparatuses, have turned out to be extremely dangerous and at the same time increasingly unpredictable. This combination makes it ever more difficult for journalists to navigate the terrain to stay safe while informing the public.

We do not want to minimize the dangers and problems faced by journalists working in authoritarian states controlling the media. However, state bureaucracies tend to be somewhat predictable. It is often possible to anticipate how state censors will react to pieces of journalism. As several chapters in this book demonstrate, in many regions of the world the environment of journalism is increasingly characterized by *unpredictability*. This of course also poses challenges for researchers trying to understand causes and consequences of self-censorship in journalism caused by inadequate safety.

Causes and consequences

Bringing together scholars and practitioners from around the world, the various chapters provide new and updated empirical insights into issues concerning the safety of journalists and self-censorship that may affect patterns of self-censorship and in turn affect free speech. The chapters document the multitude of factors depending on contexts, pushing journalists to self-censor out of fear of repercussions. These include causes internal and external to journalism, within and beyond digital domains, including self-censorship due to government pressures, police brutality, social violence, corruption, misogyny and gendered stereotyping, surveillance, and economic issues. The range of causes of self-censorship are grounded in the actions (and perceived future actions) of a variety of actors, including state and government officials, commercial enterprises, civil society groups and citizens in general.

First, the chapters document the continuing importance of *state actors*, including governments, the military, intelligence agencies and police in both causing and dealing with the safety of journalists and self-censorship. Across countries and regions, state actors implement measures and engage in actions that serve to restrict freedom of the press. As documented in several of the chapters, one important aspect is the judicial system, where different rules and regulations serve as obstacles to a free press and free information flows. For example Aytekin Kaan Kurtul, shows in Chapter 5 how lèse-majesté laws are used by the Turkish government to prosecute journalists that "insult the president of the republic", thereby causing Turkish journalists to self-censor to avoid prosecution. Similarly, Florence Namasinga Selnes shows in Chapter 11 how efforts to restrict political opposition include closure of independent media, destruction of journalistic tools and arrests of journalists. Moreover, Sadia Jamil's Chapter 3 on self-censorship among Pakistani journalists shows how digital surveillance laws push journalists to self-censor. Here, surveyed and interviewed journalists say that they not only anticipate government pressures and other perceived risks in framing actual news stories, but also that digital surveillance impacts the extent to which journalists seek out and gain information in the first place. In other words, digital surveillance laws prevent journalists from seeking out information and communicating with sources.

Second, the chapters document that a variety of *non-state actors*, including economic enterprises, religious groups, organized violent groups and other civil society actors also are important in causing self-censorship among journalists. Through different forms of repression such as violence and economic sanctions, non-state actors hinder critical journalism. For example in Chapter 3 Sadia Jamil notes that Pakistani newsrooms and journalists avoid reporting critically on organizations on whom they depend economically. Moreover, in Chapter 2 on Guatemala, Honduras and El Salvador, José Luis Benitez underscores that journalists avoid reporting on topics concerning organized crime, drug trafficking and youth gangs.

Third, the chapters also point to causes of self-censorship rooted in broader (infra)structural issues. In particular, the chapters highlight causes related to gender and to the digital media environment. First, several authors show how the digital media environment may serve to add new challenges pertaining to the safety of journalists, possibly leading to a harsher environment for journalists and increasing self-censorship among them. These challenges seem, in particular, to be related to digital surveillance and to general hostility towards journalists online where journalists receive threats and harassing comments, and more or less organized attempts at discrediting journalists' legitimacy. Second, focusing on women journalists in particular, Marte Høiby and Signe Ivask show in Chapters 7 and 8 how social media constitute a hostile environment for women journalists, leading some women journalists to avoid writing about topics that they know will cause negative feedback. Moreover, Aisha Sembatya Nakiwala, also employing a gender lens, shows how gendered stereotypes and aggression towards women, hinder women in covering political demonstrations (Chapter 9).

In sum, the analyses document how self-censorship due to perceived risk hinders (critical) reporting on a range on topics of societal importance, including corruption, organized crime, politics, religion, sex, homosexuality, minority groups and human rights violations in general. Moreover, although self-censorship certainly includes withholding of information, the analyses point to how risks associated with publishing also entail that journalists avoid *seeking out* information out of fear of knowing. In addition, the same factors that cause journalists to self-censor also lead potential sources to self-censor, like the recent example from Brazil where four persons were detained, accused of being the sources of the digital platform The Intercept Brazil. Actions like the Brazil detention create a chilling effect that might prevent sources from sharing information with investigative journalists. Thus, attacks on sources has become an increasing preoccupation that could be linked to self-censorship in further research.

In the literature on self-censorship of the type we discuss here, it is quite common to envisage self-censorship explicitly or implicitly as something that happens when journalists know something of public interest but refrain from publishing it because of safety concerns. In the future, however, we need more research on how and why journalists might refrain from knowing in the first place in order to stay safe from unpredictable safety concerns.

Responsibilities and solutions

The chapters in this book illustrate how self-censorship due to safety risks delimits free speech and the free flow of information. As discussed in the Introduction, an important question is thus, how self-censorship should be dealt with. Should responsibilities, and expectations of finding solutions, primarily be directed at journalists and the news media? Or should the responsibility to find measures and solutions be placed elsewhere? The chapters underscore a variety of responsibilities and solutions, ranging from individual journalists to broader structural issues well beyond single newsrooms. Given that causes are grounded in a variety of factors, from laws and corruption to information infrastructures, possible solutions are also many, multifaceted and directed at different actors and different levels, from the individual to the societal level.

First, the chapters point to various measures that can be taken by journalists and newsrooms themselves in order to minimize risks and decrease self-censorship among journalists. These encompass journalistic safety training related to both off-line and online risks, including training in digital safety and encryption; organizational and psychological support to journalists that have been part of traumatic events; more active moderation of online comments sections; gender policies in newsrooms, and collective journalistic efforts where journalists share information and "speak out" against prosecution, harassment and other safety risks. For example Michelle Betz suggests in Chapter 10 that reporters collaborate and share information with each other within and beyond news organizations, to minimize risk and ensure that important stories are told. In terms of "speaking out" Florence Namasinga Selnes, for example, foregrounds how online mobilization against violations against journalists can pressure authorities to better ensure freedom of the press.

Second, the chapters point to solutions *beyond* journalists and newsrooms, including NGOs and other civil society initiatives supporting journalism; laws protecting journalists' online and offline safety (including reform of existing laws hindering freedom of the press); efforts to improve netiquette, gender equality – and more broadly, to ensure that democratic governments promote and adhere to principles of freedom of speech and the media. Related to NGOs, Gerald Walulya, in Chapter 12, highlights how NGOs, by offering training and legal services, for example can play a key role in building resilience among journalists and so minimize self-censorship. Moreover, in terms of the responsibility of governments and state authorities, José Luis Benitez write that "State authorities need to assume their responsibility to prevent, investigate and punish aggressions and killing of journalists, and effectively support the implementation of protection mechanisms for journalists and media workers." Furthermore, and in line with our argument in the Introduction that social media can be seen as a double-edged sword in terms of the safety of journalists and self-censorship, chapters in this book not only foreground social media as a challenge, but also point to how social media may serve as tools to avoid and mobilize against suppression, engage in collective efforts and avoid unsafe physical scenes.

Finally, building on the findings of the chapters of this book, we hope to see more research in the future on what journalists do and can do to build collective resilience and thereby mitigate self-censorship caused by inadequate safety. Self-censorship in journalism is not a static, unchangeable phenomenon. It can be affected by collective efforts by actors outside the media to improve the safety of journalists as well as by collective efforts by journalists to build collective resilience.

References

Çipuri, R. (2015). Reasons of self-censorship landscape for journalists. AAB College.

Jungblut, M. & Hoxha, A. (2017). Conceptualizing journalistic self-censorship in post-conflict societies. A qualitative perspective on the journalistic perception of news production in Serbia, Kosovo and Macedonia. *Media, War & Conflict*. https://doi.org/10.1177/1750635216673283

UNESCO (2015). *Towards a research agenda on the safety of journalists*. Retrieved from: www.unesco.org/new/en/communication-and-information/freedom-of-expression/safety-of-journalists/unescos-research-agenda-on-safety-of-journalists/

INDEX

Abdülhamid II, Sultan 67–68, 71
absolute monarchy 67, 77
abuse of journalists: online 8, 101, 106, 111; by politicians 140–142
academic research 13–14, 198
Achol, A. 166
Action for Development organization 135
advertising by governments 18–20
Afghan Journalists' Safety Committee (AJSC) 154
Afghanistan 149–150, 154–156, 160
African Freedom of Expression Exchange (AFEX) 182
Ahmed Hussein-Suale 182
Akena, J. 166
Al-Ani, B. 185
Althusser, L. 52
American Psychological Association (APA) 185–188, 193
Amnesty International 81
Anthonissen, C. 154–155
approachability of journalists 116
army, Ugandan 183
Askay, D.A. 91
assaults on journalists *see* attacks on journalists
Associated Press 150
Atatürk, M.K. 67–68
attacks on journalists 137–145, 158, 166–167, 173, 176–177, 183, 190–191; responses to 141
Ausserhofer, J. 103
Austria 72, 103

authoritarian regimes 83, 91, 178, 199; *see also* military dictatorships
avoidance by journalists: of certain people 123–124, 173; of some topics 5, 15, 20, 51, 85, 89, 115–116, 124–127, 132, 139–144, 164–165

Baldetti, R. 17–18
Baluchistan 29
Banda, F. 178
Bar-Tal, D. 21, 115–116, 124, 152, 157
Barwe, R. 59
basketball 123
Bean, H. 186, 193
Becker, L.B. 182, 193
Beighley, P. 11; *co-author of Chapter 10*
Ben Khalifa, M. 182
Benítez, J.L. 10, 13–14, 199, 202; *author of Chapter 2*
Berger, G. 182
Besigye, K. 130, 166, 177
Betz, M. 11, 202; *co-author of Chapter 10*
"blacklisted" words 67
Borciani, A. 69
Boyd, J.E. 153
Bozkurt, M.E. 68
Brazil 201
bribery 57, 60–61
British Broadcasting Corporation (BBC) 150
Brooks, D. 5
Bukeke, N. 13, 18
Bulathsinghala, F. 133

Cambridge English Dictionary 3
Cannon, W. 150–151
"capture" of the journalistic profession 58
Caruana Galizia, D. 9
Caruana Galizia, M. 9
Castells v. Spain case 72–73
cautious journalism 7, 40, 90–91, 199
censorship 1, 5, 177; forms of 199; long
  history of 32, 39; soft 51; *see also* self-
  censorship by journalists
Central American countries 15–21, 24–26
Charlie Hebdo (magazine) 4, 7
Chavhunduka, M. 48
Chen, G.M. 106–107, 110–111
Chewning, L.V. 185
"chilling effects" 83–85, 91, 133, 182, 197
China 6
Choto, R. 48
Çipuri, R. 50
civil society 26, 49, 202
Coleman, S. 49
Collaboration on International ICT Policy
  in East and Southern Africa (CIPESA)
  83, 168
Colombani and others v. France case 73
Committee to Protect Journalists (CPJ) 1,
  6–7, 21–22, 81, 148, 182, 187
community building 159
complicity in self-censorship 47
concentration of media 14, 19, 184
conflict resolution 159
conformist journalists 58
content analysis 118
Cook, P. 4, 115, 124
Coronel, S.S. 15
corruption 7, 13, 61–62, 120
Cottle, S. 108
Council of Europe (CoE) 4, 7, 66, 76
Coyle, K. 103
Craig, R.L. 184
critical discourse analysis (CDA) 53, 61
Cronau, P. 168
cross-case analysis 169
Cruz, C. 103–105, 109

death penalty 69–70
decision-making about reporting 3–4; *see also*
  editorial policies of media organizations;
  media organizations; news media
defamation 49, 69–75
Demirel, S. 73–74
democracy: *insecure* 10, 14, 16, 25, 199; and
  journalism 15–16
depersonalization 153

derealization 153
deterrent effects 83, 91, 139
developing countries 184
*Diagnostic and Statistical Manual of Mental
  Disorders (DSM)* 151
digital divide 178
digital media 7–8, 201
Digital Rights Foundation 34
discrimination, sexual 109
documentary analysis 149
Doerfel, L.M. 185
Doyle, G. 184
Doyle, S. 106
dress style 137
Dworznik, G.J. 151
Dzamara, I. 48, 56

East Africa 134–135
"echo chambers" 104–105
economic constraints on journalists 19–20
Edip, H. 67
editorial policies of media organizations 51,
  55, 62, 84
Egypt 6
El Diario (newspaper) 9
El Monitor de Parral (newspaper) 9
El Salvador 10, 13–22, 25, 199
embedded journalists 108
encryption 171–172
Eon, H. 75
Erdoğan, R.T. 66, 69–71, 75
Erem, F. 69
Eritrea 184
Eserski family 19
Espinosa, V.V. 9
Estévez, D. 14, 23
Estonia 11, 114–127; ski scandal (2019) 124;
  study of journalism in 118–124
Estonian language 119
Estonian Midwives Association 117
ethical considerations 3–4, 20, 50, 56, 62,
  157–158, 193
Ethiopia 6, 182
Europe, press freedom in 7
European Convention on Human Rights
  (ECHR) 69–76
European Court of Human Rights
  (ECtHR) 10, 66, 71–77
European Union 48
Everbach, T. 109

Facebook 24, 38, 53–54, 61, 122, 175, 181
Fadnes, I. 11; *co-editor and co-author of
  Chapters 1 and 13*

206 Index

Fahmy, S. 84
Farawo, T. 58
fear 5, 9, 56, 153–155, 158, 176; definition of 150; discourses of 184, 190, 193
Federation of African Journalists 134
Feinstein, A. 150
feminist scholarship 103
Ferganchick-Neufang, J.K. 102, 109
Ferrari family 19
Ferrier, M. 8
first responders 151
Flaubert, G. 65
follow-up stories 126
"forced silence", culture of 91
Fox, J. 103–105, 109
France 73–76, 80
Fredrickson, B.L. 186
freedom of expression 6–7, 14, 18, 26, 29, 39, 42–43, 48–49, 72–77, 80–81, 88–92, 117, 131, 134, 143–144, 156–157, 165–168, 175, 177, 183–184
Freedom House 167–168, 182
Funes, W. 153

Geidner, N. 85
gendered differences 132–133, 143, 145
Gerbner, G. 105
Ghana 184
Gicheru, C.W. 178
Glaser, B. 149
Global Impunity Index 81
Gökalp, Z. 67
Gonzales de Bustamante, C. 108
González, A. 19
Gordon, T. 65
grounded theory 149
The Guardian 4
Guatemala 10, 13–25, 199; Public Ministry Unit for Crimes against Journalists 22
Guerrero, M. 15, 18
Gül, President 70
Gulf wars 108
Gutiérrez, R. 9

harassment 8, 11, 101–110, 114–116, 119–122, 133–134, 139, 176; aim of 122; avoidance of 116; definition of 114–115; forms of 115; online 101, 104, 106, 110; reaction to 116; *see also* sexual harassment
Hassan II, King of Morocco 73
Heil, B.H. 103
Heilmann, C. 4, 115, 124
Hem, M. 178
Henrichsen, J. 40

Hernández, J.O. 19, 23
"hierarchy of influence" model 31–32, 42
Høiby, M. 10, 102, 109, 153, 201; *author of Chapter 7*
homosexuality 61–63
Honduras 10, 13–25, 153
hostility towards journalists 182, 201
Houston, J.B. 132, 144
Hoxha, A. 3–4
Hughes, S. 16, 131
human rights and human rights organizations 13, 22, 43, 48, 60, 66, 71–72, 77, 82, 134, 175, 184, 187
Human Rights Network of Journalists-Uganda (HRNJ-U) 181, 186–192
Human Rights Watch 154, 167–168
humour, use of 125

imprisonment of journalists 6, 16, 183–184
independence of the media 88
"information war" 108
Institute for Economics and Peace (IEP) 156
interaction between journalists and the public 126
Inter-American Commission on Human Rights (IACHR) 15–18, 22–23
international correspondents 149–150
International Covenant on Civil and Political Rights (ICCPR) 30
international criminal law 69–70
International Day to End Impunity for Crimes against Journalists 2
International News Safety Institute (INSI) 107, 133
International Press Institute 116
International Women's Media Foundation 133
Internet resources 7, 71, 84, 91, 102–105, 110, 165, 168–171, 176–178
interviews, use of 5
intimidation 29–30, 80, 130, 134, 173, 176
investigative journalism 13, 16, 19–20, 25, 154–155
Iraq 185
Islamic State 150
Italy 68–69
Ivask, S. 11, 201; *author of Chapter 8*

Jamil, S. 10, 200; *author of Chapter 3*
Jayawickreme, E. 186, 191
jihadi groups 108
Joanne, L. 40
journalism seen as public service 48
journalistic practices 15, 33, 49, 62, 143

journalists: behaviour towards 115–118; loss of status as neutral observers 107
Jungblut, M. 3–4

Kainerugaba, M. 166
Karachi 29
Kenya 184–185
killings 21; of journalists 6, 9, 68, 81, 107, 133–134, 148, 165, 182, 202; of politicians 170
Koroley, M. 117
Krøvel, R. 11; *co-editor and co-author of Chapters 1 and 13*
Kunelius, R. 84
Kurtul, A.K. 10, 200; *author of Chapter 5*

Lai, C.-H. 185
Larsen, A.G. 11; *co-editor and co-author of Chapters 1 and 13*
La Rue, F. 81
Lee, C.-C. 84, 91–92, 167
Lee, J.Y. 103–105, 109
Leedo, V. 117
legal constraints on journalists 17–18
legal services 189–190
lèse-majesté laws 65–68, 71–77, 200
Liu, X. 84
local journalists 148–150, 153, 158
Löfgren Nilsson, M. 122
Lofty, D. 59

Mabweazara, H.M. 49
McChesney, R. 184
McLellan, T. 185
McMahon, C. 185
McQuade, B. 91
McQuail, D. 183–184
McRobbie, A. 105
Maireder, A. 103
Mama FM 134
Mark, G. 185
Marlin, R. 50
Márquez-Ramírez, M. 15–16, 131
Massanari, A. 103
Masten, A.S. 185
Mawarire, E. 48
Mbabazi, A. 177
media freedom 183–184, 187, 193; in Europe 7; violations of 191
Media Matters for Democracy 29, 33–34, 82, 84, 154
media organizations ("media houses") 41, 139, 141, 144–146, 158, 164, 166, 170, 175, 184, 189–190, 193

Megarty, J. 106
mental health 159
Merriam-Webster 2–3
metadata 88
Mexico 7, 9, 21, 150, 155, 199
Mgombeyi, P. 48
Mhiripiri, N.A. 10, 61; *author of Chapter 4*
Michelle, B. 40
military dictatorships 6, 199
Miller, D.T. 3
misogyny 121–122
Mkono, Pride 60
Mlilo, M. 60
Mnangagwa, E. 59
mobile phone numbers 122
moderating systems for media outlets 126–127
Mohatt, N.V. 148–149
Molina, O.P. 17–18
Le Monde (newspaper) 73
Morales, J. 19, 23
Mortensen, M. 124
motivations for self-censorship 3, 6, 10, 13, 29–31, 41–42, 47–48, 56
Moyo, D. 178
Mugabe, R. 48–49, 52, 56, 59–60
Mukoko, J. 48
Muleya, D. 59
Museveni, Y. 130, 165–166
Mužiková, D. 32–33
Mwesige, P. 184, 188, 193
Mwesigye, J. 190

Nadadur, R.D. 191
Nakiwala, A.S. 11, 201; *author of Chapter 9*
Naluggwa, J. 166
Nangbatna, O. 182
"narrowcasting" 105
Nassanga, G.L. 184
negative influences on journalists 116, 123–126
Netherlands, the 76
networked media environment 7–8
networking 187
New York Times 4
news media 15, 17, 51, 158, 164, 169, 171, 175–176, 202; suppression of 176
newsroom cultures 57, 62, 126, 138
niches 105
Nigeria 10, 80–92; Press Council Act (1992) and Amendment Bill (2018) 81–83, 88–91; study of journalism in 85–99
Noelle-Neumann, E. 84

208 Index

non-governmental organizations (NGOs) 11, 66, 181–182, 187–193, 202
North, L. 133
Norway 76
Nusser, N. 182
Nyathi, J. 59

Octavian 65
Okuyan, K. 71
Ombudsman for the Defence of Human Rights 22
Organization for Security and Co-operation in Europe (OSCE) 100, 148
organizational constraints on journalists 20, 31–32
organized crime 7, 108, 153
Orgeret, K. 144
Örnebring, H. 122
Otegi Mondragon v. Spain case 74
Ottoman Empire 65–67
Ottosen, R.O. 153
Owens, K. 23

Pakdemirli, E. 73–74
Pakistan 10, 29–43, 154, 200; Investigation for Fair Trial Act 30, 38, 41, 43; journalists' self-censorship in 33–34; Prevention of Electronic Crimes Act (PECA) (2016) 30, 38, 41, 43; study of journalism in 34–42
participation in public discussion 110
partisanship and party politics 58
password protection 38
patriarchy and patriarchal structures 101, 104–106, 109
Patton, M.Q. 169
peacebuilding 149; implications of self-censorship for 156–157
peer pressure among journalists 20
Penney, J.W. 80
"pillars of peace" 156
Piskorski, M. 103
planning ahead 186
pluralism in the media 133
Poland 76
police services 173, 183; confidence in 24
political constraints on journalists 18–19
positivity 186, 193
post-traumatic stress disorder (PTSD) 148, 151–152, 155, 159
Poveda, C. 24
Powley, E.H. 185
Press Freedom Index 6, 21–23, 82, 134, 182, 191

privacy, protection of 8, 91–92
professional constraints on journalists 20
"Protect Female Journalists Online" initiative 100
protection mechanisms for journalists 22–23, 26, 38, 89–90, 108–111, 131, 140–145, 181, 189, 202; *see also* Committee to Protect Journalists
pseudonyms, use of 67, 71
psychological considerations 155, 158, 205
public sphere 156
Pudephatt, A. 156–157

queer sexuality 61–62

readiness to report on certain topics 139; *see also* avoidance by journalists, of some topics
Reese, S. 31–32, 42
religion 5, 32, 34, 57
Relly, J.E. 108
Remmy, B. 130
Reporters Without Borders (RSF) 6, 21–23, 82, 134, 182
research needs 25–26, 143, 145, 160, 201–202
resilience 125–126, 148, 158–160, 181–182, 185–186, 192, 202; definition of 185; individual and collective 131–132, 142–146
Ressa, M. 8
restorative justice 159
risk 5, 8, 40–43, 131–145; definition of 131; faced by women journalists 133–140, 143–145; forms of 6; mechanisms for negotiation of 139–140; perception of 131–132
risk assessment 140–142, 145
risk awareness 137, 141
Rozumilowicz, B. 184
rule of law 16, 48
Rwanda 185

safety for journalists 1–2, 5–6, 14, 26, 29, 38–43, 132–133, 143–145, 148, 150, 164–165, 169, 172, 176–177, 197–199; conference on (Oslo) 2, 197–198
safety measures: using social media 173–177; for women 144
safety skills 158
Sarkozy, N. 75
Schauer, F. 83
Schiffrin, A. 185
Sejusa, D. 170

self-censorship by journalists: application of 185; challenges posed by 6–8, 157; concept of 198; context of 197–202; definitions of 2–6, 50–51, 59, 115, 132, 199; earlier studies of 197; effects of 50, 199; empirical insights into 198; extent of 36–37, 89–90; factors with the greatest impact on 24; implications for peacebuilding 156–157; moral justification for 152; public and private 4, 115; reasons for 33, 51, 62–63, 167, 199–200; in relation to censorship itself 14, 32–33, 50, 53, 152, 198; and responsibility 8–9; and silence 106–107; sources of 184–185, 188–193, 201; theorization of 50; and trauma 152–153; typology of 5, 167; use of the term 198; *voluntary/involuntary* 51–52, 57

Selnes, F.N. 11, 200, 202; *author of Chapter 11*

Seman, B. 185

sexism 103–106, 109

sexual harassment 22, 101–103, 106, 133, 138

Sezer, President 70

Sharia law 60–61

Shing, E.Z. 186, 191

Shoemaker, P. 31

Simon, J. 7

Skjerdal, T.S. 3–4, 51, 56, 152, 184–185, 190, 193

Smyth, F. 24

snowball sampling 169

social capital 185, 192

social media platforms 7–8, 25, 81–82, 85, 91, 102, 105, 115–116, 122, 164, 168–178, 201–202; anonymity for users of 175–176; and physical safety 173–176; as safe spaces 171–172; tax on use of 178

social responsibility 51

Socio-Economic Rights and Accountability Project (SERAP) 82

sociopsychological characteristics of journalists 21

"softer" topics for journalists to cover 137, 143

Sohn, D. 85

Solove, D.J. 91

Soonvald, U. 117

Spain 73–76, 80, 199

speaking out 140, 144–145, 202

Spielberg, S. 84

"spiral of silence" 84–85

sports journalism 109, 120–125

state bureaucracies 199–200

Stecula, D. 182

Stoycheff, E. 84

Strauss, A. 149

Suler, J. 104, 110

Suraj, O.A. 10; *author of Chapter 6*

surveillance 7–10, 30, 34, 41–43, 47, 80–81, 84–92, 168, 178, 200; and free speech 87–88

Sustainable Development Goals 26

Sweet, D. 182

"symbolic annihilation" 105

Syria 149–150

Taliban regime 154

Tapsell, R. 33

team working 142, 144–145

terrorism 4–5, 41

Thrall, A.T. 182

training programmes for journalists 42, 141, 144–145, 188–189, 202

trauma 148–156, 159–160, 185–186; definition of 151; effects of 154–155; historical 148–149, 155–156, 159–160; and self-censorship 152–153

traumatized journalists 149–153

Trenchard, J. 65

Troll-Busters.com 8

trust in journalists and journalism 127

Tuchman, G. 105

Turkey 6, 8, 10, 66–77, 200; Penal Code 68–70, 76–77

Tuşalp, E. 74–75

Twitter 24, 38, 80–81, 103, 106

Uganda 11, 130–146, 164–172, 175–178, 181–93; civil disorder in 134–135; Communications Commission (UCC) 183; Computer Misuse Act (2011) 168, 183; constitution of 134; *Daily Monitor* closure 166, 169–172, 175–176; Journalists Association 183; media industry in 134–135; Media Women's Association 135, 141, 181, 186, 189, 192; Public Order Act 165, 177; studies of journalism in 135–139, 169–171, 186–187

unions for journalists 39–40, 158, 193

United Kingdom 76

United Nations 22–23, 26, 92, 148

United Nations Educational, Scientific and Cultural Organization (UNESCO) 1–2, 15–16, 24, 40, 80, 84, 100–101, 133, 148, 164, 182, 197

210 Index

United Nations Office for Drugs and Crime 21, 108
United States 48

values, journalistic 63
victimization and "victim" identity 55, 130
Villalobos, E. 9
violence against journalists 14, 23–25, 56, 82, 106–107, 132, 164, 182
virtual private networks (VPNs) 71
Vlad, T. 182

Waisbord, S. 20
Walugembe, M. 181
Walulya, G. 11, 202; *author of Chapter 12*
war correspondents 150
Wasserman, H. 61
"watchdog" role 15, 18, 25, 124, 127, 149
Waugh, C.E. 186, 191
WhatsApp 38, 53–54, 61, 171–172
"whiners" 109–110
White, A. 5
Williams, K. 47
Willingness to Self-Censor Scale 160

women journalists 10–11, 21, 24, 34, 54, 100, 105–111, 114, 120–126, 187, 201; attacks on 107–111; earlier studies on safety of 132–134; effects of risks on 139–140; in Estonia 120–122; levels of threat faced by 109–110; reaction to attacks on 122–126; in Uganda 130–135, 139–140, 144–145
World Health Organization (WHO) 114, 119
World Press Freedom Index *see* Press Freedom Index

Yesil, M. 14
young women, risks faced by 138, 144
Yugoslavia, former territory of 107

Zamora, J.R. 17
Zanardelli Code 68
Zanu-PF party 58–61
Zelaya, M. 19
Zimbabwe 10, 47–63, 184; national crisis in 52–54, 63; studies of journalism in 53–57
Zindoga, T. 60
Zvayi, C. 59